SO NOW WHAT?
One Foot in Front of the Other

SARA ROSE

Written by Sara Rose
Edited by Kelly Allistone
Author Photographs by Aaron Ritter
Cover Design by Sara Rose

tellwell

Tellwell Talent
www.tellwell.ca

ISBN
978-0-2288-2912-6 (Hardcover)
978-0-2288-2911-9 (Paperback)
978-0-2288-2913-3 (eBook)

SARA ROSE is a 24-year-old Canadian-born singer-songwriter and author. She began writing her first book, *So Now What? One Foot in Front of the Other,* between the introduction of her debut album, *Until Now* (2018), and the release of her second album, *We Could Be Beautiful* (2019). In addition to receiving awards for Emerging Artist of the Year (2019), Local Musician or Band (2019), and the 25 Under 25 Award (2018), and nominations for the Reader's Choice Award (2020) in Orangeville, Ontario and The Voice (NBC) Closed Auditions (2020), Rose also holds a Bachelor of Social Work (Honours) (2018). She has served as vice president on the board of a not-for-profit hospice dedicated to providing compassionate palliative care, and has offered her skills as a performer as host of *Hope Through Harmonies,* a founded (2017) benefit concert. She is currently working on a country-pop album and fiction novel.

for and in loving memory of my grandma,
Shirley Rose

for and in loving memory of my loving friend,
a beloved mother, daughter, granddaughter,
great-granddaughter, niece, cousin, and one
of the strongest people I'll ever know,

Ashton Kimberley

A percentage of proceeds per book sold will be given to
Luca, Ashton's four-year-old son, in trust for his future.

Contents

Foreword

ara Rose asks "So Now What?" and it's a question that can be posed in many tones: with exasperation, with dread - or - in Sara's case, with hope.

Hope is the gift that we all need in our lives and one that has been in short supply for so many in 2020. And yet, here it is in the story of a young woman with a rare talent for sharing her music, her poetry, her life's many challenges; it's a tale of optimism and clarity veritably set to a song that has only begun to be written.

When Sara asks her title question, I am tempted to answer: "Whatever you set your sights on, my friend." Her gifts - not the least of which is the ability to be vulnerable - are opened by the reader on every page in this funny, touching and very real story of a life that will be a joy to watch in its living.

So Now...*I hope* you enjoy Sara's story as I most certainly did.

Erin Davis

Broadcaster, Author "Mourning Has Broken: Love, Loss and Reclaiming Joy" (#1 National Bestseller HarperCollins Canada 2019)

Prologue

$\mathcal{J}$ could feel my heart thumping against the wall of my chest and in my ears as I pulled open the door and walked into the unfamiliar building toward which my friends and I had just spent two days driving. Thrilled, a touch angst-ridden, and enthused all at the same time, I pulled open the door and walked toward the man sitting behind the long registration table. It's here, I thought. It's finally here.

"Name and ID please," the security guard said.

"Sara Rose," I said as I set my guitar case on the ground and handed over my passport and driver's license. He had a stern but laid-back air about him.

"Canada, eh? You travelled a long way to get here. Best of luck in there."

"Thanks," I said.

He passed my ID back, pointing me in the direction of the dressing room. I made my way in to tune my guitar and await my call with others who had been

1

cast for these NBC The Voice closed auditions. I went over the songs in my head and breathed, thinking back over the miles that had brought me here, to this very moment. I was sitting up straight, felt the strap of my guitar secured around my back, and planted my feet on the ground. I felt good. Focused. Hopeful, but at ease in knowing that it was all going to turn out as it was meant to. All I had to do was have fun and do my best.

"Sara Rose?"

I looked up to see a young lady standing at the doorway, signalling that it was my turn.

"Ready?" she asked, smiling with her hand on the door handle to the audition room.

"Ready."

I doubt very much that every person on the planet finds total ease in untangling and distributing the nitty-gritty details of their life for an array of reasons, including the uncomfortable inevitability of making us consider our very existence. Sharing the depths of emotion and truth that reside in our stories sometimes isn't as easy as tucking them under the rug with silence, a drink, or a treat – set aside to gather dust; I look up to those who give a voice to theirs.

This book wasn't written with the intent to provide all the answers to anything, just as there is no novel in and of itself that can span the subjective extents of joy, distress, love, pain, gratitude, and grief experienced over the course of a lifetime. I simply wanted to write the book I found myself wishing I had in my hands as I moved, and still move, through certain experiences that have shaped my life thus far. Surely, some pieces were difficult and still don't quite feel like talking about what I had for breakfast, while others were cathartic enough that I can now, gratefully so and metaphorically speaking, take their book off the shelf without the whole bookcase falling over. Nonetheless, I quickly learned that this isn't about me; rather, it's about helping that one girl, boy, woman, man, or non-binary person feel a little less alone in the things I think we as human beings all come to face. If even one sentence resonates with one person in some way, shape, or form, I will forever consider it worthy of being written.

So, just as I stood in a small, low-lit studio room in Boston, Massachusetts, facing a blank, yet encouragingly curious face while placing my shaking fingers on the right frets of my battered guitar, I ask myself, so now what?

ballet shoes

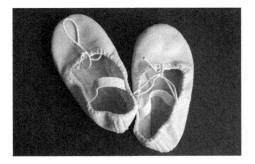

1999

ven when I think things are the same, they're not. Some days I feel there is no part, piece, or portion of my life or self that has remained unchanged over the last few years. I'm glad for this in some ways because it means I'm moving forward in my life. It means that some time-worn doors are closing, even some I really want a few more minutes with, while new ones are opening, providing the opportunity for variation and adventure. It also means the way I live my life has departed from the fairly destructive, somewhat dull routines and ways of thinking that were, as I would begin to recognize at 21, pulling my heart apart thread by thread and slowly robbing me of the sense of wonder and muse I had as a kid.

It's sort of wonderful and strange at the same time to retrace the steps that have been taken as we're paving the paths of our lives. We see where change has moved throughout who we were, where we've been and may or may not want to be again; how we looked and how we perceived, and we better understand the details of the moments it carved out to sculpt where we may end up tomorrow. Some miles fill me to the brim with gratitude, leaving me as elated as strolling through a garden of fresh roses or accidentally walking into a Krispy Kreme when I meant to head to the health food store. Others are as near to full-on panic as fighting to get unstuck from a dress in a change room (they had to cut me out of it: Spanx, dignity, and all). Of course it also includes those particular stretches of time forever marked with the treads of life's blunt realities and scattered with the various stones and potholes that ultimately tell the beautifully unique, sometimes difficult, and always intricate stories of our lives.

I don't remember a whole lot before Grade Three. Based on home videos, I spent most days walking face-first into things, eating, and trying to figure out how to balance an oversized, basically bald head with my rumpled, dimply body; most of those things haven't changed much. I had hardly any teeth or hair until I was about two and for reasons I'll probably never understand, my parents were puzzled as to why I never won the beauty contest at the fall fair.

"Come on, I really don't understand why you didn't win," Mom said not long ago, still a bit shocked, while we were going through old photos. "You had so many dimples and rolls—you were like a walking little bread basket."

1998

One certainty, I've been told, is I was on the move all the time, like a curious bull in a china shop. I didn't seem to be concerned with impossibility, lack of time, or worry that the trek from the kitchen to the living room or across the front yard would be rife with obstacles or hardship; I was a pretty confident kid.

January 5, 2019, 9:47 p.m.

I came across an old pair of ballet shoes today. They've faded to a light, washed-out pink and by the look of the worn-out toes they've seen many hours of use. Mom had tucked them away with other mementos from my childhood she's been saving to bring out when I'm older and maybe have kids of my own.

Picking up these shoes was like holding a piece of the past in my hands, like some sort of time capsule from the days when I was young, carefree, and viewing the world through a lens full of wonder.

Getting pulled back through the years that have gone by since they last fit my feet, simply by holding them in my hands and running my fingertips over the laces was bittersweet. Who was that girl with the ballet shoes? She feels kind of far from here.

-S

How change weaves its durable and at times abrasively unpredictable patterns into the details that shape us has recently garnered my interest. I realize I'm not the only person wandering this earth who has felt completely out of sorts when change inevitably inserts itself into each breath and step, the type that barges through the front door and leaves us no choice but to adapt to a new, regular stride against that with which we're so familiar. Figuring out how to move with it when it gives no other option than for decisions to be made, whether I'm prepared or not, feels similar to what I imagine learning to walk again would be like. Perhaps it's more like being thrown into the steps of a dance you've never studied before. In considering this parallel, I'm reminded of two moments.

I was invited to a wedding shortly after beginning my first year of university. I lived on campus and hadn't brought any heels with me but my friend had a pair of six-inch stilettos. Never having been one to wear much other than Converse sneakers and Birkenstocks in the past, we met up the night before to learn a walk of elegance.

"That was good. This time, let's try to not walk like we've just gotten off a nine-hour horseback ride across the prairies and have had to pee all day." She was such a kind teacher.

We started out trying to walk our homemade red carpet in the heels while holding a glass with poise and balance (gray-carpeted, ten-foot hallway with pinot grigio in red Solo cups and with dictionaries on our heads). Supposedly, the latter helps with balance but I didn't find it overly effective in my attempts at oozing sophistication. We ended up using the book as a coaster, the carpet as a seat, we drank the wine, and belted out "My Heart Will Go On" until all pride was restored. (I danced barefoot at the wedding.)

It also brought to mind the Saturday morning ballet classes for which Mom and Dad signed me up when I was about four. A large part of passing the class involved showing up to the studio in leotards and tutus with hair in buns, and learning the details of one step which would lay the foundation for building the next one; eventually, we would be taught an entire dance. At the end of eight weeks our class got into costume, ready to perform at the recital. Eager parents settled in their seats and even though, despite going to every class, I didn't know the final dance any better than the bottom of a stranger's shoe, my parents would always show up with extra camera batteries. The reason I most likely hadn't a clue as to what I was doing was because I spent most classes doing summersaults and trying to deal with a seriously sideways tutu wedgie. A few others in the class lived the *Weekly Wedgie Hour* and by the look of the home videos, the gold quests seemed to be embraced quite well. Thank heavens the ballet dream didn't hold for much long thereafter.

True to form, when the curtains opened on recital day and the song started playing, I hadn't a clue what I was supposed to be doing. It would've helped were I on stage with the right class, but the panic and hesitation about everything I'd known around me minutes before felt just as unnerving as coming face to face with change, at any age, has felt in the years that followed.

As the thought of dancing ballet remains completely foreign to me, it parallels quite nicely with moving and morphing with change; not so much the kind that doesn't quite surpass wishful thinking, but rather unanticipated change, heart-filling change, heartbreaking change, irreversible change, needed change, or life-altering change. All of these can actually end up being quite beautiful as each is a different dance that draws out various degrees of emotion, and most don't come with prep classes or manuals. Change wears many masks and is determined that you acknowledge it in the most unexpected times and places. Sometimes it's suddenly in our hands or in front of our faces like the offence of a football team. It will fit through the tiniest of spaces, drawing all the breath from your lungs and casually rewriting plot endings. It will break you open and put you back together, but never in the same way. It will lie in the centre of your road and have you trip and scrape your knee 100 times just to impart a single pearl of wisdom and test your resolve to get back up, solider on, and survive. It will blunt all terrible things and illuminate that which is breathtaking, though not always right away; sometimes it will wait until your faith or strength reaches the edge of the abyss before it comes zipping around the bend to provide some kind of exquisitely warped mercy. Change can be a real ass.

The range of emotions that pirouette through my head and heart when change blows across my path, sometimes taking me miles off course, is kind of surreal. Newness can be frightening but the more I see the intricate details, the more prominent one truth becomes: regardless of whether there's a sense of readiness to work with what is in front of us in this very moment or not, the doors that may now obscure the unavoidable that is change, will ultimately open. Floodlights with the potential to shine on every blush of confidence, every blemish of fear or imperfection, faith, and sureness will finally illuminate your way. (You may want to make it somewhat of a priority to pluck your eyebrows as much as your mornings will allow, though. You'll thank yourself later.) If you don't know which kind of lights I'm talking about, look into one of those two-sided, lighted magnifying mirrors that make a pinhead-sized blemish appear the size of a softball.

No matter how strong of a wall you've built in order to keep those comfortable ways of life safe, when change is ready to come, it will.

Change, I'm starting to like you more.

Then somehow, some way, we magically adapt. Even if it shows up wearing the worst of masks, we never fail to maintain a state of movement. With grace in our hearts or tears in our eyes, we figure out the steps to the new dance.

20 years later, as I revisit that recital day and recall that rush of hesitancy, I'm hearing Lee Ann Womack's song, "I Hope You Dance." When we're blown away from everything we know or are turned away from anticipation, sometimes the best thing to do is just take the chance, have a little bit of faith in ourselves, and dance with it. You can sit it out with the intent to better prepare for the next one, but it's impossible to foretell everything. I'm a believer in preparedness, but I also understand not all that unfolds can be planned for and mapped out to the nth degree. I need to remember this more often because I want to be like the little girl who didn't know the day's choreography but danced anyway with no doubt or explanation. Despite the moves I pulled off that couldn't have been more opposed to what was happening around me, I danced my heart out that day. I'm dismayed to report that if I found myself in that same situation on that same stage tonight, waiting in this very moment for the curtains to open, choosing to *plier* and *sauter* wouldn't be the first thing to come to mind. To be perfectly honest, I'd probably freeze like a deer in the headlights and then *jetter* the hell out of there.

I'm growing less fond of how steady this truth holds itself and considering the direction I'm trying to head in my life, it's sort of odd it even exists. I've often wondered at what point the fearless dancer in me dissolved into the fainthearted girl I sometimes feel I am today. I'll find her again, of that I have no doubt.

Embrace the dance, even if you don't know it all too well. Invent new steps on every new beat if you have to. Every moment after it is going to change and bring you to a new spot on the stage anyway because transformation is inevitable. Try not to resist the resultant opening and closing of doors due to uncertainty or the possibility of having to twirl your own version of faith into the centre of an unknown. Working with change is sort of like a relationship—you have to move together if it's going to succeed. Above all, enjoy the wonder and unknown of it all. We can't always have a say in the change of music played for us, but we can choose whether to give ourselves a fighting chance in opening the door and moving with it anyway.

I hope you dance.

scraped knees and grown trees

2008

Edna Jaques speaks so elegantly of the beauty that dwells in the heart of childhood; those oh-so-precious years when we thrive on imagination and wonder. These traits are easily replaced with cynicism and routine if we're not careful, but if we are mindful they can also make adulthood much brighter.

The majority of my upbringing as a kid was spent in two small Ontario towns: Alton and Mono. When I say small, I mean if you blink twice, you'll nearly miss them both. I loved everything about our Alton house—it was a bungalow set right where the road started to climb and was the epitome of home. It was a place of sanctuary, belonging, and relief that wasn't built in a day, where home-cooked meals often turned life's raw ingredients into something warmer and *more* palatable, a place where cold hands and feet were made toasty, and wooden frames captured moments that only grew sweeter with time.

I drove through Alton not too long ago on my way home from playing a set at The Hillside Inside festival in nearby Guelph with the acoustic duo I was in at the time. I'm not sure what sparked the idea to visit—it had been years since I was there last. A wave of memories and emotion rushed from my head and broke through my entire body as I turned the corner onto the weathered and cracking road on which my old house had been aging for the last 13 years. It was the road I learned to tie my shoes and ride a two-wheeler on, ran away from a bully after school on, chased the ice cream truck with a handful of sweaty change on, and on which I scraped my knees hundreds of times. Many of my childhood memories were created between its two stop signs and the mere thought of it never fails to make me smile. Oscar Wilde said "Memory is the diary we all carry with us," and I've always loved that.

We spent so much time chasing the sun on our bikes, trying to keep our legs up with the pedals and hold the handle bars straight, roaring with laughter. It didn't matter how cold the water was, we would swim until our teeth were chattering, our fingers and toes pruney. We wanted precisely what we had and every little thing that filled our worlds was celebrated in the largest of ways. Everything was a learning experience, everyone was a possible friend, and we could be anything because every day was bordered with immeasurable imagination and possibility. A sunny day was hardly seen from indoors. Even rainy days felt bright. Kids are so great at all of this: feeling joy and adapting to adversity or tragedy. They're valiant and resilient. And if you love them hard, they'll love you hard back. I see these characteristics in some of the kids I have come to know over the last few years and I hope they always carry as much of these traits as they possibly can. It's everything. As a child, there's inestimable value in having wide-open space to learn and play and to be surrounded by people who believe in you to do and be anything in this world. Who am I kidding, there's inestimable value in these things for EVERYONE of EVERY age. I've also been catching myself stopping to ask myself what my six- or seven-year-old self would say during those times where life feels a little too complicated and I'm sailing adrift. *Have you been in a tree fort lately?* We should all wipe the lens through which we see the world to start viewing it with beautiful clarity as a child does.

I've often wondered how time has blown change into the lives of old friends. I'd never dare to assume, but I seem to have reached that sort of awkward age where half of my friends are getting engaged, starting families, and getting vacuums for Christmas and the other half are either still living at home and working to pay off debts or figuring out what they want to do with their lives.

The sheer volume of history that's settled within the cracks of the road has surprised me. I remember being worry-free, healthy, and very simply happy here. I lived under the roof and between the selfless hearts of two parents who did everything they could, always with the best of intentions and their strongest feet forward, to give me a good life. In that world, friendships and relationships only grew stronger, people were always going to be around, and life was always good. Life is precarious now, or perhaps it always has been and I'm just beginning to notice it more as I'm figuring it out. Whatever "it" is.

Times weren't better back then, just different. Those were the days where my biggest worry was getting back home when the street lights flickered on, who was going to be "it" for the next game of Manhunt, or that panicked feeling when I lost Mom in the grocery store. I still panic when we're a few people back in the line to cash out and she says, "Oh, darn it, I forgot broccoli and there's jam on sale in aisle eight! Just one second while I go get them..." as the conveyer belt brings me ever closer to the cashier. The anticipation is basically the scene from *I Am Legend* where Will Smith is running full-tilt toward the sunlight.

I pulled over in front of the house and looked down at my worn red boots stepping onto the asphalt.

My feet were a lot smaller the last time they trod on this ground.

It was a bittersweet feeling, standing there. Pressure built behind my eyes as I recalled the myriad details that made up who I was back then. A lot of those good memories seemed to have gotten boxed up and packed away, buried beneath a pile of meticulous worries, stresses, and regret. I felt a bit like the road itself: cracked, a bit lost, weathered but also wise enough to see I still have a lot of life left in me.

The front of the house looked like an old painting. Funny, I could picture my younger self running through the white screen door I had opened and carelessly let swing shut behind me hundreds of times. It was still there. I could see the spot where I sat barefoot in grass-stained dresses with a butterfly net and simply marvelled at the world. It was the same spot where my first dog, a rottweiler named Rosie, used to play and push big rocks around with her nose. She was the most loyal dog I've ever known. She sat with me if I was happy, sad, mad, or confused. Dogs are so great at just being there. I could see where I got in my first argument with Mom and Dad, where the garden underneath the window of my old bedroom was, and where the living room met the corner of the garage. I wonder if the pen marks on the door frame are still in there from when the heights of my friends and I were marked year after year? I looked behind me and a favourite memory popped into my head—after Dad would finish cutting the grass with his souped-up riding lawn mower, I'd hop on the dirt bike and we'd race up the road. I can still smell the freshly-cut grass mingling with exhaust fumes and hear the distinct sound of, "Ready! On your mark, get set, GO!" yelled with pure joy and anticipation over the revving of the engines.

Life seemed bigger, but in a smaller, more conquerable sort of way. When you fell and scraped your knee you got up, wiped off the dirt and tears, brushed the hair from your eyes and kept going. I guess that's one of the many glories of being a kid—there doesn't tend to be a whole lot of room outside of determination and resilience. Simplicity really brings a great sense of relief and victory into the finer details of things.

I tried thinking back to when my outlook was set adrift from those small things, the anchors that kept me calm and grounded. For a quick minute, I was able to invoke their heft and value once again. I can't pinpoint the exact moment I stopped soaking in the endless blue above us, really feeling the sun hit my face as a gentle reminder that everything might just end up being alright, but I did find a huge sense of relief in the simple act of standing still for a second. Like taking in a good, full breath after losing it from a big, ugly cry or five-minute belly laugh.

There are moments I'm glad to have only lived through once and there definitely are some I wish I could visit again and again. Maybe that's the beautiful, ambivalent thing about time, realizing it's ever-forward. Literally. It will never allow us to repaint that same canvas anew, but will allow for reminiscences, revealing the versions of ourselves we've long grown out of. Ultimately, they will help propel us onward like nothing else.

Dec 1, 2018, 11:49 p.m.

Change and time go hand in hand. They coincide like coffee and cigarettes, like lemon and tequila. Like hearing the laugh and feeling the embrace of a longtime friend not seen in ages. Like grilled cheese and tomato soup on a cold day.

This dynamic pair has borne out many a variation: love and loss, birth and death, age and wisdom, passion and fulfillment, disaster and gratitude, experience and reason...I feel them in the gusts of wind that ruffle my hair, through the changing seasons, in times of loss and good fortune. I can hear their steps leaving footprints across my heart when I'm lying awake at night reflecting on my day. I can feel their desire to be recognized sneaking into the songs I write. I can see their reach in my friends and parents when we've gone a long time without seeing each other, and in my dear grandmother as each passing day gives life to her illness by pulling away another piece of hers.

I've lived in angst and, by word of Adele, "raged on rolling seas" when they've shown little-to-no mercy. I've loved them honestly and fully when I've tried letting them into my step and seen how they can teach priceless lessons, bringing freedom and opportunity into that severed part of me struggling to find meaning.

Visualizing the places they will carry us isn't easy, but I'll keep growing more comfortable in their presence because they're devoted. I like that together they're the one thing that can be counted on in this gigantic, floating, predictably unpredictable, spinning ball on which we live.
-S

Remembering this little girl who marvelled at the little things, ran barefoot with flowers in her hair, and drew goodness onto the pages of life that from time to time can surely be cause for gloom yet bore a silver lining I didn't realize I was needing to feel again. Sometimes, it's little reminders such as these that bring what was once so predominant back into view. I suppose that's just a remedy of looking back on yourself from a different time.

I fell asleep smiling that night, feeling as if the Me I'd been reminded of was sitting in front of me. She'd put her hand on my knee, smile, and nod in reassurance and encouragement that I was doing ok and would be ok. Not because of the hundreds of mistakes, setbacks, and tiny failures I've experienced since I last frequented this road, but because over the last two years I've started changing the direction of my travel, making a conscious effort to keep going and become a better version of myself. She probably wouldn't leave without telling me not to take everything so damn seriously, and to just have fun and be myself.

Go outside. Feel the sun hit your face. Learn from others and see everyone as a possible friend. Hang on to the miracle of being on earth. Dance in the rain, be silly, and for God's sake, laugh aloud. It's the greatest feeling and it will make you feel young and alive. You can tell how much time an older person has spent smiling and laughing by the wrinkles near the corners of their eyes. My grandfather has a lot of them and I hope to develop lots of them, too.

2004

grains of sand

I haven't officially explored my family's lineage, though at some point I'd like to try one of those ancestry tests. The amount of history to be found by spitting into a cup and sending it away is fascinating. From my understanding, the surname Rose originates with English, Ukrainian, Irish, Scottish, French, and German origins. Mom's maiden name is Church, her mother's was Fisher, and held within are Mohawk and French-Canadian roots. The Mohawk are a tribe of Indigenous People of North America with the three animal-named clans being the Wolf, Bear, and Turtle. The percentile I have is lower than what legally deems a person a Status Indian, so I haven't been able to attain mine. I feel proud my background connects to this culture and I know who I am, but sometimes a larger principle piece subsists.

It wasn't until I sat in university lectures learning about the history of the Indigenous culture that I came to know more about how our home nation was treated and still is to some degree. The Indian Act was enacted in 1876, granting the federal government control over most traits of Indigenous life. People were stripped of their homeland culture and separated from their families while children were administered an education reluctant to teach from a place of cultural respect, inclusivity, and diversity, all while statuses, wills and band administration were controlled. The last federally operated residential school closed in 1996.

This reference doesn't paint near the entire portrait of these oppressive wedges of difference and "us versus them" that were enacted and entrenched deeper between cultures and humanity, but it must continue to be acknowledged. The privation of acknowledgement of how our home nation was treated in the past and of what a lot of those children and families went through as a result, leave me in a sad, sickened, and embarrassed state. Who the hell do we think we are to impose docility upon other human beings? While it didn't directly affect my family in the same way it did others (aside from most likely being a part of the reason some of the culture faded along the lives of previous generations) it beleaguered a human right and cut the freedom of many to live within their culture. To this day, many both inside and outside this culture live in that oppression's wake, resulting in a lingering distress. They continue to bear its weight emotionally, physically, financially, and spiritually; my heart breaks in the face of that inequity.

Changing what courses of action were pursued is not an option, but coming to terms with the fact that remaining blind to its historical existence, leaving it unacknowledged, doesn't work either. When in doubt, human decency means choosing kindness, empathy, humility, and love. We are but grains of sand on an infinite, cosmic beach.

three-piece set

University Grad, 2018

"Take care of the nickels and dimes and the dollars will take care of themselves."

-My mom paraphrasing Benjamin Franklin

J'll bet I've never met anyone more economical than my mother, and my mother in labour for certain. From what I've been told over the years, Dad was about to park the car in a spot nice and close to the entrance of the hospital on my birthday when Mom's reluctance to pay what was probably about five dollars back then meant they ended up in free parking a block away.

"What can I say, hospital parking is expensive!" she said when I asked why on earth she opted to park four kilometres, a bridge, and a gas station away from the hospital.

Based on the relayed story, she stayed in the car while passing the hospital so she and Dad could go in together. It's sort of sweet, wanting to go through the whole experience side by side. I'll tell you this much, though—if that were me and my vagina was starting to transform like Optimus Prime does in the *Transformer* movies you can bet your bottom dollar I would not be taking the scenic route. Fast forward to midnight on April 8; I was born and did not fall out in the parking lot. They named me Sara Holly Rose: Sara, after Mom's childhood best friend Sarah Holmes and Holly because Mom always loved that name. It took until I was about 18 to realize my name is 70% plant-based, but I digress. If we're going by stripper names based on your first animal and the first street you lived on, I could've been Shirl Timberlane (or Zesty Italian Teal with white polka dots if it's your favourite salad dressing and the colour of your underwear). Either way, neither strikes me as being particularly saucy, though they do suit how I'd likely look trying to dance on a pole.

Mom and Dad met in 1991 and from where I stand, they've seemed to always share a life pretty well without hesitating to be themselves. That is, after the first fart happened. I'm pretty sure every man goes through a phase of believing women don't fart. WE DO. Why are things like that so awkward? We literally all do it. Anyway, I only recently learned that before moving on to be a mechanic and then a supervisor at a major transit company, Dad was one of the city's greatest tow-truck drivers dealing with transport truck roll-overs. It's interesting, the things you learn about a person even when you've known them your whole life. Mom's a sales coordinator and has worked for the same company for 32 years. Anyone who knows her knows of her optimistic point of view and that she'll share her heart with everyone else well before stopping to consider sharing it with herself.

I've often been asked whether I enjoyed being an only child growing up. Undivided love, hanging out with friends a lot and a view of the adult world from my spot at the grownups' table were nice. It was a little lonely at times and, while my parents cheered on nearly anything I put effort into, I feel like some added pressure comes with being an only child given you're usually the sole person being watched. Predictably, when it came to doing things as well as can be, when I got older it did become more stressful, as I never wanted to let them down.

I was a decent, well-mannered kid with a few reckless drunken party nights and unacknowledged speeding tickets. Overall, though, I was pretty up-to-par with what is expected of a "good" teenager...I think. I always said please and thank you and never said I hated them, told them to fuck off, or got myself in any illegal trouble. I did go through a phase of not being as pleasant as I should've been and i gave a lot of small things the power to interfere with what really should've mattered in the larger scheme of things. I think as teenagers it's normal to look outside the sphere of life with your parents, believing they don't always know everything. This doesn't make it acceptable to be unpleasant or rude, but I think it's part and parcel. You want to be your own person, to live your life and be treated like an adult, but still need mom to schedule your dentist appointment and dad is still who you call when your car starts making a noise that even the radio can no longer block out.

Upon reflection, I think most people will agree that around the age of five everyone thinks their parents are everything and have all the answers, around 16 they don't understand what you're going through and don't know a thing, then in your late teens it becomes clear that they probably know a bit more than you'd originally thought. Once you reach your twenties and beyond, they're among your most cherished friends.

I love my parents; a lot of who I am is thanks to them—they're authentically good people with big hearts and I want them to feel proud of how they raised me. What I saw as nagging was often them just being parents doing what parents do and I was too immersed in my own drama to see it. At that point I hadn't lived long enough to realize the best parents are the ones who openly admit to imperfection and how while we're getting older, so are they. Only in the last five-or-so years have I found myself thinking about how when they pass away, which I hope to god isn't any time soon, as an only child I'll be forced to go through it alone. It doesn't make losing parents any easier, just different. While I'll hopefully have a family of my own, I imagine siblings ease the weight of such difficult events.

Kids also don't come with instructions and I interpret each phase of a child's life as a learning process filled with decisions felt to be the best, most wise choices at the time. I know everything they did while I was growing up was because they wanted me to be the best person I could be. Mom once said, "We want you to be so much better than us. To be healthy, successful, get a good education, have good relationships, be financially stable. Surround yourself with good people and fun times. Good friends are a good support system and you have them." In the rocky times they still came to every show they could, did everything they could possible to support my hopes, dreams and life, and I would say without hesitation that they're still my biggest fans.

Why is it, I wonder, that we hurt those we love the hardest. To say no one knows what goes on behind someone's closed doors is to recognize that every family deals with their own issues. No family lives a White Picket Fence life, even though it may appear so from the outside. Mom and Dad's feet haven't always fit seamlessly in every pair of shoes I've worn (in fairness, whose does?) and they'll be the first to agree that we bicker and yell over things trivial and not so trivial, but the love remains. I'd sooner see us frustrated with each other than meet a silence that screams "nobody cares!" anymore. Doing the best we can with what we know is all we can do.

"We're a three-piece set," Mom would often say. "We don't work so well without all of us."

As I get older, I find I've grown to really appreciate how involved my parents were and I relish the fact they're still with me now. I'm listening more to the little things they pass down, tucking them in my back pocket for future reference; from sayings such as the one above from Ben Franklin to adages like "always give more than you take." I know I cherished them then too, but in a different way. I never considered a parent may not always be there until I became a young adult trying to figure things out. It was then I realized the countless details that weave their way into making a life as we go about the business of growing up and living our own lives; our parents' stories lay the foundations of our own. So be patient when they're asking you about technology and what "an Instagram" is.

Who You Are

You share your whole heart
With everyone else
But do you ever share it with yourself
You're running around
You do not sleep when there is pain
And you will never, ever complain

Chorus
It's who you are, who you are,
who you are, who you are
It's just who you are

You leave the light on
When I am not home
But do you know how far I've gone
You fill your soul
With faith that this shall pass too
And you still live a life full of gratitude

Chorus
All the little things we thought we big
Fell off our shoulders and now are obsolete

Chorus
Sara Rose, Until Now, 2017

candy red and the Beatles

$\mathcal{J}$ spent a fair number of weekends hanging out with one of my aunts when I was young. I loved how special she made each visit, regardless of whether we were just hanging out and vegging or travelling somewhere like Niagara Falls. It was quality time. I was ten when a visit in 2006 would plant a seed that hasn't stopped growing since. I don't think it ever will.

I got an impromptu guitar lesson from her roommate at the time who had offered to show me a couple of chords, which led to me practising *Blackbird* by The Beatles all night. I can still picture the pages of sheet music scattered across her living room floor. We stayed up until two in the morning and, as the story goes, my eyes were bloodshot and drier than cardboard because I'd been in such awe of the guitar. I'd barely blinked all night.

After that she decided to take me to Long and McQuade, the music store just a few blocks away. I had a total of twelve bucks in my bag, with which I had been planning on buying popcorn and candy. I remember sitting at the back of the store on a tiny carpeted stage when the salesman brought out a candy red Fender Stratocaster electric guitar and plugged it into a small amp. He was a former member of the glam heavy metal band Slash Puppet and had toured with Canadian singer Lee Aaron.

"Go ahead, rock it," my aunt said.

I was unsure and nervous about the whole thing and played the handful of chords I knew over and over again in a completely off-time version of *Blackbird*. After breaking out a wide grin, she made a decision that would forever impact my life in the fullest of ways. She offered me a deal: if she bought me the guitar for my birthday I wouldn't get anymore birthday presents. I felt like I'd won the lottery. We were talking about this not too long ago and she said, "I picked it up two weeks later and gave it to you on the 30th of January. I couldn't make you, or me, wait months until your birthday. I figured if it sits in the corner of your room for ten years and you only play it once, that's fine, but I wanted you to try it."

Mom and Dad enrolled me in guitar lessons and I play mostly acoustic now, but that guitar immediately became my everything. I started writing that day, seldom walk by my guitar now without picking it up, and haven't really stopped since. I'll forever remember sitting in my aunt's living room after dinner and learning *Blackbird* as the time when music and writing became a refuge. I'll be forever grateful for it.

the furthest thing

June 13, 2019, 10:23 p.m.

I've always thought of life as kind of unwarranted in and of itself. There are some things that suggest no explanation nor give the leanest pinch of reason. Laughter and moments are sunken deep into hearts and memories are made and edged into their soundest places as life unfolds one day, hour, minute, and second at a time. Families and friendships are built by blood and by choice and while some last a lifetime, others dissolve into the abyss as a result of life's general ebbs and flows. Loved ones often leave this world to embark on their next adventures much sooner than we'd like, and to say it's been hard and jolting wrapping a heart around a fraction of an understanding of any one piece would be an understatement. Laced within this precariousness though, is a certain connection between living and dying; it's a lane seldom walked until an end is met, finding permanent living space in a heart's corner.
-S

*J*t's fascinating how the road one takes in life, or presumes to take, will inevitably shift, introducing various cliffs, slopes, and obstacles. Experiences reveal themselves in our dusty footprints and await our actions while perceptions are observed and noted with each mile we travel. Fate-based or not, some bring about wonderful things: a realization, friend, new connection, mentor, or perhaps an unexpected experience. Others may bring enough devastation, fear, or sadness that they pull the rug out from under you. Perhaps someone dear to you has been given the diagnosis of a life-limiting or incurable illness, you receive some devastating news, or a major loss just opens up in front of you; sadly, the list of possibilities is endless. Each one, no matter how large or small has the potential to take everything you thought you knew and turn it inside out like laundry. All it takes is One Thing.

In the fall of 2016 I was starting my third year of a Bachelor of Social Work degree. A requirement of graduating the program included completing two student placements at an organization(s) of interest. During a meeting with one of the school's faculty consultants, I was asked which fields sparked my interest most. Mental health and addiction support came immediately to mind, though I wasn't ready to make any solid decisions.

"You'd be ok with anything?" the consultant asked.

"Yeah, but I'd prefer to not have a hospice if possible," I said.

"Why is that?"

"I'd just like to keep my distance if I can," I said, unwilling to budge regardless of her curiosity.

As if I would reveal the real reason for my reluctance— then I'd have to face it! For as far back as I can recall, the discomfort and fear I felt regarding the harsh reality that with life comes death has held steady. Even as a little kid, hearing of someone growing ill or passing away sent gigantic boulders dropping into the pit of my stomach. The more I heard of people dying, the more I blocked out this distressing fact of life, believing that as long as I didn't think about it too much, it would somehow spare me. Yes, you may feel the need to state the obvious, that dying has a lot to do with the unknown and one never really knows where our souls venture once they're no longer confined within their earthly bodies. Ultimately, I plan on living as fully as I possibly can while I'm here, despite that unknown.

"Hmm, ok leave it with me. I'll be in touch," she said.

I would soon receive a call letting me know a spot at a hospice had become available for me. I then reminded the faculty consultant that I was the student who had hoped for something different.

"I know," she said. "Here's their number."

That date now stands out as my first step down a completely unforeseen road I had been actively avoiding, but is now one I will forever walk with great appreciation.

Just off the main drag in Orangeville, Ontario (population: 29,000) you'll find Centre Street. The town's only bowling alley was located there until a few years ago when, sadly, it closed its doors. The renovated building became a community centre filled with various agencies, including this hospice.

I went in for the interview and wound up accepting the offer for a social work student position. I had experienced a hospice environment once before, but felt degrees of unease and uncertainty around whether or not I could again. I knew death and dying were going to be a large part of the focus of my placement. My understanding of the breadth of palliative care barely went beyond thinking that hospices were places where people go to die and this stretch of time would end up being a year packed with extreme sadness and death. The negative undertones associated with hospice palliative care are felt by many.

From the moment I showed up at their door, full of goosebumps and nerves, the welcoming vibes of acceptance, respect, community, and warmth were impossible to miss. Contrary to my earlier assumptions, I quickly picked up on the truth that hospice palliative care isn't simply about dying. An interdisciplinary approach balances comfort, compassion, and peace with dignity for those facing the end of their lives.

Part of the student role I filled was initially shadowing the hospice's social worker in peer-support based groups and in one-on-one psychosocial therapy sessions for individuals living with life-limiting illness, for individuals nearing end of life, for caregivers, and for the bereaved. The group programs were full of examples of the positive benefits of peer support; it was nice to see feelings of isolation in an illness experience often decrease as a result. In addition to the advantage of these programs allowing the time, space, and resources for clients to communicate with others living similar experiences, the operation of these groups allow time for caregiver respite. These are the people who are often consumed with supporting their charges both emotionally and physically, and such relief allows for the restoration of energy, patience, and balance so the care provided and the relationship at hand remain well.

Over time I moved on to handling my own caseload and it was an honour to walk alongside those dealing with this part of their journey. I've yet to find the words to describe what I felt supporting someone as they explored their personal beliefs around life and what the beyond may be like, while tapping into things like forgiveness, acceptance, meaning and hope along the way.

Hope is a bit of a flowing construct when it's shone against the context of a progressing, life-limiting illness. I think as one's realities change, hope echoes and transforms, too. A cure may be counted on initially, whereas with time that hope may evolve into remedial control of symptoms, which may then become care for one's family after their loved one's time has come.

Feb 13, 2017, 12:02 a.m.

The other day I was sitting at hospice's dining room table playing guitar and singing with clients while they were crocheting for a Christmas craft sale. Life was radiating off one person in particular as she was bopping along to my rendition of "Bye Bye Love" by the Everly Brothers. I always think of my grandma when I hear this song; it's certainly a favourite.

It was one of those moments where life isn't just seen, but felt. While I was taking this in, I wondered how they could be so happy and seem so hopeful when their illness trajectory realities are swaying like a pendulum? I suppose the obvious answer to my question would be this: you live in the moment. You don't wish time away. You make the best of the time you have left.

-S

Every person with whom I crossed paths impacted me in some special way, but the person referenced in the above entry made an indelible mark on my life. She had a stride that didn't falter in the face of adversity, an armful of reasonable hope to contribute to her quality of life, and a certain kind of grace that made even the thought of not fighting for existence seem unacceptable. I admired her for not allowing herself to be defined by this one aspect of her story. She was one of many who demonstrated that life can be lived well and with quality despite misfortune or any form of hardship. Her illness was but only one piece of her being—she didn't allow it to diminish the joy that radiated from her wherever she went, raising the spirits and hopes of others.

An area that really sparked my interest was the use of music in care. It was this interest that resulted in me creating a pilot music program while completing my second placement with the same hospice. I was enrolled in a relative certificate program at the same time, and I learned that music as care rests on the basis of either music as healing content or a healing context (Room 217 Foundation, 2016). As healing content, directive focus is placed on using sound and music as a curative agent, whereas healing context is used to support natural balance (Room 217 Foundation, 2016).

The foundation upon which my program was built utilized music as an additive care component in one-on-one sessions with palliative, caregiving, and bereavement clients. While each person's program was tailored to their needs and interests, general areas drew on environmental sound with regard to entrainment, timbre, sound in common care spaces, and techniques to alter environmental sound. The use of the breath and the voice were explored in respect to pitch, tone, and contour. Breathing intentionally, humming as presence, singing and writing, choosing, sharing pieces significant to the individual and analyzing lyrics to meaningful songs, and building playlists to match or induce certain emotions were also explored. All techniques were used with the intent of enhancing the therapeutic and clinical support being provided.

Bearing witness to music's impression and influence as a vehicle for human beings in such moments and experiences that often overflow with vulnerability to life, was incredibly insightful. The most eye-opening piece, to top it off, was how much those without a musical background whom I worked alongside in this program were able to get out of it.

Aug 3, 2018, 8:19 p.m.

This week was one that made me take a step back and look at everything again. I spent time with someone who had gotten shattering news. No doubt exists in the heaviness that comes bucketing in with illness some days, no matter if it touches you through work or family. It makes me cry, but also reminds me to count my blessings.

I feel selfish to have gone through a period of time not recognizing the value of living life to the fullest. I was glad for what I had, but merely infrequently recognized the value in the little things (which were typically the larger things) hiding in plain sight that, when leaned into, allow life to be lived and valued fully. Embracing the blessing it is to share intimate conversations with people who teach me to treat every day as the gift it truly is, lends a reminder to this. I'm counting this blessing today.

-S

Upon my graduation and my opting to stay involved with hospice in some voluntary role for a few years after, I found myself suddenly fielding many comments and curious questions. Many were disguised with tonnes of reason such as, "Oh, that place must be so sad; you know people connect with hospices because they're dying, right?" or, "Really? I don't know how anyone could do that kind of work in any role. I couldn't." In all earnestness, I can understand why people are drawn to working and volunteering in hospices, I can appreciate why burnout exists with healthcare providers and why in general people may choose to avoid such an environment: building connections through intimate conversations about life and death up to one's last breath is impactful but daunting. Both the social worker and executive director I had the pleasure of learning and growing from kindly offer the following quotes, which couldn't respond to such queries any more authentically.

"I feel blessed to work in hospice palliative care. It is truly an honour and a privilege to walk alongside individuals during the most difficult time of their lives. It is often in the most profound moments when I am in fact not a "social worker," not an "expert;" in these moments, I am just a human being sitting with another human being, connected in the experience of life. I don't take it lightly when someone chooses to invite me into their story. To work in hospice palliative care is to experience humility daily."
-Natalie Talma, RSW, MSW

"Hospice is a place of love, compassion, and patience. The hospice mission is to foster life. For the client that is dying, we help them live fully through recognizing and respecting their emotional, physical and spiritual wishes to their very last breath. We want to support the grieving family throughout their journey so that they can emotionally, physically, and spiritually connect with their life while recognizing their experience. In return, staff and volunteers are

given a reminding gift from the dying and their families that life is to be lived with appreciation."
-Maureen Riedler, Hospice Dufferin Executive Director

Quality is such a key ingredient in the fulfillment of a wish to die with dignity. I witnessed how hospices humbly help clients move through illness and loss by tending to emotional, spiritual, and physical needs and desires. Dying, care-giving and grieving are three of life's greatest challenges and deserve kind, caring support. How we meet what is often a very vulnerable time of life reflects the compassion of our community and without this care I think we would see a lot of people going through a difficult journey in distress, impacting the quality of life of the individual living with the illness and their families after death.

Since connecting with hospice and having fulfilled social work roles and sat as vice president on their board of directors working to help their community thrive in providing quality care by collaborating as a team, the manner through which I look at living and dying has been enormous.

In the face of illness, life's realities are drawn to the front of our hearts and minds, demanding we acknowledge them. In resisting the urge to block them out, I've come to realize that the end is just as an important part of life as being born and living. Whether we admit it or not, it's a journey everyone ponders at one time or another and will experience in any of a number of forms.

April 3, 2017 6:19 p.m.

A comment someone made today has me thinking about how the final days and moments of our lives are approached and how generally, people want to participate in decisions regarding their care. Changes and improvements in areas such as medicine, legislation, and subjective goals of care have provided room for increased control, but in order for such decisions to be carried out, conversation needs to happen. While the conversation about end of life decisions is not necessarily an easy one, it smoothens the process.

With hospice care in general, a common feeling is that it's a sad, dark, end of life experience. In reality, it's a warm, friendly, peaceful environment with appropriate medical interventions in place, all of which rest on the connection between living and dying that allows one to live the remainder of their life fully, hopefully pain-free, and with their loved ones present. In reference to a caregiver and her loved one being connected with a hospice, she shares, "I think of those who have gone through such experiences without hospice care and all the days that could have been spent that much more preciously had someone, be it a family member, friend, or healthcare provider, started that conversation just a little bit earlier."
-S

I wondered, and still do at times, where I'd be had I not been connected with hospice. If it had been up to me at the time, I may have briefly considered it but doubt I'd have taken the initiative. Serendipity is a powerful force with a funny way of bringing what we need around the bend just when we need it; fate occasionally gives us a push to stray off the beaten path and try something new. People cross paths and are thrown together, sharing experiences for reasons that may never be known. I, for one, only need to remember with profound appreciation the lessons learned from the experience. I'm going to keep the gates of my heart open to let the universe do its thing from now on. The adventures that may result can lead to some pretty wonderful, life-changing and defining things. I now realize, gratefully so, that it's often one moment, person, or encounter that can colour the lens through which you perceive the world, challenging you to rework all of which you once believed to have known.

Little did I know that knocking on the door on my first day of placement would take the initially dreadful feeling I felt fill my body and begin turning it into one of gratitude, humility, and in some ways, fulfillment. I'm grateful to have been at a place that touched my heart every day I was there, forcing me to re-evaluate my perspective and thinking; I did not expect to meet so many beautiful souls. I also don't mean to sound trite when I say I have never seen a group of people working so passionately and whole-heartedly towards providing quality care and service. I met people who taught me more than I can inventory about gratitude, quality, inclusivity, passion, community, dignity, innovation, and inspiration and to always remain teachable and humble. I was there to obtain an education and provide a service to a population, but I left having learned just as much from them as they did from me. Everything about spending time with those facing end of life or going through an illness, hearing people's stories and their feelings about life and death taught me more about living in a state of now. The insights, experiences, and lessons heightened my awareness about the value of appreciating life, connections, and love. Ultimately, the daily thought-provoking question is one I believe every human being needs to ask: Are you living each day like it's your last?

In any capacity, hospice palliative care is an honourable ground to walk. Margaret Paan, executive director at a local hospice, shares: "Bearing witness as someone journeys through end of life is understood by the many clinical professionals, staff, and volunteers who give of themselves in service to those with palliative care needs and the ones they love. Our purpose is to support the whole person to enhance quality of life and address suffering."

It's refined my understanding of the connection to see it as the universal street that runs through all of us. This connection is one that once realized, will never part. (Talk about irony with this hospice actually being on Centre Street!) The way it has folded itself perfectly into the creases of everything I thought I knew has given a new face to life and death like nothing before and has enriched my life beyond measure. As a result, I almost feel like there's a fence separating the conversation of living and dying and the connection between them. Despite the adjacent proximities of the two, I tip-toed over the surface of the relation among them before finally walking the road that connects to their centres.

There is nothing more human than the concept of living and dying; it's totally and inevitably relevant to everything, like breathing, yet it's the discussion from which society most often tends to turn away. This belief that suggests there is no connection among the two must be dismantled if we want to grow more comfortable with moving around the rigidness that currently lingers around this topic. How wonderful it would be, should we try to open our hearts a little wider to recognizing this in the same way that hospice's doors are always open to us. Suppressing this connection until it becomes bad blood in our own bodies doesn't do anything other than encourage the idea that life is a fight against death when in reality, it's the furthest thing from it.

24

Sept 9, 2018, 11:09 a.m.

At the thought of the unknowns ahead, I'm not sure how I feel. Excited? Overwhelmed? Scared? A tad insecure? Ready? All of the above? Undeniably, whether I've been ready for a shift in direction or not, there always seems to be a few feet of open space leftover, a reliance on the certainty that a new normal will form as life shapes me with every minute, hour, and day that unfolds.
-S

*W*hile never belittling what a gift it is to be here, it's a tough thing to shoulder, being alive. Figuring out who you are and becoming the person you're meant to be, building your circle and finding your feet. Overcoming a lack of patience in what can be an otherwise impatient world. Drawing mercy out of seemingly merciless situations. Living with loss. Becoming full-on, decent human beings. Realizing your purpose and then finding a career that not only reflects but hopefully fulfills that purpose is ultimately what keeps you afloat. The entire process is a rhythmic operation and the fact that occasionally a beat comes down directly in our chests, allowing us to fully experience it is surely gratifying.

As the last few years have passed, I've started feeling as if all the puzzle pieces of my life lie scattered across the living floor in front of me. Some pieces are bits of time, experiences, lessons learned, and emotions and memories from places I've been, while others are still in the box—dreams, aspirations, and worries that have yet to take on enough of a tangible shape to determine whether or not they'll be a good fit. I've been lost, torn between scrambling and just staring at them, head in my hands, trying to figure out how they all fit together. Despite being just a year shy of 25, I can't seem to help but feel a pull, a dire need to hurry up and finish the puzzle so I can see the final picture and get to where I eventually hope to be.

At 15 years of age I remember watching *The Notebook, Highschool Musical, and Twilight* with my friend in her parents' basement, talking about where we wanted to be by the time we reached our mid-twenties. We imagined having finished school, being well into our dream careers, and living off steady incomes. We were going to be in the best shape of our lives, figured we'd be engaged or at least in serious relationships, one of which would realistically be with a Hemsworth or Zac Efron, and possibly beginning to think about starting families. I laugh a little now because all of those predictions lead straight to happiness and victory. No turns, pit stops, or bumps, no room for unexpected dead ends or shifts in direction. Little did we know the years to follow would bring the realization that those seamless lives we dreamt of weren't exactly realistic. True, the actual road beneath my feet has been all but unswerving, but there's a meme that is never far from my mind: "You spend your early twenties thinking you'll have everything together by 25, but by 25 you realize you're still a child who likes to eat cereal for dinner and sing along to Disney movies, except now you have bills, taxes, anxiety, and can't sleep." Whoever originally wrote that, you sure hit the nail on the head, man.

May 2, 2018, 7:14 a.m.

For the past two years, we've put on a benefit concert for hospice called Hope through Harmonies. It was there, standing on the upper landing last week, when a thought hit me, and I'm talking HIT me, like a bag of potatoes right to the heart:

After four years of university I'm starting to question whether I see myself pursuing a career as a social worker. I chose this field since to me, there's no better feeling than helping someone along part of their road. I also wanted to one day be the kind of social worker I didn't have in high school because I can understand and empathize with the feeling that comes pouring down on one as a result of baring one's soul and having it left invalidated as a result.

I love working in hospice, but existing in this environment also confronts one with thoughts of their own quality of life. Music and writing are two things for which I live and breathe and I don't know if looking back on my dream one day and saying, "I wish I'd have gone for it," would sit well with me.

So, I've been second guessing a lot and have no idea what I'm doing at the moment. I also drove away with my favourite coffee mug on the roof of the car this morning. That's about it. I guess it's true, how just when things are going well, something comes out of nowhere to keep life from being boring and either test us or keep us on our feet.
-S

As I move into my mid-twenties, I'm finding that becoming a full-on, well-versed human being takes time. This reality has frustrated me because of how fast time is seeming to slip through my fingertips like tiny drops of rain—I don't particularly feel there's room for long detours. This overwhelming feeling is justified when the clock seems to be turning at an unprecedented speed while I race to build a career, pay bills, attempt to maintain a social life, and most importantly try to stay sane in the face of feeling lost more than found sometimes.

Last year I had somebody ask how it was that I could be 23-years-old and not have started my career yet. Bearing in mind we live in a society where at 18 we're supposed to have an idea about the direction we want to steer our lives, I still maintain there exists no "correct" way. There are more than six billion people on earth and not all of us could possibly do everything the same way, in the same order, or at the same time. I know of others who have been certain of exactly which profession they saw themselves in since they were kids while others have redirected their path, sometimes more than once. Some had children young while some are starting families in their thirties. Some marry young and are with their soulmate for life while some marry young and get divorced or meet their soulmate at 60 and still manage to spend 30 years with them. Pave your own way and remember: there is no cookie cutter timetable to be followed; a shift in direction or change in destination is totally fine.

Halfway through completing my degree, second thoughts about just exactly what I was chasing started coming at me and by graduation, they had elbowed their way into the front of my mind with a certainty I could've sworn was more set than cement. I did graduate in 2018 but realized a few letters after my name doesn't always secure happiness or a career. I lost myself in depression and anxiety again, each of which tend to come back and visit every so often to test my mettle. I took a big financial hit, moved back home, and went back to working the minimum-wage jobs I'd had at 18 while once again working to build a career from the ground up because I now know what makes me feel most alive.

My friend went a different route, opting to take an extra year of high school, is stressed over not having started her career yet, and spends more time studying and working than sleeping. Oh, and we still find ourselves sitting in her parents' basement at least once a week, feeling like adulting is soup while we're forks. At least we're studying, writing, and motivating each other to keep pushing forward and make something of ourselves.

Sept 20, 2018, 3:05 p.m.

On a short layover in Vancouver yesterday, I was sitting in the airport with a coffee in hand, listening to Sam Smith and Ed Sheeran. God, I love them. Simply brilliant. I took out one of the journals in the ripped bag hanging over my shoulder and flipped to a random page.

May 5th, 2010: "I feel lost sometimes and I'm struggling but I think that's ok. I'm not the same as I was yesterday and that's a good thing, I think. I'm finding me."

There isn't anything wrong with wanting to find yourself. I think it's something that can really centre a person. The levels of personal growth your head, heart, and hands can achieve when one embraces solitude rather than resisting it is surprisingly large. I'm definitely not the same person I was yesterday. I should listen to my 14-year-old self more often.
-S

My grandmother always had a puzzle on the go, spread beneath whichever hand-made tablecloth was being used on the dining room table that week. I remember peeking under the tablecloth to see how far along she was and being confused as to why, despite how large the puzzles often were, finishing them seemed to take her so long.

"Why does Grandma Arlene always do massive puzzles?" I asked one night after our usual homemade sundae desserts.

"Well, she enjoys seeing the picture at the end," Mom said.

"Why doesn't she just buy a picture in a frame and look at that instead?"

"Because it's not just about the final picture. It's the experience and joy of creating it that matters to her."

Right up to the unforeseen heart attack that lead to her death in 2008, she was inspired by the art of doing puzzles. I didn't fully grasp what it meant then, but I appreciate it now. This was a woman who firmly believed in fulfilment over instant gratification, in the joy of the journey over the destination, and puzzles stood as a symbol of the beliefs that shaped the way she lived her life.

The secret I've been somehow blind to so far is that life is observational; you don't need to know exactly where you're going or get there by the time your morning coffee's finished in order to enjoy the very moment you're in. I think evolving as a person is a lot about learning to be resilient and identifying the fact that we're constant works in progress. It's about finding what drives us as individuals and cultivating personal happiness based on those passions. It's not as much about obsessing over the end goal or crossing the finish line as it is about the experiences and lessons throughout the journey. Being alive is a process, just like a puzzle, and there are many stops, turns, doubts, missteps, speed bumps, victories, setbacks, lessons, and joys to be had throughout; each gives us another piece of the puzzle that make for the intricately unique stories and truths of our lives.

I don't know what my final puzzle picture is going to look like and I'm ok with that—being lost has value and the not knowing is actually kind of exciting. Figuring it out just means I'm living my life, trying to trust that instead of being hard on myself for not landing exactly where I'd hoped to be by now because I don't have all my pieces yet. I'll find a few each day and some will fit right away while others will have to be rotated, possibly be crammed in, and may not even be a seamless fit in the end.

Not long ago I received a kind tweet that read, "Cut yourself some slack and remember that life is a learning process. Only appliances come with manuals—the rest is ours to discover, love, cry over, yearn for, regret, remember, & most of all enjoy."

Take heart in that. My grandmother's love for puzzles is a humble symbol of this. I was 12 when her last physical puzzle was left incomplete but the picture of her life became whole. I wish I could sit at the table and do a puzzle with her again. I wish I could tell her *I understand it now.*

a grudge never held

2000

Feb 13, 2020, 2:14 a.m.

January 10, 1999, following a big bang, the dashboard is getting closer. I can hear glass shattering, but I can't see dad. Then, nothing. Flash forward, I'm looking around the back of an ambulance and notice dad's hand. Then, nothing. Then I'm sitting on dad's back as we're being rolled down a hospital hallway. I still haven't heard his voice. Now a nurse is carrying me by the underarms and trying to give me a god-awful, terrifying looking teddy bear that looks like it would probably come alive at night. Flash forward again to the bathroom, getting the extent of my injuries—a nose bleed and two black eyes—cleaned up. Considering Dad was thrown far out the back windshield, I find the extent of the injuries I endured as a little kid to be quite fortunate. Either someone was looking out for me that day, or Dad managed to do something to keep me as safe as he could. Or both.

Years later, after learning we'd been t-boned by a few kids trying to pass us, I was told, "Even if his legs had been broken, he would've run back to the car for you."

-S

My dad has taught me many things. How to change a tire, ride snowmobiles and dirt bikes, to forgive and to do so without call for settlement, how to drive a standard. He taught me to stay grounded and while always encouraging me to keep at the things that bring me joy, to remember how sometimes in life you just have to get out and try whether it works out or not. Of all of it, most importantly what I've been shown is how not to hold a grudge. I've been shown the precise opposite of this, actually. If I told him any of that, he'd probably say it's because he forgets things. He doesn't really give himself much credit or believe in himself as much as I think he should. Neither does Mom.

A grudge is a keen thing. Its persistence is uncanny and with resistance its spite will harbour past hurt like nothing else. It holds the potential to drink forgiveness dry and the more time that's given to it, the more its resistance to budge is as sure as a sinking anchor. Sometimes they're deserved, but holding one will only aid to sink your ship.

For years when it came to certain circumstances, my frustration towards Dad drove a gigantic wedge between us. He'd say things like, "Let it go, time will heal," and would flat out say he didn't want to make empty promises, and still I let time tick by in anger, sadness, and confusion. To think of this now makes my heart hurt since I understand his position a little more, having seen similar struggles myself over the years. Instead of being bitter over some habits or characteristics my naive eyes saw as selfish, I wish instead I'd said, "I know, but I love you no differently." It would've likely meant more and not damaged the relationship as much.

Not necessarily related to how I've handled situations with family, I do also have regrets in general; the worst kind are those with tiny sharp teeth that make letting go nearly impossible. Hence, a grudge actually fuels resentment. I recall a saying implying the freedom that resides in letting go, with a photo of an injured hand tightly hanging onto a rope, above the same hand letting go of the rope, reading, "Sometimes holding on does more damage than letting go." But, how does one make the decision whether to hold on or let go when both hurt?

After being asked whether some arguments or frustrations would matter if one of us were not here tomorrow, the answer was usually "no." I do my best to hold on to this outlook when those aggravating circumstances creep into my life because holding on to grudges makes me restless and unhappy. None of us is perfect, we're all human. We all screw up royally at times and when we do we should learn from those mistakes, not repeat them.

Throughout it all, we accept those we love for who they are despite the frustrations; when something doesn't sit right, we strive to keep the lines of communication and understanding open. So, shed the regret and the tedious "you done me wrongs," keep the good and let the rest go because the past can never be rewritten. It's an imprint on cement that will never remold. Pieces may linger but other than that the future is all that exists. It's like the writer Iain Thomas says: "It's up to you to yank your hand back, put it on your heart and say, "No. This is what's important."

Nov 29, 2019, 11:14 a.m.

I asked Dad how doing the gratitude journal was going. He said he had tried yesterday and could only come up with family as everything else was immaterial. Begrudging someone something you may not fully understand overwrites a lot of the good things; good things that make me proud to have those in my life, in my life. Looking at what we're grateful for sometimes refocuses us back into the bigger picture.
-S

chest press

Everybody's got their most embarrassing moment and I'm pretty sure I'll never forget mine. My friend and I were in the middle of our workout at the gym when I decided to have a go at the chest press machine. I sat up after my first set to see a guy standing there, who may I add was quite handsome, looking at me from *the* worst possible angle possible. Instead of my regular two chins, I had at least four and a half and probably looked like I was on the last stretch of a race across the city, exhausted and trucking towards the granola bar and Dilly Bar table at the finish line.

He was smiling and went on to say something, which I thought was, "what are you doing?" It would probably have made sense, given I didn't really know what the hell I was doing. Not thinking of taking my headphones out or even pausing Cher, I blurted out "Chest press!" with a confidence even I didn't even recognize. His eyes went wide and he kind of looked at me with a crooked smile, underneath an "I'm going to nod and smile, and slowly back away" look.

A few minutes later, my friend came up and smacked me up the back of the head with her headphones.

"What did you just do?" she asked, laughing.

"I was doing the chest press. What did it look like?" I said.

"No, with that guy. Why did you do that? He was a hunk!!!"

"Do what?"

I came to learn that he actually did not ask what I was doing, he'd asked me what my name was. Yikes, why am I like this? And yet, a few days later I was on my way back to brave the scene. *Nah, he won't be there. What are the odds?* I thought. Well, I thought wrong. He was there. And I looked like a dish rag, so I stayed on the stair-climbing machine for an extra 42 minutes until he left. As one might assume, we're getting married now. Kidding, that ship sailed before it anchored. Oh well, sometimes you just gotta laugh. Like the other day when my friend and I were out for breakfast, I accidentally ordered a vegetarian omelet with ham.

Find humour in the little things. Laughter is the best medicine and is sometimes the only way through.

11,000 seemingly insignificant feet

2017

Sept 29, 2017, 3:12 p.m.

Planning and preparation are noble things, but there's something beautiful about spontaneity. Outside of spur-of-the-moment decisions that may lend themselves to destructiveness, spontaneity is proving to be an avenue to serve current needs and demonstrate the awe of living in the centre of a moment.
-S

There's a certain kind of bittersweetness that comes with really living in a moment. I find it to be such a difficult, yet rewarding task to achieve. Tending to only what's currently happening and absorbing the details of exactly where you are. I try, but it's not something that comes easily. Somehow, worries about the future pull on one pant leg while bygones pull on the other. Autopilot mode carries many through their days, chipping away at general mindfulness. I can't tell you how many times I've pulled into the driveway and thought, *I don't even remember most of that drive home.*

On the other side of the coin, I wonder whether the mindfulness it sometimes takes to hold steady in a moment makes me not necessarily live in the moment. Does the success of it mean consciously placing and holding yourself in one at all times, or just sometimes? Does the focus it requires mean you're not really living in the moment at all? I don't know. It hurts my head. Regardless, I do think there's a tendency for humans to dwell more on the past or to look far into the future; they're much easier things to focus on than the exactness of where we are right now.

The part that both breaks my heart and sort of repairs it at the same time is that everything is really a series of moments. I used to get hung up on the fact nothing in life felt permanent but now I know when moments reach their conclusions, they just open up space for new ones to present themselves, leaving behind memories and feelings to cherish.

One thing I'm certain of is in early fall of 2017 I finally felt what it's like to be wrapped in a moment, to see the world from a totally different perspective. I'd just spent the day at hospice, which was fulfilling as always, yet that morning I'd awoken with a heaviness I couldn't shake. I knew what depression and anxiety felt like and while there was some degree of that happening, something else was mixed in that I couldn't quite put my finger on; it felt sort of like taking a sip of a drink and only recognizing what two of the three ingredients were.

I was walking across the parking lot, not headed anywhere in particular, and couldn't help but notice how thick the air felt for a September night. The sky was a grey gunmetal colour mixed with the slightest tint of blue, as though threatening rain. It took a minute before I realized the person I'd been walking with had stopped long ago. I strolled back over with one hand in my pocket, guitar case in the other.

"Maybe you need to do something to make you feel alive," she said.

"Yeah, maybe I'll go jump out of a plane," I responded lightheartedly.

With a smile she said, "Maybe not that extreme. Just something to get your body moving a little and remind you you're alive."

I put together enough change from the bottom of my bag for a coffee and headed to one of the locally owned coffee shops in town. Thinking back to the last time I felt alive, and I mean heart-beating-against-the-walls-of-your-chest-no-words-to-do-life-justice and also-might-pee-a-little kind of alive, I grew saddened at how far back in my memory I had to go. Spinning the coffee cup around on the table, one of the presenters from a conference I'd attended entered my mind. She encouraged everyone to table the things they hadn't yet done but wanted to do—an impromptu bucket-list build, if you will. I figured why the hell not and started composing one on a napkin. Interestingly enough, as I was writing, I began to notice an emerging theme: fear. It made me ask myself if I thought I'd ever be content living life exactly the way I was, without marking any of these off. The answer was a resounding "No."

I started feeling this growing need to just DO something. Anything. At that moment, it didn't matter what it was, as long as it would show me I wasn't an empty version of my list; it would also serve to remind me that I was alive, sort of like when I see my food coming at a restaurant and I'm really hungry.

So, I hopped on the moment. Not being particularly fond of wind, falling, or any height much above eye level, the closest thing I'd ever gotten to an adrenaline rush in my life apart from performing music was jumping off a three-foot diving board with my eyes closed and wearing my dinosaur water wings when I was six. I figured a skydive was the best, most realistic and logical option.

In just a few hours, I started warming to the thought of this adventure. It was something new that would surely make me feel alive and it was a fear I wanted to prove I could face. It didn't have anything to do with the fact I got an email confirming the jump time with a list of associated risks above big, bold letters that read: DEPOSIT NON-REFUNDABLE.

It was pouring rain while I was waiting to get suited up at a small airport 45 kilometres from my home. After being told the likelihood of the jump happening wasn't looking good, Dad and I went for lunch with the hope that by the time we finished the sky would have cleared. In case it did, I kept it light, ordering a cheeseburger with onion rings and a strawberry milkshake.

Rain was still coming down, suggesting this may have been the universe's subtle way of telling me I could feel just as alive on the couch in my Christmas onesie watching *Suits*. I wasn't sure if I was content or upset. How easy it is to talk ourselves out of doing things outside of our comfort zone. I've managed to dissuade myself from many things in the past: taking risks, travelling alone, speaking up in a room full of people, plunging into the unknown, giving a voice to a story—it goes on. Interestingly, on the drive home, the sun broke through the clouds like a child running down the stairs on Christmas morning, the sky turning a cerulean blue. We turned around.

The instructors were cool guys. They even said (jokingly) the duct tape on the inside of the plane was only there to make people actually want to jump out. Thanks to them I was more concerned about not remembering if I had flushed the toilet at home before I left. It's funny, the things that come to mind when you aren't sure if you're going to survive the next twelve minutes of your life, and it were those thoughts that really made me catch my breath. I couldn't remember the last time I told my friends and Mom and Dad that I loved them.

As we took off and were climbing higher into the sky, we got strapped together so tight I practically ate my onion rings again.

"Ok, well this is good, right? We could probably just go from here?" I said, looking out the window.

He laughed and said we had just a little further to go.

"Is this the most extreme thing you've ever done?"

Play it cool, Sara. Play it cool, I thought.

"Pfft, no..." I said.

He looked at me.

"Ok, yeah."

Everything on the ground was shrinking to the size of pin heads and eventually blended into a beautiful landscape. Again, what in the flipping hell was I thinking? Well, to be exact, this:

What happens if I pee my pants? I hope we don't hit a bird on the way down. What happens if my heart stops? What happens if I pass out or throw up all over this guy? Maybe it will be fun. What happens if we die or land on top of someone because the parachute doesn't work? Why would anyone think this kind of anxiety is fun?

At the same time, my gut feeling was encouraging me to follow through, to find enough courage to tell fear to screw off, get on the plane, and just damn well do it. I knew if I didn't find that internal fortitude I'd be too awkward to ask the pilot to land the plane and I didn't want the good looking instructors to think I wasn't a bad-ass, even though with the helmet I looked like a nervous walking pylon. Or maybe there was something else going on deep inside me: like a plant reaches for a ray of sunlight, the quietest part of me is steering me towards where I truly want or need to be.

We reached altitude at 11,000 feet and I could feel my heart rate picking up, my hands starting to sweat. The camera guy went out and hung by one hand off the plane's wing, letting his body swing freely, while we moved to sit on the edge. The 80-kilometre winds pulled my cheeks back to my ears, so very attractive. The instructor pulled my head back and though I don't remember, I apparently asked if we were going to be ok and told him not to forget to pull the parachute. *You can do this, you can do this, you can do this*, I thought to myself. We rocked forward: one, two, and three and when our feet pushed off, I felt us flip forward and then back to level out.

Strangely, skydiving doesn't really evoke a falling sensation or stomach twist that often happens when you're riding a rollercoaster; it's more of a warm sensation. Like friendship and sunshine with a bit of peeing your pants thrown in, which might be because you're falling out of the sky with your life dependent on a parachute folded into a tiny backpack. The instructor shook my arms and I opened my eyes. I felt like I saw everything. Every meticulous worry slipped away, leaving only the sound of my beating heart. The weight of the world lifted and not one sorrow or regret could have taken me out of that moment. Well, except maybe if the parachute hadn't opened. Other than that, there was nothing. I saw the way the clouds contrasted with a sky I didn't even know could be so blue, I felt the wind rushing against the front of my body. I knew we were falling at 200km/hour, but it felt like we were floating. I tried to smile for the camera without losing my cheeks and looking like a doorknob, but I didn't care. It was the best feeling ever, happy and on top of the world, like I could do and be anything. I get the same feeling when I write songs or perform on stage.

When we landed, the heels of our feet were extended out in front of us and skidded across the grass. We landed on our butts and as the wind slowed, the parachute fell behind us. I felt light weighted and full of an overflowing amount of energy. Kind of like I'd just jumped out of a plane – go figure – and took a huge breath. It wasn't like one of the thousands of shallow breaths taken throughout any given day, but rather the kind that causes your chest to swell and your mind to clear. At that moment, in all of its 30-or-so minutes, the blinders I hadn't noticed I'd been wearing came off. To see the world from a whole other perspective, quite literally, was a truly significant circumstance for me. It showed me that I had been standing in the way of myself and made me realize that placing myself in the moment is good and why I'll do my best to repeat that more often. It serves to remind me where I am and that I'm ok right now. It actually reminds me to breathe, too. I still get sucked into the past from time to time and sometimes that's helpful when thinking back is a means of getting through the present moment. Anxiety still tries to push me into worrying about the future, and I know I've wasted time investing a lot of energy into small, trivial things, which has only served to take away from the here and now. Worrying, while sometimes justified, is a waste of time and energy. We're so busy filling the days of our calendars and rushing off to the next thing that we seldom stop to take stock of right now, when there is so much to be savoured from it.

I wanted to get up and do it again. If it weren't for the cost, I would have.

Who'd have thought that 11,000 feet in the air would be the catalyst that tipped me out of the wagon and into the moment, realizing that everything is temporary but that makes rejoicing in what is and was, that much sweeter. It spurred me on to start writing my first album that same night and feeling like I could finally move forward. I think what I needed was to see and feel something outside of the bogged down state I'd been stuck in and be reminded of how big the world really is and how much life is out there to be embraced. It's filled with so many more possibilities than one could ever imagine. The profound contentment I experienced that day hasn't really ever faded away. In fact, as I'm writing this, I'm reminded of the old sayings that imply how life is about doing as many of the things as possible that, upon even lending thought to, bring a faster beat to your heart and a brighter glow to your eyes. A mentor once spoke of "clearing the deadwood" from our lives that serves only as blockage to the creation of as many of these moments as possible.

So, go. Jump. Right into the moment and savor it. It's almost like a habit—the more you do it, the greater ease it brings. Let the fuel that holds the brightest, warmest, most passionate flame inside you help spur you on to do what often feels out of reach, and then keep doing it. Because when you live for the moment, it's harder to drop it inside the past or throw it to the future. Never underestimate the reach of a blue sky. It's a tremendous thing.

Until Now

Losing track of time, I hardly recognized
The reflection in this mirror as mine
I take flight when the winds blow
Half-empty glass stronger than any backbone

Chorus
It's all part of the road
Every turn and stone
Being bold, holding your heart in
the palm of your hands
A weight has lifted
Until now I've resisted letting go
Of every bent and rigid sorrow
Got a feelin' I could be someone

Threw away old maps and signs
Dared fear to bend, let me drive
Challenged black and white dreams
Painted in fading lines

Chorus
Sara Rose, Until Now, 2017

how many times?

"It's supposed to be hard, all the challenges in life prepare you for your future."

-A.D Dolphin

April 14, 2017, 6:12 p.m.

A light blue wooden decoration was placed in front of me this morning that read, "If you could attempt to do anything and knew you could not fail, what would you do?"
I stuttered.
-S

Maybe victory is just as much about recognizing how far you've come as it is about having the tenacity to get up after being knocked down. I find failure to be such a misused, often misleading word. Surely, for as much attention as success and the good side of the coin gets and how few failures are admitted to or posted on social media, one may come to the conclusion that failure is something to be ashamed of. Truth is, we all fumble and hope we'll ultimately make decisions that will get us somewhere, but sometimes we don't. We make mistakes and fall down, but if we look closely, we may find we've also succeeded in our own little ways.

The vibe often associated with failing at something can easily denote feelings of disappointment, humiliation or shame. When I was told not to expect to be successful in my craft because I'd never have a vocal range as large and beautiful as Adele or Celine Dion or a way with words like J.K Rowling or other renowned best-sellers, I started seeing most of what I did as a disaster. When I messed up and fell back into habits I was trying to break, I saw failure. When a relationship would hit a rocky point, when I didn't reach a goal in time or get the hang of something right off the bat, I saw failure. This response lead to me internalizing those negative feelings and brought me close to giving up on multiple occasions. The only thing is, I was overlooking the crucial point at which this negative vibe shifts toward one of growth and progress...

Failure and victory can coexist.

Once this insight is processed, failure stops deflating success: which, in my humble opinion is ultimately self-defined. In regards to my music, the main thing has always been that I want to be believed. It's not about "making it" to the top and raking in millions of dollars. I'm sure everyone's dreamt of something similar and maybe I'll make it someday, or maybe I won't. I don't have a crazy vocal range or knack for writing, I only know my way around creating a song by taking an experience and expressing it from the heart.

It comes down to this: I make music because it makes me feel good, it's fun and liberating, and it's gratifying knowing that it may make someone's day a little better in some way.

If while failing or falling down you're persistent in rising up again while taking personal responsibility, that's saying something. It shows the difference that exists between throwing in the towel and simply falling a few steps back. When you quit something, you leave it where it is and it never moves. When you take a rest after failure knocks you down, you can take the time to assess and then return with more knowledge. I'd always found the rebounding part to be the hardest until I realized why—I was forgetting to be my own biggest fan. When I failed or wasn't doing well at something, I wasn't cheering myself on to get back in the saddle. I was picking myself apart for not being good enough and that tore my strength down and held me under failure's thumb.

I remember a high school vice principal once mentioned there is no louder self-critic than oneself, so don't forget to be your own biggest cheerleader, too. The way I see it, if you've done your best, don't punish yourself for mistakes or failures any more than celebrating the things you've done to get where you are. Remind yourself you've done well and that small things, too, come around to bring huge victories.

It feels good to get things done or succeed in reaching a goal, but even if you fail it just means you're getting out there and trying and that in itself is pretty fantastic. As such, I think failing with grace is about having the courage to bounce back despite it. Its presence, as frustrating and challenging as it is at times, feels strangely good and motivating because it sits at shoulder height with growth, learning, resilience and achievement. Show me a person who has failed countless times, still continues to work hard because they've checked the facts, and hasn't learned a thing or grown an inch from it—I don't think you can. Look at our ancestors. It took years figure out how to paint their stories on walls and I'll bet they saw failure a few times before it worked out the way they wanted.

I'm listening less to the part of me that sometimes considers throwing in the towel and more to the part telling me to rise up. To overcome. To not let a setback overcome me or not leave things unfinished even when I find myself a few steps behind. I will conquer my doubt and defeat my fear of failure by continuing to see it as an ally; it's in my own fiascos that I'm seeing failure isn't a hindrance to success but rather a necessary part of becoming a better version of yourself. When failure knocks you down eight times, what matters is that you stood up nine times—even when there are a million reasons to give up, find the one reason that's suggesting otherwise.

So, my answer to the question on that wooden decoration a few years ago is now quite simple: Everything. I'm going to put everything I have out there, despite knowing I will probably fail and mess up a whole lot along the way because while the query of "what if I fail?" is loud, persistence and passion are much louder. I'd much rather keep taking the risk of failing and learning than live with the question of what life may have looked like if I'd taken action.

Onward.

day ones

1999

O ne of my favourite things about being a kid was never being bored. Grandpa often brought Josh and Adam over on Saturdays and we cousins were always sure to keep busy building forts in the living room, playing outside, sledding at the hill, or making a slip and slide in the front yard. Adam probably wouldn't be quick to confess to the princess dress-up days now, but since Day One, even when they'd tease me in good fun, the two of them have been some of my best friends and the brothers I never had.

In 2005, to our family's shock and disbelief, our family would become one less: Josh passed away in a biking accident at 14 years of age. I wish he could have had the opportunity to grow up and experience more of life. I still wonder why such horrible things happen to genuinely good people. He had such a gentle soul, like his brother, and the mark he left on everyone was nothing short of love and light. I miss him. A few years passed and, at about 13 years of age, I picked up my guitar and wrote "Taken So Young" in Josh's memory. Almost ten years later it was recorded and put on my first album, *Until Now,* and I was honoured to find it's been used at a few Celebration of Life ceremonies.

As Adam and I have grown and as life happens, we've gotten busy and don't see each other as much as we used to. I remain grateful in the knowledge that, if I ever need anything, distance won't disrupt the fact that we always have each other's backs.

The two of us have now spent more time without Josh than with him, but I look back on the days we had together with a smile. Never forget that those around you are a blessing—there's always someone out there who wishes they had it as good as you.

They were and will always be my Day Ones.

1999

Taken So Young

Looked at a picture hanging on my wall
A flood of memories rushed in I could not forestall
A gentle soul walking a life with love
I think of the man you were going to become

Chorus
But I hope that you spread your wings and fly
And I hope you're dancing with angels in the sky
Maybe God had a plan that I my
heart just can't understand
You were taken so young

Catching butterflies and building
forts in the living room
Mom said kids look at their wings
Watch them fly
They are free

When loss strokes our hair
And wraps its arms around our hearts
Your absence here is tearing us apart

Chorus
When life has shown no mercy and
collected precious time
It's like always living a long goodbye

Chorus
Sara Rose, Until Now, 2017

pot of gold

Feb 1, 2019, 12:13 a.m.

I'm not embarrassed or ashamed of what I do and do not have. Materialism has never really defined fulfillment for me. I was raised with the perspective that true bliss isn't money-oriented or found in one's belongings, but rather comes from experiences, love, laughter, a willingness to contribute empathetically, and the people around you.

A five dollar sweater from Walmart and a 200 dollar sweater from Michael Kors will both keep you warm. Hell, you can find happiness in a shoebox if you're with the right people.

-S

Very little is required to make a happy life. I say that as if I've successfully tracked down the famed pot of gold that many spend days, likely even years, chasing down. I'm not, though. I'm actually sitting under a ripped umbrella at a rusty metal table and chair on my lunch break, working a minimum-wage job that couldn't be further from my degree, I'm wearing old, ripped jeans and have $34 to my name. I don't have money or whatever else is rumored to be in that pot but I have a job, a home, and a friend. And I'm happier than I was.

The firmer the grip I thought I had on true happiness and the more I chased what I thought it was supposed to be, the more it became this idea of nirvana, an oasis that just grew shinier while moving further away. I've longed for it with every ounce of my being, to the point it almost could've been mistaken for an addiction. Looking for and overpromoting that kind of happiness with such intensiveness, actually made me profoundly unhappy. As a result, I seemed to have been walking towards eternity, blindfolded and filled to the brim with frustration at losing sight altogether of what was being pursued. Statements such as, "just be happy" and, "happy up now, girlfriend" didn't help the quest, either.

"I don't know how!" I felt the urge to yell back.

I don't think it was one single factor that brought this feeling to the surface. Apart from the fact depression often tempers the genuineness of contentment, I think when we're young we're inherently happy simply because we've not yet known negativity, grief, tragedy, and despair. It isn't until we see the news, experience family dysfunction, profound loss, or hurt that we then go on to feel those things. If we could live in a bubble, we would be forever happy but that isn't reality so we have to find our own happiness and coping mechanisms to live a fulfilled, "of the moment" life. Not having considered this, I previously thought we were supposed to feel happy all the time and that other people must just be stronger-willed than I. I was wrong. They weren't happy all the time, nor are they meant to be.

May 4, 2017, 2:13 a.m.

If you're unhappy, then change whatever it is that's making you sad. If you can't change it, change how you look at it and move forward. If it's killing you, let it go. Sometimes holding onto certain things does more damage than good; there is little worth more than compromising your inner peace. (Moms are usually good at pulling optimism from messy circumstances and making the best of a bad day.)

I don't want to complain. I know what makes me happy and challenges me but also fulfills a sense of purpose. I think I've just avoided diving in because I'm scared of having something to lose.

-S

I've never been, nor will I ever be, an advocate for war, sickness, hatred, or immoral living. We have this world that knows (or should know) better and during the times when that isn't the case, bad things end up happening. Just turn the news on and you're guaranteed to feel the tug away from optimism hearing of something new giving strength to the feeling that our world is in a state of melancholy. There should be a news channel that only focuses on the good. I once asked a mentor why bad things have to happen. While agreeing the world would be a better place in their absence, she also referenced the inherent value of balance.

I believe greatly in that concept. Apart from the fact that everyone and everything would likely be the same without it, the thought of a universe that turns without it makes the hairs on my arms stand up. If difference were of no value, would we ever understand or appreciate true gratitude and goodness? Would there be love, or just hate? Or neither? Would peace be distinguished from evil? Would we recognize the blessing of wellness? Would goodness and gratitude be as tightly wrapped around us in times of pain and loss? Would it be possible to lean as hard into love and joyous moments without having felt the tugs of hate, pain and loss? If there were no bad days, would good days exist? Without their opposing counterparts, would the value of peace, wellness, love, happiness and good days be as authentically known? Even more so, would we recognize them? Feel them in the same ways? Appreciate them as much?

Everything is relative. We know how grand a limitless blue sky is because we've been caught in storms, we know about kindness and benevolence because our hearts have ached upon hearing of evil, disaster, and sin, and from war and suffering we come to understand the amity and tranquility of peace. We know what laughter is because we've shed tears, we know joy because we've gotten to know pain and we know about living because we know about dying. I'd like to think now I've got the sense to understand that just like what comes up has to come down, bad days come and go, and that there's no timeline for achieving utter delight. A good day is a bad day's companion, after all; the bad ones help to add value to the good ones. The ups and downs are what make life, life. And this is life:

You get the ups, the downs, and the in-betweens. It's what you make of those ups and downs that dictate what you get out of life. When I'm having a bad day, I pick up my guitar. I write. I exercise. I breathe, which sounds so simple yet is the number one thing I forget to do. I remind myself that not every day is going to be filled to the brim with joy and happiness. Some days are just bad days, not a bad life, and tomorrow is always a new day.

Oct 14, 2017, 9:13 p.m.

Simplicity is complexity's best friend. The latter just might not know it yet.
-S

Happiness isn't a destination that is met once things become less complicated or easier. I'm learning that there will always be some extent of complexity or messiness to life. Happiness's founding does not rely on, nor equate to, a life strife with complete perfection and an absence of difficulty. Rather, learning to rejoice in the moment encasing you right now. Today is a good day to be glad for what is and take control of your own joy by making the most of what is had right now. I mean, when the replay of your life is seen at the end of everything, are you going to be happy? Do things you enjoy because you enjoy it, even if you don't think you're good at it. Write. Paint. Dance in the rain. Stop waiting to lose the weight or gain the weight to wear a bikini. Donate not just monetary things, but your time. Help somebody. Listen to somebody. Hear somebody. Realistically expect the good. Sing at the top of your lungs with your best friend in the car because you can and because it feels good to laugh and be silly. Dance in the rain at a concert, but maybe reconsider peeing in the bush on the run back to the car because the headlights on the road will light up the bush in which you and your friend are crouching. Take stock of what you have. Tuck the good times away for safe keeping; for the days you need them to carry you. Mostly, remember what my friend says about materialistic things: they may bring temporary happiness, but it's not real. Happiness is family and friends and being with them. Laughing with them. Sharing your time with them. Having a huge house and a fat bank account mean nothing if you don't have family and friends with which to share your life.

A good laugh with a good friend helps. Life is so much easier this way.

2016

2014

a companion like no other

June 26, 2019

They say whoever believes that diamonds are a girl's best friend never owned a dog. That has surely been the case in my life. Many more of my years have been spent with a dog beside me than not and when Rosie, our first rottie, came home with us 14 years ago this whole diamond thing started to make sense. Over the years we heard a bit of hassle around the breed we chose, mostly revolving around how supposedly vicious Rottweilers are. It's not so much about the breed than it is about how they're trained. Both of our Rottweilers were petrified of mice—killers, eh? They were the best, most loving dogs and brought so much joy to our lives.

One of the first songs I learned to play on the guitar was "The Lion Sleeps Tonight" and it was quite funny how no matter when I played it or what was going on, if Rosie was around and heard it she would almost instantly lay down and fall asleep. She would also wake from a dead sleep and howl when "Big Yellow Taxi" by Joni Mitchell came on the radio, and her favourite toy to play with was an empty, unused jerry can. Dogs have such unique personalities. So very loyal, too. The fact that they can't say anything, yet can so easily pour love and build a relationship like no other, is simply amazing. I don't, and will probably never, understand how it makes sense for some people to harm an innocent animal or inflict any kind of pain or neglect upon them. They've got souls and know how to love and feel emotion just like we do. People can really suck sometimes.

Rosie was diagnosed with bone cancer at six years of age and when it was time to let her go, the vets came to our house. They had such a kind and compassionate way of moving us through the process; it was as if she were a human being passing away. I think all living beings should be treated this way. While I played her song on guitar, Rosie was let go on her favourite hill outside the house, the same hill where many chipmunks had been chased and tennis balls caught.

The house felt empty without her. The presence animals bring to a space is fulfilling and it wasn't long before the hollowness caught up to us that Mom and Dad welcomed another rottie into our home. I was in Grade Ten when we went to Sarnia to pick up our sweet girl, Cedar. Our cat Smudge bullied her constantly, walking on his hind legs and swatting her bum when she would trot away down the hallway. She, like Rosie before, had such a gentle manner about her and was a protector and companion to us like no other. We were lucky to have had her for eight years; once she was diagnosed with bone cancer, it all happened so quickly. We took her for a Timbit in the Tim Horton's drive thru near the vet, she was spoiled with treats and a huge meal when we arrived, and she went peacefully in our arms.

After Mom and Dad left the room to get the truck, I shared a conversation with the vet who'd cared for Cedar her whole life. Not that her answer would have changed anything at that point, but I asked her if we'd made the right decision in letting her go. What she said was something that will forever inform the profound appreciation I have for dogs and the loyalty in which their companionship is founded.

With tears in her eyes, she said, "Dogs are stoic. If she reached the point of not being able to walk anymore, she'd still have crawled to you if you called her. They are the most loyal beings. She wouldn't have let you see her pain. You made the right decision."

The loss of a dog, or any pet for that matter, is a hard one to take. They're family and can fix us in the absence of a single word. I will always talk to my animals as if they're humans even though they probably only comprehend a portion of what I say and sometimes look at me like I have eight heads. They are, as noted by our vet, stoic and loyal beings. I will forever miss and be grateful for the unconditional love, companionship, and silliness brought daily by my girls. Even the thefts of Kleenex and stolen bites of toast.

A few weeks later Mom, Dad, and I took Cedar's ashes and spread them in the spot we felt was her favourite place to run like mad and be free. The view was quite breathtaking—we were standing at the highest point and could see for miles. The trees were full of life, the sky was blue, and the hills rolled on forever. Sometimes I think I take where we live for granted. After Mom said a few words I opened the lid of the urn and, let me be clear here, there had been absolutely NO wind ALL morning, but as soon as I tossed them an enormous gust of wind picked up and brought the majority of what was just let go squarely into our faces. I thought that only happened in movies but apparently, timing and weather say not.

One last lick.

perfectly imperfect

Sky Kintsugi, Rami Shami, 2020

"To all the girls who think you're fat because you're not a size zero, you're the beautiful one, it's society who's ugly."

-Author Unknown

Dec 29, 2016, 3:14 p.m.

I wish I could go back to the young girl I was
And tell her I'd be ok, tell her I was loved
That this world is yours and this world is mine
Dream big and hold your head up high
When I was eight there were monsters under
*   my bed*

Now the biggest ones are inside my head
And the grass stained dresses I wore as a little
girl
They're neatly folded in an old dresser drawer
They say the world sees us as we see ourselves
I guess I'm still learning to love myself
-S

When I imagine perfection, I picture the kintsugi bowl. A traditional Japanese form of art, these bowls are created by the joining of broken pieces and fragments of pottery. No two are alike and the cracks from the repaired breaks are seen as part of their history. The lens through which the bowls are seen is tinted with the perspective that beauty resides in imperfection. Ironically enough, I first heard of them in the midst of a long-standing trek to perfection.

Whenever I hear about perfection equaling beauty, it makes me want to poke my eyes out. The actual definition of perfection is, "The condition, state, or quality of being free or as free as possible from all flaws or defects." So, does this tendency mean if somebody wants to be perfect, they can't be real? Every real human being I've met isn't perfect and that is the most beautiful aspect about them. I must mention, based solely on history, that I don't know if I'm really one to talk; at some point as a teenager, I developed a real knack for being extremely hard on myself. I started walking around with the unjust belief that if I wasn't achieving the dictionary definition of perfection, whether it be in my music, academics, or life's generalities, that I wasn't good enough. I never felt pretty enough to wear my hair back, go out without makeup on, or be myself. My body became more of an enemy rather than the real ally it is, getting me out of bed every morning and allowing me to live my life.

I don't even know who I was trying to be perfect for—it certainly wasn't for me, given the great concern I placed on the opinions of others. Perhaps my overall drive was partly related to one of the many facets of human nature: the quiet, underlying drive to apply attention and energy to what others think of us. We've all wanted to be liked by people. Many are afraid to find their feet due to their worry of what others may think and personally, the amount of energy I wasted over the years in this fool's errand bugs me because what others think of me is none of my business, shouldn't sway who I am at a basic level, and I'm willing to bet people are too wrapped up in their own lives to really give a damn anyway.

I applaud everyone who puts their shoulder into living without fear of judgement. To live without it is a really bold and confident thing to do, though not the one of the easiest. I try not to compare because I know, as I'm sure you all do too, that self-sabotage will surely follow. When you compare yourself to someone else's gifts, all of your magic is left, ignored, on the back burner.

May 13, 2018, 3:14 p.m.

I don't know why we question our ourselves, but we do. Just ask someone to talk about something close to their heart and you're guaranteed to see them fall into their purpose and worth, which is

*often so much more than they're even conscious of,
but see them fidget when you ask them what they
love most about themselves. If they do manage to
answer, a "but" is likely to follow. We need to just
say thank you and not seek reasons to make those
truths unjustified.*
-S

Overwhelming doubt is just a part of what it is to be human and everybody needs reassurance and validation sometimes. However, it's when the direction you face isn't dictated by you and the reflection in the mirror is shaped by way of others that we forget why we were even reaching for the bar in the first place. It's also hard when you consider what society communicates to young people about mental health and physical appearance—this fabricated idea that unless you don't have flaws, you're not perfect. If somebody dresses well, they're showing off, if they dress plainly they must not have money, or if they back down they must be a coward. If somebody drops a pile of weight or puts weight on, they're either struggling or unwell. Criticism is everywhere and I don't think we always realize it.

I admire those who are authentically and unapologetically themselves and have realized that you'll never be at your happiest under someone else's light and certainly not while living through the haze of worry about what others think. Being someone I'm not and trying to be liked by everyone by shaping my life in a way that pleases all but myself has never actually gotten me very far. In fact, it only landed me in a very chaotic place; skin crawling, feeling like I was always walking around with that sideways tutu once again.

I personally believe that perfection is a hollow state of being with constantly-moving goalposts; it can't be defined without bias and subjectivity. Since no two people are the exact same in every way or are put back together after being broken in the same way, much like the kintsugi bowl, how can anybody be perfect? Who decides what does and does not illustrate perfection? What is the defining point at which something, especially something as real as a human being, is deemed flawless or defective? Nothing real is either of those two things. Yet for some reason we strive for it and all it does is make us undercut ourselves, ruining any chance at inner peace.

What one sees as "perfect" may also differ from the perceptions of another. I like the amount of subjectivity involved in making a person who they are. If there were one single definition of perfection, life would be so terribly boring.

Feb 28, 2018, 3:12 p.m.

The vocals for "Taken So Young" were being recorded a few weeks ago and I think we had gone through about 20 takes by the time we finished and it was sent along with the rest of the album to the producer mastering the album. I was being so critical about one part not sounding perfect that I got really down about the entire song. Instead of listening to the whole song, I was focused on this one part as the overarching quality of the whole song. The producer mastering the album sent me a note a few days later expressing how that exact part of the song caught his heart strings because that was where I was most vulnerable and connected. It left me dumbfounded, wondering if he was listening to the same track I was. His note continued on to say something I'll always remember, which was that we're human. Those tiny mishaps that stand out more to the artist than someone listening from their own frame of reference rather than solely as a critique are often just the thing that makes the whole piece perfectly real and raw.

I guess it's sometimes in our own criticisms, insecurities and vulnerabilities where beauty rests from the perspectives of others. We ended up keeping the track as it was.

-S

In Japanese, "kintsugi" means "golden joinery." Rather than being threatened by difference, we need to thrive on it by coming together and empowering each other, emphasizing the differences in one another that make us unique because we make each other fuller and better. Striving to reach perfection has been a waste of time. Take worth, self-esteem, and value, for instance. They're big words and are all things ultimately shaped and decided from within. Whatever you think your worth and confidence is, is what they will shape up to be. When you walk through life with the belief that you don't possess those values, it's a slippery slope into bad decisions and depression. Focus on your own definition of worth—it's the one that matters most because it lays the groundwork for where we go and how we live. It's sort of like making a garden in your front yard, but in your head. First, you have to figure out where you could use one, then you pull out all the weeds so there's space to plant the flowers. Then you water the flowers, let the sunlight shine down on them, and watch them grow. Initially, I figured this idea was horseshit but it's not, it's really just about having the courage to be kind enough to accept ourselves and not run from the love we deserve. For me now, it's about how much I censor myself and as such, whether I decide to hide or use the voice that makes me unique in this world.

I began to realize this as I reminisced about a time in my teens when I'd been head over heels for this particular guy. He ghosted me after "the deed" was done and I remember automatically asking if it was because I wasn't skinny enough. Not even a full minute passed before, "yeah, sorry" came through. I was mortified but because I internalized it and how I started seeing myself both physically and emotionally changed. Ironic, given this situation wasn't related to the kind of person I was at all. Nonetheless, I had been motivated to try to be someone I wasn't, eating less and working out more, all with the intention of being good enough for somebody someday. How is it that even when we hear ten compliments and one negative one, more often than not we will focus on the negative one. I should've recognized from the jump that he wasn't good enough for me.

I'm not perfect. Far from it, actually. My weight fluctuates, I have stretch marks, I'm not sure where exactly my purpose lies, and I'm still learning to love myself. I mess up, make mistakes, bite my nails when

I'm overwhelmed, and rarely please everyone. I have scars, but that's just because I have a story. However, I'm doing the best I can to let go of who I think I should be and instead I'm trying to hold fast to who I know I really am. I don't want to wake up years from now looking back with regret on all of the things I wish I'd done in order to live a big life and the inner peace I'd compromised in the name of perfection.

If I could write a mantra for every person, including myself, who has ever felt a sliver of doubt around perfection equating to worthiness in any degree, I would write this: Throw the idea of perfection out the window, accept and love yourself as nothing less than the real, beautiful human being you are. Unconditionally. Do your best every day and let your best be satisfactory without any concern of what others have to say about it. Drop the idea you need to be perfect. No one is. Drop the negative self-talk, pick up the worth. Drop the past, keep the lesson. Eat the Kit Kat, wear the bikini, and just enjoy the sun's rays. And for God's sake, be yourself and own it. Always. Not because there's a point to be proven but because there will only ever be one of you, and you are who you'll spend the rest of your life with. Let the things you may see as signs of imperfection illuminate because from someone else's point of view that may be exactly what makes you perfectly unique. Imperfection is beautiful.

parking garage

*J*nspiration's timing is impeccable and weird. It's the best when it comes by surprise and you find yourself scrambling for a scrap piece of paper and a pen, your computer, or a napkin in your car to get it down before the bright idea carries on past you and into another pair of hands. I was sitting in a parking garage in Toronto one evening in late 2017 with no phone, a broken-down car, and a guitar, when this happened.

I had heard Jann Arden was coming to town for a concert a few days before. I've looked up to her as a singer-songwriter for a lot of my life. She was going to be playing at Massey Hall in Toronto and there were only a few tickets left, one of which was in the front row; I splurged last minute and bought one. Oddly enough, I have only been to a few concerts, none of which were by myself but I can, without a shred of doubt, say this concert changed a lot of things for me.

She was so authentic. Funny. Candid and bold in the bravest, loveliest of ways. Going alone felt kind of weird but it was also really lovely to just take in the music and get wrapped up in the emotions in the room. To this day, it was one of the greatest performances I've ever seen.

A memorable concert transports you, and I have huge respect for artists who are unapologetically authentic and versatile. Artists who are able to create a real connection with their audience, regardless of size, taking them on a journey to beautiful new places with each song. People love going on adventures to new places, especially if those places, according to speaker Tierney Thys, "Outfit us with new lenses to see the ordinary in an extraordinary way...enrapture us and engage multiple parts of our brains simultaneously." Though I've yet to see them in concert, P!nk, Shania Twain, Ed Sheeran, Trisha Yearwood, and Sarah McLachlan are other artists whose music has touched my heart in ways I cannot explain.

It was about 11 o'clock as I was standing on the street realizing I hadn't the smallest clue which way to the parking garage and my car. I found my phone in the bottom of my bag, which ended up being useless as the battery had died halfway through the show. It was snowing and bloody cold out, and I was quite sure I would be telling Mom the next day that she was right in badgering me to wear a warmer jacket.

When I found my way back to the car, in the opposite direction of where I had walked, it wouldn't start and the tea pot light in the dash was flashing at me. No one was around and every scary movie I'd seen was now playing through my head. As often as things seemed to go wrong with that car, I still loved it; it was a 2010 standard Mazda3 and the first car I ever owned. I put about 250,000 kilometers on it between commuting to school and co-op in the three years I had it. My friend went through the same thing with her Rav4. We'd talk on the phone while we were commuting and could hear the banging and clanging of each other's cars. I usually just turned the radio up. If a tree falls and nobody's there to hear it, does it really make a sound?

I figured I may as well make use of being stuck, so I got my guitar out, pulled the crumpled concert ticket out of my jeans pocket, and started writing a song on the back of it. "Not Alone" was penned that night. Ironic, given I was definitely alone. Well, maybe I wasn't, who really knows. Regardless, those 45 minutes ended up being nothing short of extraordinary. Art runs on its own clock, I suppose.

You can have all these signs flashing in front of you that something is off or needing to be acknowledged, but if what needs to be felt is ignored long enough, you might break down and tend to it in order to move forward (and get home). Just like the teapot light in the dash, which I learned is not a teapot but an oil light. Sometimes you don't need much more than a few minutes alone with yourself to figure out where you are (though a GPS may have sufficed in this particular situation), and sometimes it takes pausing for just a moment to begin realizing just how long you've been avoiding whatever it is you're running from.

I felt so much that night, from hearing an incredible musician connect with some five-hundred people who were brought together through music, laughter, stories, and tears and made to feel like they weren't strangers, to sitting alone in a parking garage with a guitar, pen, and the back of a ticket. It's not always such a bad thing to see where you are and be there sometimes.

Don't ask me why or how my car suddenly ended up starting because I have no clue, but it did and I made it home. It could have gone much worse in about a hundred different ways, but it didn't. I got lost, realized it wasn't just on the map, and found my way back in more ways than one.

Not Alone

Hear a familiar song playing on the radio
I breathe in a dusty old memory
I wasn't just lost
Could've sworn my heart stood still
From the truth that hung all afternoon

Chorus
I don't know where I'm going
But I've been running away
Had to believe things would be ok
Just a little longer a few more miles down this road
Honey you are not alone

Bear the weight of the world
Then wonder why your knees grew
weak and it hurt to breathe
Well it's taken just as long to heal as it did to hurt
It's quite strange how against the light
All the broken bits light up inside

Chorus
Sara Rose, Until Now, 2017

107

not backing down

Dec 12, 2019, 3:09 a.m.

If something's not going to be given the power to bring me to a halt, why would I allow it the power to be a nuisance? Seems simple enough.
-S

I 've always wanted to be the person who never backed down in a fight, but I was the kid who rarely spoke up in middle school, high school, and most of university. I kept my head down for the most part and was always off to the side, just writing journals or songs. I did wonder when in the name of Mars I was going to find my confidence like all my peers and family members seemed to have found theirs. Odd, given I had no problem singing in front of people.

I never imagined my name lit up on anything more than the phone screens of the girls who found their fun in going out of their way to make my life hell for a little while. Getting pushed around and being picked on didn't help.

I thought I was weird and that being weird or different wasn't wonderful at all and I hated that. I wanted to be bold and brave and wear my heart on my sleeve with strength and without hesitancy, to have fun while not being the shy one anymore. See, I couldn't understand how being weird can actually be a beautiful thing in this world. I saw just how deeply I felt and analyzed the world as a flaw. I loved the idea of being the exact opposite of who I was.

It's a terrifying thing, being bullied or having your worth be outwardly challenged or undervalued—even witnessing it can be scarring. Thinking of those who live it every day, and in more extreme cases those who have lost their lives to it, makes me heartsick. There is no reason to tear others down. If you feel there is and it makes you feel better with your own problems, I don't know what to say other than to seek help.

If I could go back in time, there would be a lot of situations I'd approach and handle differently. To some degree, I think everyone would love a chance for a "do-over" with a past event of theirs if they could. In all sincerity, there are things I'm now confident enough to say and do that I would have never dreamed of saying or believing in ten years ago, and I'm certain those feelings will be even greater ten years from now.

This is not to say I think I'm great; there's a difference between being confident and walking around with your head up your ass. I won't apologize if I'm told I'm not enough or too much. Someone who refuses to be bullied and won't allow their worth to be stolen has realized their value. Stand up for yourself, don't back down from your worth, and be proud in doing it. You must.

a difficult mile

"One of the most significant realizations you can encounter that can make a difference between light and dark is knowing you are not alone."

-S.R

It's almost uncanny how good feelings, experiences, and memories are at creating harmony or dispute between the head and the heart. I've been finding that some of life's recollections show up, breeze through like the wind and are forgotten with time while others are steadfast, returning to pull the rug out from under my feet. Then there are the ones that see themselves in gradually, almost unnoticed, until I find myself shoulder deep in the heart of them either going, "so much has grown or changed," "well, fuck," or "how did I fall so far?" Or even all three! Those are the ones that feel, like the ink on my skin, almost unequaled in their permanence. They're tender at times, yet the details they capture reveal our truths and stories that are forever evolving in meaning.

Over the last eight years or so, one particular mile I have travelled has gradually coloured the lens through which I see the world, ushering in a darkness I've struggled to accept, let alone imagined myself ever facing. This stretch of my life nearly became an empty spot in my history, like a book with faded and smudged ink on its middle pages.

A shroud of hesitancy and trepidation enveloped me when Ico life. Apart from the unease that the process may stray from being a cathartic one, the risk of essentially reliving certain life experiences gave rise to a feeling of apprehension that often accompanies opening oneself up to vulnerability. I felt rigid and anxious to turn the playback volume up because doing so contrasted the general quietness I've become comfortable bringing into the world. There was also pride, that very shame-propelling thing that does its darnedest to sever vulnerability and pull us back from exposing and giving dialogue to some of the very things that simply make us human.

I also worried about "outing" a corner of the healthcare system by voicing an encounter that wasn't so grand; a corner which exists with an intent to be a dependable safety net but which actually proved to be a net with a gaping hole in it. Eventually I was held up by it, thanks to a few outside factors.

These apprehensive feelings only reassured the need to continue writing. A great quote by Erin Davis, kindly forwarded to me by Lisa Brandt, kind of says it all, "You can't be brave without being vulnerable." In equal measure, I'm a firm believer that the more acceptance, patience, and conversation that are had around the honest realities of mental health, the more we combat the stigma that silences and undermines so many stories, voices, and fatigued souls. The less we close off paths to healing and the more we help hold one another up the further we move, in unison, toward the greater resilience of humanity and society. I'd like to live to see a world where dishonor or shame towards a completely human experience doesn't exist, or at least know I contributed a little bit to the ongoing creation of one.

I'm surely not an expert on depression and anxiety, despite feeling like they were a fog that plagued me for a number of years and still find their way into my stride or catch my breath. A diagnosis was given in university, though their start line is inked much further back. Various degrees of each have hovered over many hours, days and months of my life from when they began rearing their heads in high school up to this very day.

Bear in mind, I consider myself to have had a charmed childhood. We weren't rich but I was never made to feel worried about it. Mom and Dad always worked hard to live humbly and do that which brings joy—I admire them for that. I had a roof over my head, food on my plate, and things to look forward to. I've known that I am loved. I have parents who would move heaven and earth to ensure my happiness and friends who'll always have my back, yet the sorrow snuck in and began shading my mood and perspective on life like cataracts. I was a happy-go-lucky, healthy, and outgoing kid who went quiet when I hit adolescence.

I remember noticing the ease my friends had in letting joy carry them through their days, in accomplishing tasks I'd typically be digging my heels in to even start. They seemed effortlessly happy, further underscoring my struggle to be that way too; everyone knows how very hard acting joyful can be when you're simply not.

I didn't know how to be happy anymore.

As I struggled to find purpose while dealing with life's realities, those things I previously loved and enjoyed doing began to fade away. Mom used to say, "these are supposed to be the best years of your life." I know she wished for nothing more than for me to be happy and live the most fulfilled life I possibly could. I wanted that too but I couldn't see how being a usual teen fit in with what I was going through. The simple act of facing people and upholding a conversation felt like a challenge because I was horrified at the thought people would know something was up the minute they saw me; there were also days when I was surrounded by others, yet somehow managed to still feel very alone. I was just so down and out and couldn't understand why. It was sort of like having a stomach ache on a near-constant basis and not really knowing why or what the pain is, just that it's there and it hurts. I lost sight of who I once was and the ability of imagining my life without depression faded. I used smiling as a Band-Aid to mask the emotional pain I was in and the sadness I felt, whose volume I often didn't even understand. My appetite bounced from bottomless to nonexistent. Constant exhaustion filled me, yet sleep was barricaded by worry and, at times, contemplations on how I was going to end my life only to realize I didn't care whether I lived or died. I saw myself as a failure at best either way, and was existing as a result of not knowing how to live anymore.

Years later, when a diagnosis had been linked to these feelings, I learned that depression is much different than sadness. It's smiling and feeling good with friends in the afternoon but feeling numb throughout the night. Sometimes it's halfway through a good belly laugh with a friend. It's not loving or caring at all or loving too hard and caring too much. It's feeling ok one day and seeking out a fake fix to fill a paralyzing hollowness a day later. J.K Rowling expressed it best when she said, "depression is the most unpleasant thing I have ever experienced... it is that absence of being able to envisage that you will ever be cheerful again. The absence of hope. That very deadened feeling, which is so very different from feeling sad. Sad hurts but it's a healthy feeling. It is a necessary thing to feel. Depression is very different." As for what lights its flame, everyone is different. Sometimes it's genetic, sometimes it's situational, an event or experience that changes you. Other times it comes on when you hit adolescence and life's realities become more "real."

Regardless of the onset, sometimes being able to give something a name, relating to an experience from another perspective, or identifying the origin of a pain makes it less abstract and more concrete. As I would come to learn, mine was mainly due to a genetic vulnerability—an imbalance of the serotonin and dopamine chemicals in my brain, stress, and situational factors. I was prescribed medication to balance my mood and therapy to learn the coping skills that when applied would allow me to manage my wellness.

Depression clings to my ribcage like a lost, heavy breath trying to find its way back to a pair of lungs, albeit wearily and unsuccessfully. It makes me feel emotionally and physically weak, as one may feel while treading water with weights around their ankles. It tries to convince me I don't matter, tiptoeing into my day or grinding life to a halt by expanding itself into every minute of every day. Then, because the two are often quite good at building off one another, anxiety pushes its way into my head and I begin to overthink every word, move, and niggling thing. It wastes positive energy, swelling to create more space for worries and wrapping those worries around things that either haven't happened yet or that may never happen.

Together, depression and anxiety grew into an antihero version of Batman and Robin in my story, changing nearly everything about the way I viewed myself and life in general. They thrive on rumination and on sticking around to watch you try and get up and out from beneath their thumb while they nip away at sole purpose. Alone they're strong, but together their symptoms can become debilitating and fierce. The one common trait they share, the very one that buckles their knees: neither are fond of being acknowledged or fought.

a difficult mile:
one breath at a time

---

*"You might think that you don't matter in this world,
but because of you someone has a favourite mug to
drink their tea out of that you bought them. Someone
hears a song on the radio, and it reminds them of you.
Someone has read a book you recommended to them
and gotten lost in its pages. Someone's remembered
a joke you told them and smiled to themselves on
the bus. Never think you don't have an impact. Your
fingerprints can't be wiped away from the little marks
of kindness that you've left behind."*

-Anonymous

There are degrees of everything. There are degrees of feeling downhearted or sad, of feeling depressed, and then there is the nth degree, the feeling of not being able to continue.

I grew up taking swimming lessons and always enjoyed being in the water. When I was about four years old, one of my lessons started with most of the class standing on a big metal stool in the shallow end, listening for direction from the instructor. We were going to be practicing treading water and because we were short, the stool was there so our heads could keep above water while we rested between drills.

As we got older and moved up in levels, the drills became more strenuous. The treading water we'd done in the shallow end years before moved to the deep end where we were instructed to tread for a certain amount of time while holding flutter boards high above our heads. I'm a strong swimmer, but I remember fighting to push through on this particular day years later. Minutes had been ticking by and I can still remember the heaviness and burning sensation that overtook the muscles in my arms, lungs and legs. A few of us started bobbing under the water while I watched the gigantic digital clock on the wall, wondering when the instructor was going to blow her whistle, indicating the end of the drill. Growing steadily more exhausted I soon started focusing on where the life preservers were located, where I would have had to move in order to touch bottom, and just exactly what happens to a body when it runs out of air. Will I sink? Drown? Make it out in the end? What if I ask for help and fail the lesson? What I remember longing for most, though, was relief.

No matter the circumstance, it's unsettling to feel like you can't breathe. Not long ago, there was a period of time I felt like I was right back in that pool, depleted, defeated and fighting to keep my head above water. Due to exhaustion or not, the only difference this time around is I was much older, treading in depression and anxiety and yes, this time I did sink to a painfully dark and emotional rock bottom.

In the weeks leading up to this, one of my oldest friends and I were sitting on the brittle old picnic table in my backyard. I don't recall the occasion, though it's safe to say it could have very well been an impromptu visit. Unplanned, on-the-spot get-togethers seemed to be the most convenient for us all during the years we were going through school and working part-time jobs with finicky hours. Our schedules contrasted like night and day 90 percent of the time, so when a window of opportunity opened we'd do our best to take advantage of it. It was summer and Cedar was running around the yard in complete heaven because she not only had one person to throw her ball for her, but two. Plus, she loved showing off for company.

I don't remember what we were talking about, but I do remember how I felt. Trying to hold a conversation while gathering all the backbone I could muster simply to jumble a sentence together. Just one single sentence to tell her, one of my best friends of nearly 15 years, how I was feeling. Frustrated, I was thinking to myself that I could have said it (whatever "it" would have come out as in that moment) 12 times by now if I could summon the courage to do it. It was like pushing a piece of string—not overly productive. Whatever was holding me back, I wasn't sure. Being judged by her? Doubtful. Thinking about it? Unlikely, considering it had been on repeat in my head. Fear of how it would feel to acknowledge it, name it, and say it out loud? Perhaps. Saying things out loud tends to make them more real. While doing so may diminish some of its power, often we're reluctant to talk about it because for some weird reason we think it may increase the likelihood of it happening. So, I didn't say anything.

August 16, 2017, 10:02 p.m.

> *I'm a lover of simplicity*
> *But sometimes it's hard to breathe*
> *It only hurts when I breathe, but I'm up off my*
> *   knees*
> *And if I go, will I sink like a stone?*
> *-S*

A few months later, days filled with depression and anxiety were outnumbering the good ones each week. I felt an overwhelming loss of control in my life and despite feeling worse off alone, I chose solitude and promptly dropped off the face of the earth. My friends said I'd become a shell of myself, and looking back now I believe I was. Distance had definitely grown between friends and family, and even I felt numb to my feelings. Locking myself away, metaphorically speaking, was the avenue I saw as a way to cope and it caused the good things in life to pass me by.

Anxiety pulled on one arm, wanting to lead me to a place where I felt scared to die and depression pulled on the other, trying to convince me that taking myself out of the equation was the only way of relieving my pain—a tough brawl to host. I was depressed, which heightened my anxiety, which in turn made me feel more depressed.

So went the rampant wheel-turning fears, persistent feelings of sadness and emptiness, and grief, every rotation nicking at the corners of my ability to see and reach out for important lifelines like hope, self-worth, love, inner courage, fighting spirit, and purpose.

The idea of things getting better was obviously only perceived from the outside, given that I was on the inside and could only wonder if they would. No matter how much I wanted to find a way back to serenity, light, and positivity, no matter how frustrated I got, the path there seemed about as clear as looking at a faded memory through rose coloured glasses. Or mud. It was the type of numbness which grew to envelop a person's entire soul, radiating pain from all angles, yet can only be described as a black hole I hadn't a clue how to fill.

And here was where I met my rock bottom moment. The resolve I had to live bent until it broke, finally reaching the point at which I saw the great escape that is suicide as the only option left to ease what felt to be unbearable suffering. There I was, head resting in my hands, within arms' reach of an irreversible decision. I remember the incredible weight of my eyelids and how each breath I drew suddenly required a Herculean effort. It's interesting how something as innate and straightforward as breathing can become so easily compromised while under depression's thrall.

Death seemed easier. Life seemed harder. That's a difficult thing for me to say. I wanted to fight. I wanted to be alive, just not this way anymore, drowning in a race with no finish line in sight. I had drawn up an impromptu will outlining my wishes, given a few things away or sold them and said it was because I needed the money (which wasn't totally untrue) and some important letters had been written. With that, a sense of lightness came, which these days brings such a wave of sadness upon reflection. I think it was because I knew the fight was near its end.

I don't like that I felt that way—that lost. It also wasn't as if I wasn't eternally grateful for what had made up my life and for the people around me who brought love and light into it. I recognize the gift we're given to be alive in this universe and that it should be cherished by living it fully and purposefully. I was frustrated and felt guilty to seem ungrateful for lacking the capability to wrap myself tight enough in gratitude, to recognize the choice I had to keep living while for many others that's simply not an option. I say that especially thinking of Josh, my cousin who had passed away at the age of 14 in a biking accident and never had the chance to grow up and experience the rest of his life. I also thought of those who were fighting for just one more day of life on earth but losing it to other diseases while I was contemplating taking mine. They'd have likely traded spots with me in a second if they could have. I had a means to live and couldn't see it.

There was also the rather isolative component of worrying my situation wouldn't being taken seriously because I had a good life. I did and do have a life many, as well as myself, see as fortunate. That's the thing about depression: it doesn't discriminate or back away easily.

It found a tear in my genetics and did what it does best: seeped through to find its way to the softest, often most fragile parts of us. It doesn't care about your age, what your story is, where you come from, the talents you bring to the table, how the world sees you, if you're homeless, or live on a $400,000+ salary. You could be a queen or the founder of a multi-million-dollar company and still be affected by it. It doesn't give a damn if you have a future, potential, a family, an exciting day awaiting, have a lot of life ahead of you, or have barely even lived yet. It. Does. Not. Care.

And I couldn't play host to it anymore.

February 18, 2017, 9:46 p.m.

> *Hell-bent on the hope*
> *That a break will pay its dues*
> *From the grounds that are always hinting and*
>   *giving reason*
> *To not feel good enough*
> *No soul should go unloved*
> *- S*

Feeling so much and not quite knowing how to express what you feel is strange. I mean, what is there to say when all the words have either been spoken or there's just so much smoke in the room that you fear if you take a breath to try and talk that you'll sputter and choke? Depression makes putting words to emotions challenging, and effectively silences one's capability to reach out. Later, I was advised on an excellent coping technique: basically, there's a picture of a stoplight and beside each colour is a definition of a feeling. Where green may imply a state of feeling good with mild-to-low symptom intensity, red may imply feeling very low with strongly intense symptoms. Orange would be somewhere in the middle. It was a great way of explaining how I was feeling if finding the words wasn't possible. Before I became aware of this strategy I would default to silence and stubbornness, adding yet more resistance to any chance of my admitting I wasn't in a good place and did truly need somebody.

If I was going to reach out, I didn't know what I'd even be asking for, how I'd explain myself and where I would even begin. Hell, at that point I didn't know if I'd even wanted to be saved. I'd also been so rotten to myself that I'd become equally rotten to those around me and, as such, felt guilty asking for help. The idea of reaching out felt futile anyway, which was all the more reason to do so. I knew if I hadn't, the night may have ended with me opting for a decision that may result in matters much worse, so I opted to call. I could have reached out to Mom and Dad, but I didn't. I would have wanted to know if it were my child; however, fearing the pain that knowing the specifics of my situation would have caused to those closest to me, I've found greater ease in accepting the support of close friends. I also felt sad and overwhelmed at the thought of them discovering their only child was out on an emotional ledge. I didn't want them to accept blame or mistakenly believe it was a result of something they had or hadn't done.

When I called my friend, I told her I didn't know what I needed but that I was afraid I was reaching my limit and wasn't sure I felt completely at ease to be alone. Within a half hour we were sitting beside each other.

"Talk to me," she said.

"I don't want to let anyone down, but I don't think I can fight through this pain anymore. We know people who fought for many more years than I have and they're making it through. I've been dealing with this huge inner fight for almost a decade and it's breaking me," I said.

"No, it's making you stronger, you just don't see it. I think it's like you not seeing yourself as we do. You need to truly look at yourself and listen to the good, happy Sara who sees the stuff we do, and be honest with the doctor and therapist."

"I know but I can't do this anymore. None of this really matters," I said.

"Well, it should matter. You can do this. You are not on your own. You have more than you think. Fight for it, you are more loved and stronger than you'll ever think and know. You're doing yourself an injustice if you act on this moment's emotion by turning to an irreversible choice. Getting through will be hard, maybe the hardest thing you ever do, but it will be worth it," she said. "I believe in you. Can you just promise me a little bit more time?"

Being as far in as I was, I thought it was an unfair request. I knew it meant refusing to give in to the feelings that were overriding the good things in life and that felt impossible. Yet, for some reason using a pinky promise against something as big as what was essentially my existence didn't feel trivial. Had I not agreed to her request, I'd have likely attempted to take my life that night.

Something that's not been far from my mind since that evening is the question of reason. The reason why someone who may have appeared to have so much to live for left this earth by ending it all may never be known. How they were regarded by others may not have been the same way they felt about themselves. There are people who I thought had absolutely everything to live for and still they died by their own hand. This goes for intentional and accidental acts, including some overdose cases. Regardless of the foundation, it serves as a reminder that pain doesn't always show and how unspoken fragility or unsteadiness may well be lurking behind someone's smile. People don't have to look sad or seem depressed on the outside to experience depression, they don't have to look like an addict to be facing what can be a second-by-second struggle with addiction, and they don't have to be visibly or constantly restless to know what anxiety feels like pulsing through their bodies. Some of the seemingly happiest, strongest, and most confident people I know currently struggle or have struggled with their mental health and/or addiction and give a surprising voice to the number of inner quarrels they've gone and go through because of it. The truth of the matter is a lot of people are silently fighting all manner of internal battles; it also goes to show how success doesn't preclude feelings of despondency, either. Unplanned or not, you have only to look at beloved personalities Robin Williams, Kate Spade, Ernest Hemingway, Mac Miller, Tom Petty, Amy Winehouse, Heath Ledger and Anthony Bourdain.

Signs often go unrecognized, as well. Some go quiet, some spin out, some don't give anything away, some appear the happiest they've ever been. Occasionally the signs are flashing neon and nobody knows what to say because it's frightening. I've felt afraid of saying the wrong thing for fear it would be misinterpreted or may actually worsen matters. One thing I will say, phrases such as "You don't look depressed," "Why are you using when you have so much love in your life?" "What could you possibly need to escape from?" "How could you be depressed, you have a great life," or a statement such as, "I don't think you'll do it. If you were going to, you'd have done it by now," achieve nothing, while there is great potential in using phrases such as "How can I be there for you right now?" "What are you feeling?" or, "Could I sit with you for a while?" It is of the utmost importance to not minimize someone's pain. Instead, empathize, encourage, and try to understand even one aspect of it. Leave judgment behind and tear down the rear-view mirror. Be human and be kind.

If it's been awhile since you've heard from someone or you notice someone hasn't been around all that often, be the one to reach out. Let them know you're there; a call or text can make all the difference and turn somebody back around. We need to check on each other, even the strongest and happiest of our friends. If there's any indication that someone's personal safety is an imminent concern, it's ok to ask them about it and don't leave them alone. Prevention methods are often most effective when early warnings are recognized and help can then be provided. Should support from professional resources or aid be required that falls outside your comfort zone, call someone who can provide that support or head to the nearest emergency department and walk the mile with them. In the end we're all human and we all want to feel secure.

I think when psychological pain tips the scales away from comfort and solace, we become more able to consciously recognize that imbalance. I relate to it in terms of having weights piling on your shoulders; if enough weights are added, a person will eventually collapse.

If someone had been looking at my life from the outside, they would probably have seen a lot of good things happening over the couple of years leading up to my breaking point. I wrote and dropped two albums, headlining a debut release of one, did a few music videos, won a couple of awards, graduated university with honors, and reconnected and grew close with a few really wonderful people. I was teaching guitar part-time, playing shows, had a job to pay the bills, transitioned from a student doing a placement at a hospice into a vice president role on their board of directors, was shoulder deep in writing, and was (still am) figuring out in what direction I should steer my life. While trying to be a good friend, daughter and granddaughter, I was also wrestling with an incredibly raw ache deep inside. This internal strife both weakened and distracted me, causing my family and me to constantly butt heads. I was spreading myself thin. I lost my job and money was scarce for a while. I was putting everyone else first. Medications would work and then stop working. Depression was playing a strong hand, inducing a feeling of playing euchre against an adversary who was stowing away all of the high cards, yet still demanding I play. As a result, my positive mental health began to plummet, with my physical health following suit shortly thereafter.

I can't point to one specific event that acted as the straw that nearly broke the camel's back, either. My rock bottom was basically approaching complete emotional exhaustion due to years of hanging on throughout the fight; a few added nudges finally resulted in my seeing no other way to ease the pain than to take myself out of it. This black and white, all-or-nothing thinking eliminated any grey middle ground and sat like a stubborn rock on the centre of my chest.

March 29, 2019, 7:12 p.m.

Some days I feel the sun hit my face and am instilled with hope, realizing that a number of days have gone by without depression or anxiety looming over me. Other days I watch them dance out of time around my living room floor like a goddamn parade, wearing their shoes through to the floor. I'd almost rather them hit me once than tow me around.
-S

Committed is sort of an odd word to use for someone who succeeds in taking their own life, yet it's a melody that continually plays. Suicide was decriminalized in Canada in 1972, though many still use the word as if a crime has been committed. True, in some ways you're fighting for your life when you're contemplating suicide; having suicidal thoughts evokes feelings of either being stricken by numbness or wrapped in swirling vortex of never-ending pain. For someone to find the fortitude to pull themselves out of such strong emotions is both difficult and tiresome.

When depression and anxiety work together to fill a mind to the brim with negative chaos, thinking logically often becomes difficult. Perception and decision-making skills become obscured, and the ability to see any beauty in life can become blurry. Impulse can take the reins.

I came across a wonderful quote by Elizabeth Gilbert this year that reads, *"You need to learn how to select your thoughts just the same way you select your clothes every day. This is a power you can cultivate. If you want to control things in your life so bad, work on the mind. That's the only thing you should be trying to control."*

My therapist broke it down further by explaining the human brain as having two minds: the wise mind and the emotional mind. The emotional mind is the reflexive one that acts on sentiment and impulse and it's the wise mind that makes decisions based on logic and reason, outside of emotion, allowing us to not be held hostage to our emotions.

Nov 12, 2019, 8:03 p.m.

Today, while having coffee with a friend, I was asked what I thought was the most bizarre question, and I nearly ended up in a field with some cows. We were discussing the wise mind and the emotional mind, and it started off like this:

"Well, the logic makes sense. If you're driving your car, what would happen if you looked toward the ditch for more than a few seconds?"

"Well, I'd probably go into the ditch," I said.

"Right. Your thoughts become your reality. It's like how with anxiety, the more you worry, the worse you'll be. Try not to grab hold of those negative thoughts."

Adele came on the radio as I was thinking about this metaphor on the way home. I was so lost in the song and in looking at the cute but sad-looking cows to my right, wondering what they were thinking about that I didn't realize I was heading for the ditch and had to catch myself to quickly steer back into the middle of the lane. There was no one on the road except for me, and I swear I'm a good driver. Kind of unrelated now that I think of it, but nonetheless: wise minds definitely need to be in control of the wheel.
-S

In all seriousness, there is much value to be found in controlling your thoughts. If we don't, we find ourselves sitting passenger to our emotions. You are in control. You are in the driver's seat. Even when the emotional thought is more powerful and the sadness or melancholy is loud, I think the wise mind can still triumph, given that I probably used it when I made the decision to reach out for help that night. Look and steer in the direction you want to go, because when you're constantly focused on where you don't want to go, your destination will inevitably end up there.

This is not to imply we should never acknowledge feelings that aren't positive; validation is important and it goes for happiness, sadness, anger, and everything in between. I'm realizing the helpfulness residing in not suppressing or fighting off negative emotions. Accept them by identifying what they are, feel them, and then ground yourself in the moment. Ask yourself what your values are, too. It's ok to have random sad days, to feel darkness—just don't live in it. Trying to interpret how you feel all the time can become exhausting, kick starting a cycle of unhealthy introspection. When an emotion grabs my attention, I do my best to react by letting it move through me with the recognition that I don't need to become that emotion. The same logic applies to overcoming suicidal thoughts: they're only thoughts, and thoughts need not turn into actions. Bearing in mind that thoughts tend to influence actions, the technique that helps me is consciously replacing those negative thoughts, emotions or unhelpful behaviours driven by emotion by swapping them with new, healthier, and more productive ones. For example, replacing negative self-talk with positive affirmations that reaffirm worth, like "I'm experiencing anxiety, but this doesn't mean I am anxiety," or "I am loved, I have purpose, and I'm ok." Taking "I'm going to feel this way forever" and replacing it with, "this is how I'm feeling in this moment. I will not feel this way forever" is another one. A personal example of redirecting thoughts and action is by taking note of the fact that I know turning to a substance when I feel a desire to escape an emotion intensifies that emotion sooner or later. In its place, doing something productive that boosts happiness and doesn't enhance stress like going for a walk or run, seeing friends, dancing in the living room, or engaging in a creative outlet may be a better choice.

I find reflection treads more intensely when depression and anxiety are factors, making dwelling on the negatives far easier than grabbing hold of the positives. There's greater ease in operating within a negative emotion than a positive one, as a result of the fact that negative sensibilities' relative information is processed more thoroughly; some even say it's human nature to be pulled toward the negatives. I'd like to think it's just a really unwanted super power I possess. However, the general "glass half-empty" perspective is inherent, hearkening back to our earliest existence. Cavemen had a sensitive awareness to danger to keep them safe as they spent their days hunting for food; if on one day they weren't successful, that was what motivated them to keep going. Some studies have also suggested that negative thoughts are stronger than positive experiences, the reason being that our brains' flow of energy in response to negativity is larger. Still, with effort, it's possible to dampen overthinking and turn down our repetitive thoughts.

The bottom line is, it's all right to have negative thoughts. We all have them at times. They're valid and they don't make someone a failure or ungrateful. You're allowed to experience things. It makes you a human being with emotions and responses. There are going to be times when we'll stare at the ceiling, mulling over all the things we may have done wrong, or deal with overwhelmingly down days where we may not really know why we are sad, just that we are, and that's ok, too. Life will find ways to bog us down; some of the most well-off, happiest people I know have openly admitted to questioning their lives and said they've fantasized about dying or have considered suicide. The point is to not wrestle with the negatives or dwell on what could go south. We need to do our best to wrap up in the joys, focus on the positive, and immerse ourselves in possibility and in the memories that pull up the corners of our mouths. The more I water the positives and good memories reaching for the sun, the more they grow. It's taken time for me to believe it but there are choices sewn into every single day.

Perhaps it's not the situation or feeling itself but our interpretations of it that make the situation appear positive or negative. If one is always looking at the negative parts of life, it's exactly that with which will become aligned. If you search for negativity, you will see it, whereas if you look for positivity, that is what you will likely see. Now, simply choosing to look in a direction or for specific things will definitely not cure depression, but it may help to manage it. Work with yourself. Be kind to yourself. Take time to acknowledge what you're feeling and try to understand where it's coming from, but always remember to nurture the parts that are cheering you on, too—optimism is enormous. If that's too far of a reach, other options remain: friends, helplines to call or text, or hospitals.

The more I consider all of the above contributing factors, the further the myth of "willpower" moves from acting as the sole decider of what keeps a person alive when they're at their lowest point. It becomes more about overall wellbeing and safety, and getting through the minute or handful of seconds than it does to "just find the will to turn off the depression or urge to indulge" and "keep trying harder." The only thought I could muster after hearing such suggestions was, "I'm doing the best I can to find it in my heart to stay." That was a frustrating flint that definitely ignited some arguments. They say we tend to take things out on those we love and although it never came from a place of intent, I regret that I pushed away people who were trying to help in any way they could. We're only human and we all say the wrong things sometimes, especially when we find ourselves in a position where it's difficult to empathize. My friends and loved ones weren't really doing anything wrong, they were just acting out of a caring place.

In part of her introduction on the *Super Soul Sundays* podcast, Oprah says, "I believe that one of the most valuable gifts you can give yourself is time. Taking time to be more fully present." I've often reflected with a heavy heart, and heard others say, how if those who chose suicide had simply given themselves a little bit of time, they might still be here, working through that which they didn't believe they could.

In the weeks leading up to the night I nearly ended it all for myself, I had been taking into account a lot about my life in general. I remember thinking if I was going to feel the way I was in that moment forever, I'd have terrible difficulty in holding fast to the desire to live at all. So, swearing on the promise to give myself time came with considerable hesitancy. Nonetheless, I now believe it might be true that in some cases, people who follow through with taking their lives may have experienced regret in the last second.

I share this because ultimately, even though there may be other factors, the most important thing I have been in need of during my unguarded moments was time. Just time. Time to create distance between thoughts and actions, which are two very different things. Time to get supports in place and then give my medication a chance to start working. Time to rethink what's felt in the moment, to verify that what's actually going on is in fact also what I believe is sitting heavily on my mind or in my heart. Time to learn patience, self-worth, and to regain purpose. Time to recognize that the rock sitting in the bottom of my chest was actually bravery and strength longing to emerge, and that what was holding them down was fear and pain. Time to let the conversations I had with friends and my therapist sink in enough to change my mind. I still have things to do in this world, and I am worth the fight. You are always worth the fight. Time to realize that even if I think I may not matter all that much in this world, despite being told otherwise, impact is one of the very markable things that cannot be wiped away. If you're thinking what I'm thinking, you'll know of the very popular quote that sat on my university desk for four years as a reminder:

"You might think that you don't matter in this world, but because of you someone has a favourite mug to drink their tea out of each morning that you bought them. Someone hears a song on the radio that reminds them of you. Someone has found the strength they needed because you made them feel they could. Someone feels good enough simply because you praised them. Someone has read a book you recommended to them and gotten lost in its pages searching for a message, thinking you left it with that book. Someone's remembered a joke you told them and smiled to themselves on the bus. Never think you don't have an impact. Your fingerprints can't be wiped away from the little marks of kindness that you've left behind."
- Author Unknown

Above all, giving those moments filled with dark thoughts just a little bit more time to move into a place of belief that, as most situations in life are, all emotions are temporary.

My grandmother, and my mom, always said, "This too shall pass." It's such a memorable comment on how life is constantly shifting. As long as the clock ticks forward, emotions will ebb and flow, providing space for new ones to take their place. It's so important to believe that good things will come, often rising from the ashes of adversity. Even after we fall, positive things can still happen, moving us a little further along. How you feel right now is not how you will feel forever. I was hard-pressed to believe it, but over the last year I've been cast for a closed audition on The Voice, signed a book deal, developed contacts in the music industry after *We Could Be Beautiful* dropped, started a country-pop album and a fiction novel, and met someone wonderful people who've reminded me about the significance of time, hope, and the usefulness of inner faith. If I gave up, the possibility of helping someone else get through a difficult mile by telling my story would be lost.

May 14, 2017, 7:34 p.m.

I was cleaning my room and found an old letter from Mom after a fight we had when I was in high school. This part is important:

"I remember many times over the years, Gramma said "This too shall pass. Of course, at the time, I would think, Yeah, right. This is never going to pass or get better. She has no idea what I'm going through. This goes way back to when I was a teenager, up to when she died and I was 41, she still said it. She was always so positive and I know it helped. She was always happy, an inspiration, putting a positive spin on things. I am grateful to her for this. Every day someone is struggling with something. People of all ages—people we know, people we don't. Issues that stem from health/money/relationships. These struggles are what make us stronger and the people we are on a daily basis."

-S

Time is not always the cure-all for something as complex as suicide, but I truly believe it helps; tomorrows don't come without it. We may never know what is in store until we get there and live it. What if the next day is the best one of your life or a really good thing is going to happen in a week's time, bringing your dreams even closer? Don't you want to get there and live it? The morning is always a new day and every day can be a new way.

Following through with my ongoing promise to give myself time, even when it's been and continues to be hard, is usually grounding; it brings perspective into the moment. This reminds me of an older gentleman I had the honour of working with while I was in school who once shared his perspective with me.

"I appreciate time. With it, everything changes and nothing stays the same. Good things I love fold into themselves, as do the bad ones. Do you think it's about choosing to release the bad ones and let the good ones carry us?"

I'll never forget that, or how much influence, perception, and time have on direction.

There have been a few occasions over the years where leaving me with a bottle of sleeping pills and alcohol probably wouldn't have made the Top Ten on the "Greatest of Plans Right Now" list and as I'm writing this, I'm feeling this might be one of those occasions. If I put my hands down at my sides, I may even find I'm touching the bottom again, but I'll get through because the difference between now and then is that I recognize a couple of vital pieces I previously struggled to see. I know now that in the heart of these moments, depression tends to create blinders that block the view of the important angles and components that make life worth living; those seemingly small details like a hearty belly laugh, a cerulean blue sky, a good friend, love, patience, and time.

I'll do yoga (even though I can't touch my toes) or something that gets my body moving. I'll sit under the sky for a bit. I'll take part in an activity that makes me happy or lean on my support system, striving to remember what helped me through the last time. I'll "practice the pause" so as to avoid leaning back on impulse and making permanent decisions on temporary emotions by asking myself: What am I feeling? Am I sad? Am I hurt? Tired? Lonely? Angry? What is the motivation for what I am doing? Is it logical? Am I bringing safety into thought? Will I feel this way a month from now? If yes, I'll tap into the wise mind, taking a pen and writing it all out into something tangible, which sometimes helps bring the blur into sharper focus. I'll get through because even though I might feel I'm back in that pool with its darkness, gritting my teeth and doing whatever I must to push the other way into the grey is always necessary.

A friend, while in the midst of her own struggle, once asked me what she was supposed to fight for. I told her the same things I've been told when I haven't known: For you. Fight for you. And if that's not good enough, then you grab hold of your strength, love, and faith by digging deep with everything in you to fight for those who may one day use your story as part of their map to surviving this mile.

The courage and strength it must take for a person who has lost a loved one by way of suicide or of unknowingly and unintentionally taking a fatal drug, to carry on is almost unimaginable to me. It's heartbreaking and tragic and it's a precarious feeling, particularly if you yourself have toyed with ending it all. The comments arising in the aftermath of such an event mostly seem to centre around, "I had no idea," "I don't understand," or the question "Why didn't they just ask for help?" And then there's the big one, "If I had only known, I could have helped them. I would have started driving to them at 3 a.m. It didn't have to be this way."

Answers to such large concerns are often lost with that person, be through any kind of sudden loss. Those left behind are immensely sad, shocked, devastated, guilty, perhaps mad and confused. While love may come to outweigh these feelings over time, it's still the kind of hurt that just never goes away. Sadly, I'm inclined to empathize with the struggle between the head and the heart.

In truth, no pain or problem is spared through the avenue of suicide. One person's pain may end but it doesn't just go away; that pain gets passed on to everyone left behind, increasing substantially, leaving no one unscathed. The ripple effects so many people.

Those who are currently struggling may spiral and make the same decision, given that whenever I've heard of someone dying by suicide or by unintentional substance overuse, my next thought would be, *Am I next?* which then leads back to that swimming exercise.

Yes, if one treads forever, drowning will inevitably happen, but there are ways around that option. There are lifeguards. There are edges on which to grasp. There are professional supports and friends to help bear the weight during your search for renewed inner strength. There are flutter boards to help you pause and catch a few breaths, which may even have been in your hands all along. There's always a chance if you make the effort to put your feet down you may be able to touch the bottom and find some stability, even if it's just with your tippy toes. Truth be told, you've already survived one-hundred percent of all the awful circumstances you've experienced so far.

I wish there was a magic wand or fix that could take depression away from all who live with it. Unfortunately, unless I just don't know about it, there isn't. There is, however, help. Depression is not a place of no return. It can make the heaviness and weight of certain moments seem fierce, determined to remain unbreakable and unending. There may be days and nights where simply finding air to breathe becomes wearisome, making us feel stuck or hopeless or as though we've met rock bottom, and maybe we have. The bottom was made up of similar, yet totally dissimilar things each time it broke a fall, the only common thing was how it felt. And when I would achieve some height, I grew petrified at the thought of slipping back down again. I felt like the better I would get, the higher from rock bottom, but the longer the fall and the harder the crash. Nonetheless, the bottom is still the lowest you can go and remains the point where things feel they can't get any worse but, like I was told, the bottom is always the bottom. The only good things about it are that you can't get much lower, so you've already seen the worst and have been making it through. The other is it provides a platform to stand on while you begin climbing again. There will always be more reasons to keep going than not, you may just have to dig a little deeper to find them. When you do, hold onto them and don't let go for anything because the gist of it is, there will be good days along with the difficult and overwhelming days when it feels like you're not moving anywhere and can't go on. Keep going anyway.

If your heart is heavy or you're suffering under a fog that isn't lifting, reach out. See your doctor, seek out a professional, reach out to someone you can trust and take care of your mental health as you would a broken bone. It can be hard to ask for help or tell someone how you feel, especially if it's something as bracing as, "I can't go on." Never feel wrong for asking for help. It's when you don't ask that it's wrong. Ask a friend to check in every so often if needed. If you can't find the words to describe it or you can't say them out loud, start by saying you can't describe your situation but you need support. I'd bet my last dollar that my friends and family would much rather listen to someone talk for hours about how they feel than listen to a 20-minute eulogy. There is hope and there are options that won't result in making a permanent decision to what may be a temporary problem, a decision that in one second can manage to end one story while filling others' with anguish.

I'm trying to focus on the good things that are so preciously woven into every day and let them carry me. Even though it can feel damn hard to know where to pull the strength from, I will keep going. With just one day, one step, one task, one breath at a time, in through the nose and out through the mouth, we will white-knuckle it through the night. And then we will do it again tomorrow. Like kintsugi, we will find the cracks that let the light back in, some of which will come from within, and search for the light at the end of the tunnel. It's just time and patience, time and patience. Truth be told, there are so many amazing wonders and challenges ahead that haven't presented themselves yet but are worth sticking around to discover. Things do change and they do get better. My friend tells her kids that just because you can't see or feel the sun right now doesn't mean it's lost in the clouds for all of eternity. The clouds will part. The rain will stop falling. The sun will come back out and it will be appreciated even more. I've always loved that.

In the end, maybe it's in the heart of those moments that bring such strong feelings of uncertainty about keeping the pen on the page or a hand on the strings that we should indeed continue writing and playing. The clients I had the honour of working with while on placement at hospice remind me that our strides and stories do not have to stop in the face of adversity. The adversities we face are not all of us, they are just a part of us and the stories of our lives.

Just one day at a time, one breath at a time.

Life is hard, but it is worth living.
There is always something to live for.

Dec 31, 2019, 11:45 p.m.

I had a hard day yesterday, but I woke up this morning feeling glad I woke up.
-S

For 24 hour mental health and/or addiction support, call one of the numbers below. Please, call. You are not alone.

Crisis Services Canada (24/7):
1-833-456-4566 or text 456455

Ontario Drug and Alcohol Helpline (24/7):
1-800-565-8603

A Rose

When your mind is filled with chaos
Seemingly endless problems pose
And you feel life's not worth living
Reach out and smell a rose.

When you're troubled and you're anxious
And you long for sweet repose
Push your worries far behind you
Reach out and smell a rose.

If from labours you feel weary
But your eyes you cannot close
For your work is still unfinished
Reach out and smell a rose.

Let the sweet scent calm and soothe you,
It will vanish all your woes,
Life assumes a deeper meaning
If you reach and smell a rose.

- AUTHOR UNKNOWN

a difficult mile:
you don't have to be strong for me

Feb 18, 2018, 2:12 p.m.

Mom and Dad taught me how to play euchre when I was about ten-years-old. We were camping in Bancroft, a town tucked away up in Northern Ontario. The majority of my summers were spent there growing up. As soon as we pulled in, it was as if all stresses paused and worries melted to the ground. It was my favourite place to be. My friends and I were always busy swimming, having mud fights, catching frogs, dirt biking, and having bonfires which, over the years, went from roasting marshmallows and falling asleep in front of as kids, to playing music and just being typical teenagers.

Buckets of rain were falling from the sky and showing no sign of letting up so Mom broke out the cards on the front deck. The radio was on in the background and even though there weren't enough of us to play a proper hand, they offered to teach me.

Mom lead the game with a king of clubs and I looked up from the hand Dad was teaching me from to see him already strategizing.

"Hearts is trump and Mom played a club, so put down a club if you have it. If you don't, play a trump card and we'll take the king," Dad said.

"What does trump mean?" I asked.

"The suit chosen that beats all cards except a higher trump."

"I don't have a club. I only have a two of hearts."

"Yup. Play it," he said.

"It's only a two, though. Mom played a higher card," I argued.

"It only seems like a weak card because the number is low...but the suit that's trump is always stronger."

High cards may be dealt to the hands of pride and shame, but when vulnerability is trump, it doesn't matter what card is laid down, as long as it's on the table. This day seemed irrelevant then, but it doesn't anymore.

-S

hat is strong? I unexpectedly stood face to face with this question in the midst of some kind of rundown in 2019.

My friend and I were watching the sunset when the conversation hit a wall. I looked up to see her worriedly asking if I was ok. I said I was fine, when in truth I was desperately trying to keep my composure. She didn't buy it. I didn't want to seem weak or admit I was struggling again. Grief from a recent loss coupled with a build-up of suppressed mental and physical exhaustion were leaving me in a wreck every minute and breaking my emotional back. I knew if I let my wall down that the conversation would lead to me falling apart and maybe not ever being able get it back together. It was sort of similar to resisting to let tears out, for fear they may never stop.

Being vulnerable enough to answer with honesty equalled the fear that washed through me 15 years ago at a school dance in Grade Six; picture a boy leaning in for a first kiss with his tongue out, braces on, and leftover Cheezies on his lips half-way through a Coldplay song. Obviously, this was a bit different. Oh, and my first kiss was on a chair lift when I was 12, we bashed helmets and then didn't talk for the remainder of the ride.

When my friend's hand took hold of mine a few seconds later, the sentence essentially dropped itself onto the table.

"I don't know how to keep being strong," I said, quite frankly. "And I'm not saying it for pity. I just feel like I'm scraping the bottom of the barrel trying to keep it together to be strong. I'm running out."

"What's strong?" she asked.

My jumbled attempt at a reply was met by two sentences that turned out to be a significant turning point in my life.

"You don't have to be strong for me," she said. "Look at me. I'm there for you. You just have to try to give me a chance to be."

Whenever I hear the word "vulnerability" I think of University of Texas research professor and New York Times bestselling author Brené Brown. Studying courage, empathy, vulnerability, and shame, she writes, "Vulnerability sounds like truth and feels like courage. Truth and courage aren't always comfortable, but they're never weakness" (Brené Brown, PhD, LMSW, *Daring Greatly*). Moreover she says in the same book, "If we can share our story with someone who responds with empathy and understanding, shame can't survive." Soon after, I heard an interview where Oprah and Brené discussed trust being created in small moments. This was one of them.

I looked down at the hold on my hand and it was in that moment that the armour I had spent the greater part of the last few years developing to shield me from fear, shame, and pride fell away. Not a lot was said initially, but not much had to be. We just sat in the same spot while steam rose from the pot. She didn't play doctor or tell me how strong I was or that what I was feeling was only in my head. She just listened with the intent of understanding without judgement and sat with me while I felt what needed to be felt and said some things that needed to be said. Like releasing, it took some pressure off. I felt like I could finally breathe again.

I'm a bit ashamed of how bravely pride previously stood with conviction and an overbearing confidence that prevented me from really feeling dignity and worth. I must acknowledge, even though muddling some of the words together to describe what I was feeling was hard,

I saw how something quite outstanding happens when vulnerability is met with trust, wide open arms, and the presence of the right person at the right time. Most of all, by leaning into vulnerability I'm beginning to learn what being "strong" actually means.

We as a society have somehow taken the word "strength" and romanticized its narrative as not being vulnerable to what we feel. Given this, I think the version of ourselves we often initially feel compelled to present to the world is one that does not crack, struggle, fall apart, or experience fragile or soft moments; one that withstands immense stress, pain, or pressure and never doesn't have themselves together. Once we recognize this version of "strength" is really just upholding the falsehood that vulnerability is something to be ashamed of, we can then move into a place where indignity in something so human and normal to experience does not exist.

This isn't to say society's general outlook on mental health hasn't improved. It has, especially with the calls to action for increased awareness like Bell's Let's Talk campaign. However, the shame and stigma do remain; people don't necessarily want to be seen in that light and that's where pride barricades vulnerability. I've been guilty of that—I still am, to some extent. Baring my soul in this book for everyone to see or leaning on others when I've felt too weak to stand on my own has definitely required a level of intestinal fortitude I wasn't certain I possessed. I didn't want what I viewed as my weakness to become widely known and I cringed at the thought of anyone thinking *well, there she goes again* if I went through another low period. Fear of being considered burdensome or of being rejected has tempered so many of my decisions, even though no one has ever said that aloud; I was the one who wrote the pen dry writing myself off for an inability to be "strong."

Until now, I thought being strong meant never losing ground or falling apart, and certainly never letting your emotional armour hit the floor. In my mind, that meant adversity trumps bravery and wins the hand of resilience. So basically, to be strong meant to be the *Terminator* in a game of euchre. I was pretty right field on that.

Strong doesn't mean we don't have moments of weakness. We cry, we struggle, we lose our balance and the rug sometimes gets pulled from beneath our feet but that's when we pull ourselves up and keep going. Putting one foot in front of the other when times are tough has been the hardest thing, but it is the very thing that's making me so much stronger. Choosing to throw your shoulders back with your head held high when life is presenting a million reasons not to is strong and brave. Feeling pain and facing up to emotions is strong and brave. It's ok to release the pain. Inviting your struggles into the room, sitting beside them and trying to breathe in time with them instead of holding your breath is strong and brave. Choosing to move forward when you're afraid or don't want to, is strong and brave. Being vulnerable, reaching out, and admitting when you're in a difficult place is strong and brave.

Over the last year, I've become a firm believer of the significance of the concept of "strong" inherent in a good support system; it's truly an integral part of emerging from the hills and valleys of each mile a sturdier version of yourself. I feel very blessed to have people in my corner who have been my touchstones through the unsteadiness that often lives in depression, anxiety and grief. They've kept a light flickering during my darkest days by listening without judgement, always trying to understand my situation while encouraging me to believe in something more, even if I don't know what "more" is at the time. They've helped me navigate the healthcare system. They refused to let me give up and when I couldn't fight, they've fought for me, even if it meant risking my anger at them or them kicking my ass to pull myself together. Their ability to find strength and resilience in moments of weakness, to draw optimism from turmoil is only one small part of their beautiful souls. When nothing can be fixed, they've shown up and never stopped walking this mile with me.

I've realized that good friends believe in us when we can't quite believe in ourselves. They help bear the weights we carry. They use their two good legs and strong backs to let others lean. When we have a good support system, the storms and difficult moments that come with the precarious paths on which we travel seem a little calmer and more manageable and it will undoubtedly inform the kind of friend I'll strive to be going forward.

Vulnerability has become one of the greatest assets in my life since allowing myself the freedom to feel emotions, spilling my soul into song writing and to those in my circle. Every time I've kept it all in or resisted feeling unpleasant emotions it was like more harm gathered at the edges of my psyche, like far-off clouds threatening an inevitable storm. Silencing emotion does not equate to being a strong person. Running away from a feeling or problem is a sure way to ensure it will shadow you until you turn and face it.

I wish I had realized vulnerability's value and what being strong meant much sooner, but I know which narrative I now believe. Giving any truth, especially one that many walk this very moment, a voice and place to be heard is scary but it's so important because it's a piece of what helps us get through, reminding us we're not alone. The reality is, a mental health struggle is nothing to be ashamed of or embarrassed about. Being open and honest about the feelings that make you human doesn't tarnish self-image or reduce your worthiness as a person. If it does, those around you aren't holding you up. At some point, I think everyone has, had, or will have, a moment of wondering how on earth they're going to carry on. Whether it's growing so exhausted that you just sit in your room and cry it out or a thought of *I can't do this anymore*, to some extent we've all been there. The importance of remembering that even though it can feel like you're the only boat in the sea sometimes, there are actually a lot of other boats with captains who feel set adrift experiencing very similar things. When I was working as a court reporter in 2018, almost every case referenced the words depression or anxiety. We are never alone in the challenges we face and I truly believe that we can move through pain and adversity with greater ease when we feel our feelings and let out the hurt, secure in the knowledge that we're all going through similar experiences.

Asking for help and learning to let others in takes a lot, but there is much strength to be gained from it. Depression and anxiety enjoy being met with silence, becoming even more pronounced when we keep mum. Their kryptonite, though, is vulnerability; they don't stand as tall when it enters a room and puts its feet up. I still struggle with it from time to time because, well, to say reaching out is always easy no matter if it's the first or hundredth time would be untrue. I'm self-reliant, don't want to inconvenience anyone, and to some degree I still care what others think. Plus, if I've lost the support of some in the past, trusting can be tough. I had to rationalize the amount of guilt I was feeling and recognize that just because I can wear myself out trying to keep it together on my own, doesn't mean I must. Also, we can't always give ourselves some of the things that a support system provides, like coping mechanisms, perspective, a shoulder, and life experience.

I need to remember this, as well as the fact that not everyone is going to do that, and in order for people to show up for you, you have to let them. I've often reflected with gratefulness on how that's happened—it was such an important part of my continuing on when I truly felt

I could not. To not only hear, but to feel and know you don't have to be strong all of the time, that things will be ok, and that we are indeed not alone in the things we face even when at first it seems we're the only boat in the sea, brought me back from being adrift. I've since made a conscious effort to never underestimate the power and reach of words, a small act of kindness on our spheres of influence.

I came to think later on, there should be benches spread across every town to facilitate difficult conversations and help those who may not have anyone to advocate for them. In times of adversity or distress, people could go to a bench to send the message, "I may not be able to say the words, but this is how I feel today" simply by sitting there. Others could join them, listen, provide support or just be present, and by doing that contribute to the creation of more compassionate communities and a society that says "you're not alone."

There is such value in showing up. It can be life-changing for anyone suffering. Even if you can't fix the problem or take away all of someone's pain, still show up. It's ok if you don't know what to say or you worry about possibly saying the wrong thing.

Still, show up.

Acknowledge aloud that you may not have the means to stop the downpour but can definitely walk through the rain beside them. You are only one person, but that one person can make all the difference. Some of the hardest days I've had felt less impossible to get through when someone showed up and I wasn't alone while moving through the weight of what I was feeling. More than likely, the presence of another had a lot to do with it. We need each other to lift us up and we need human connection almost as much as we need air to breathe; whether it's the literal or figurative touch of a hand, a listening ear, an empathetic shoulder to lean on, sharing a laugh or having a cleansing cry, just show up.

"Always, always check in on your people and always, always be kind. In this world, you never know what someone is going through. It is so normalized to hide your pain but no one should ever feel like they're alone. Slow your life down and take it in. Sometimes we're all so rushed in our everyday lives that we forget what we're passing up. Time with loved ones, time with ourselves, time with the world. You'll never be able to get that time spent back. So spend it wisely. Before you're missing what was."
- Ashton Kimberley

The best gift you can give is neither material nor quantifiable. Perhaps it's the offering of a new perspective or wrapping a new frame or shape around something in order to shine light from a different angle. Maybe it's compassion, love, helping someone see more of what you see when you look at them, or helping someone show up for themselves. It all comes back to vulnerability—the place where the power to make a difference between light and dark, and in some instances between life and death, resides. We all want to feel understood, and vulnerability is a real catalyst for getting there. How a sliver of compassion, empathy, or presence may land in the heart of someone in the midst of a struggle may never be known.

Show up anyway.

Free

I have felt the warmth of a brilliant sun on my face
And a second later fallen to my knees
I have a whole-hearted friend who reminds
me of the width of our shoulders
And just how much we can carry

Chorus
I am free
Let go of aging hurt in me
My soul can breathe
I'm free

I have changed a lot since this
dusty mirror saw me last
I am happy with all I have
This life is not dull, it can be hard as hell
Dig your heels in it anyhow

Chorus
Days fold into themselves
And like a passing shadow I let go
Days fold into themselves
And like a passing shadow I let go

Chorus
Sara Rose, Until Now, 2017

a difficult mile:
Jenga

Mambo No. 5
September 17, 2018, 1:57 p.m.

Two middle-aged women were sitting across from me the other day. A young man walked in, talking on the phone at a volume loud enough for us to learn that whoever he came into the emergency department with was just admitted for reasons related to their mental health.

One of the women went on to speak to her friend of a supposed ridiculousness in having so many "needy," "attention-seeking" people using valuable resources and taking time away from people with "real illnesses." It's said time and time again in kindergarten classes, if you don't have anything nice to say, grit your teeth and walk away. Perhaps they thought no one was listening, didn't realize how loud they were speaking, or just didn't give a damn. But there were people sitting in that waiting room who did.

I felt like I should've had six arms for having difficulty with my own mental health, and I wasn't even there for that reason. I felt so sad for whoever this person was, and he or she didn't even hear the hurtful remarks. If it were me, I wouldn't want to know. Whoever this person was had been admitted and whatever their story may be, they were seeking out what was best and safest for themselves.

Saying someone's mental illness is just in their head and that it's not real would be like telling a drowning person that the drowning is only in their chest. Maybe I should've held back from weighing in, as what followed probably wasn't one of my proudest moments. However, the frustration over the lack of thought and regard that went into what they said washed over me like the gigantic water buckets in the Ontario Place waterpark my friends and I went to as kids.

When I was called to triage, I stopped briefly and asked the one woman if she had a broken arm and was in pain if she would seek treatment for it. She looked at me like I actually did have six arms.

"Well, yes. Obviously," she said, awkwardly.

"So, what's the fucking difference if people are seeking mental health assistance for their emotional pain?"

The elephant in the room may as well have been doing Mambo No. 5.

-S

The delicacy woven throughout a standing structure can be unimaginably huge. One piece, hidden or in plain sight, could be bearing all the weight and we might not even know it until it takes a hit at just the right time, or gets pulled out like a block in a game of Jenga and it all comes crashing to the ground.

In 2017, I sought help from the hospital. Resources I'd been using were either exhausted or not working very well anymore, and it had come down to what I hoped it wouldn't but knew deep down was the best option. My eyes remained trained on the ground while I wrestled to push my heels against the concrete floor and take the next step when the word, "next!" was called from across the hall.

"What brings you in to Emergency today?"

The nurse asked the question twice before I found my voice, as if I needed to remember how to use it. I guess I was trying to reply without having to say it bluntly, given the answer that fell out of my mouth seriously skirted the question. It's scary to reveal things about ourselves, it opens the door for opinions and, not to mention the fact that letting the truth out means meeting it head on.

"The crisis worker will be with you shortly. You can get changed over there. You'll stay with her?" she said, looking down at her keyboard and then up at the person who was with me.

If I'd broken a bone, seeking help would have been no issue, but I was there for mental health struggles and I felt ashamed for it. I was nervous and didn't want to be judged or labeled as "crazy." I was there because I didn't want to see my life end and needed help. I think that's a piece that often gets overlooked when someone feels a similar fear about going to the hospital for mental health reasons. Yes, the language healthcare providers sometimes use can come across quite blunt and a little painful, such as the ones I've been privy to. "Are you going to kill yourself?" and "If you plan to kill yourself, do you have the means to do it?" It was important for me to recognize that these individuals likely see similar cases on a daily basis and perhaps become numb or immune to it compared to how it may feel to someone who could be facing their truth for the first time or is petrified of what they're going through. The title, "crisis worker" and seeing security guards posted outside the unit sent shivers of terror down my spine. I'm grateful to have not gone through these few hours alone, especially since I knew I couldn't advocate all that well for myself right then.

I distinctly recall the two chairs and couch that took up most of the crisis worker's room, each of which were ripped and looked more ancient than the bland, washed-out paint covering the walls. I could see a layer of dust coating the top of the book shelf from across the small space and when I look back now, I had managed to blend in. I was a part of that couch that day. Some breathing, existing extension of it.

I didn't feel a great sense of ease during my conversation with the worker, but she was kind and did her job. Not having been through this before, but knowing that when a person says they have a plan to end their life and are intent on acting on it, it typically increases the chance of being admitted, I tried being honest without implying anything. It was difficult, but had I been at the point of acting on anything it would have been a mistake to cover any part of the truth.

I was sent home with an agreed-upon follow-up appointment with her one week later. Upon my return, I was taken aback by the shift in energy radiating off her. The warm, professional demeanor I'd previously appreciated had become blunt and tinged with disdain. That was about as much thought as I gave it as I was still feeling quite low and frankly couldn't gather the energy to care much.

I found being completely honest was harder than the week before. I wanted help but I was afraid of what that might mean (perhaps being admitted to an inpatient program, which I'd worked up in my head as being locked in with no way out). I didn't feel like I had all that much to lose at that point, though, so I decided to proceed without any filters.

I was asked if I'd done anything productive to help myself since my last visit and while not much had changed in terms of my mood, I had seen my doctor and been prescribed anti-depressants. The amount of convincing and positive self-talk it had taken felt slightly absurd and as much as I wasn't stoked on the idea of medication, at that point it did turn out to be a bit of a lifeline, allowing me to get things done with a little bit more ease. Telephone therapy sessions weren't doing the trick and I came to find the most effective method of treatment sometimes includes both medication and psychotherapy, as was the case for me two years later. I told her I was still holding on by a thread, but that I was trying really hard to view seeing the doctor and being honest as positive steps towards greater wellness.

The silence was deafening while she peered down at the clipboard and papers sitting on her lap; the limited eye contact and her overall manner weren't what chilled me so much as what she said next.

"Oh. Yeah, you'll be long dead before any medication will work for you," she said.

I suppose the ear-splitting silence beforehand had really been the calm before the storm. As I inhaled the words expanded into every part of my body. I had to clarify that I'd heard her correctly.

"Hmm?" she replied, while continuing to look down at whatever she was writing.

"What did you say?" I asked.

Word for word, with a seeming indifference, she once again echoed her last sentence.

Jenga.

I was still reeling from disbelief as she handed over a piece of paper. I had wondered if what she'd been writing over the past 20 minutes aligned with what I'd been trying to explain, and what her interpretation was going to mean for me going forward.

To my surprise, suggested dietary advice was scribbled across the page, alongside a copious number of vitamins I needed to be taking. Within a few seconds she joined me on the small couch while a YouTube video lecture on skin care played. When I looked up to ask about the relevance, she suggested I'd likely find myself much less depressed in life if I had clearer skin. Surely, physically feeling good helps to boost anyone's mood a bit; however, considering I was actually in an emergency department, suffice it to say my current emotional state was a bit past being fixed through softer skin. If factors like that or making my bed every morning were the ultimate remedy for curing depression, I'd buy all the skin care products I could and make every single bed in the world for the rest of my life. This is not the case, and mental health hardships are not always "fixed" at the drop of a hat.

Her remark and obvious disregard of the matters on the table hung like heavy chains on my shoulders. I couldn't seem to gather enough sense to wrap my head around why it was that a healthcare worker, a person in a position of influence, would imply to someone struggling emotionally that they were more likely to die from depression before a pill could provide a chance to save them. Moreover, how did a patient in crisis end up in a position of explaining to a crisis worker that depression isn't the exclusive result of physical appearance or not taking vitamins?

By the time the video ended, I had talked myself out of seeking help. I wanted to be honest but figured if all the workers were like this one, I'd be better off trying to save myself anyway. So I told her the information she'd shared was enlightening, I could see it being a great help to my situation, and also that I was feeling fine.

After all that I was sent home with a piece of paper and a statement that never entirely quit running through my head.

My experience that afternoon has always reminded of me a quote by Atticus: "Depression is being colorblind and constantly told how colorful the world is", which would be akin to telling a colorblind person that if they could just pick out the yellows and blues in life, they'd be a lot happier with their rainbow. When we only listen to reply, communication barriers surface and cause potentially huge and dangerous issues.

In hindsight, I should have been admitted that afternoon. Despite a wavering ability to describe and advocate to be heard, the actual emotional state I was in was barely addressed or completely assessed and thus not understood, given I was still contemplating taking my life when I walked out the door. Anyone who's tried to speak with someone who is preoccupied or not really listening knows what effort it takes to communicate and how a lack of understanding can occur as a result. Regardless, if we don't take the time to gain an understanding of a situation, story or circumstance, we may as well not respond at all; when we're not present, we miss things and information can fall through the cracks.

While I was struggling at my very low point, I still consider myself lucky to have not gone any lower. I cringe at the thought of somebody in worse shape than I sitting on that couch. A simple offhand phrase, such as the one I was privy to, may very well have acted as the wooden block resulting in a Jenga for someone, or be the catalyst preventing one from allowing themselves to be vulnerable again in the future. Words are powerful.

My heart breaks when I think of those I know who have sought support from any healthcare facility, have not always been completely comprehended, and were sent home struggling more than when they went walked in the door or later went on to take their lives. In such cases, not being heard or understood anywhere along the path of their tumultuous walk, the system failed them.

Perhaps there was a genuine intention to help somewhere in that worker's approach toward me and my situation, or at least one would sincerely hope that was the case. Maybe the timing was just unlucky and it was a one-off circumstance. Or, this is just an instance of stigmatism and of how we can be paid to do something and still show up for work but not fully be there or deliver the job fully, who knows?

I haven't spoken about this bump in the road to paint a mucky picture of the healthcare system, talk down about anyone, or make you pity me; I would actually ask that you lean away from doing that. This is only one part of one person's experience in a very large system that's still trying to iron out some of the wrinkles. There are many wonderful, passionate workers out there saving the lives of those in need every single day, and I salute them because the work they do is so very vital to the well-being of so many people.

I share this anecdote with the hope it illustrates how situations can lead to people keeping their inner truths, such as adversities related to mental health, to themselves. I mean, why would you share something personal or bare your soul if you knew there was a chance it would be minimized or not treated with the dignity it deserved?

As well, there is importance in remembering that crisis workers are human beings, too. We wouldn't be human if we never messed up, said the wrong things, or made mistakes sometimes. We grow as decent human beings when we learn from those mistakes and work to prevent them from happening again in the future.

The question I've since wondered the answer to is this: How do we justly expect people in need of help to reach out if the hand for which they're reaching will still apply the stigma or is allowed to communicate without a layer of accountability?

I don't know a whole lot about much, but I think the starting point to helping each other to stand tall and strong is by breaking down the stigma with empathy. To be empathic is to hold the ability to listen, truly hear, and put yourself in another's shoes so as to better understand and support their emotions, truth, and needs without bias. Perhaps of greater importance is that you attempt to feel what they feel because listening should be engaged in with the intent to understand, not just to reply. Taking in how day-to-day life is lived allows treatment methods to be more accurately shaped. I see these qualities in the social worker I began working with in 2019 and I see it improve through my friends and overall support system; it's truly made all the difference.

The potential costs of stigma to someone's life can be detrimental. I was "depression" in the room that day and it was a driving force behind why I found myself opting to breathe depression and anxiety in but never out, and why reaching for help when I needed it is probably one of the most difficult things I've done. I felt trapped in my depression and even though suffering in silence can worsen symptoms, I would still rather have done that than speak out, given that I'd built up such fears about returning. I needed help and, as the current system is the only one we have, I had to accept that one poor experience doesn't summarize the quality of it in its entirety. There are a lot of fantastic workers out there and I'm grateful to have since found a passionate team that is committed to meeting people where they are with compassion; they more than make up for those who have in the past made words like "anxiety" and "depression" very ugly.

These days there are wonderful calls to action that are so impactful in more ways than I could ever say, such as Bell's Let's Talk, which exists to combat stigma and raise awareness. Since its inception in 2010, the campaign has committed over $100 million to help create a stigma-free Canada and drive action in mental health care, research, and the workplace. However, a catch-22 still remains because awareness, acceptance and understanding can only take us so far. There are still underfunded crisis teams with limited amounts of time to provide services, and there are long waiting lists for assessments. The referral I received to see a psychiatrist a few years ago came with a nine-month wait. I remember thinking, how do we expect to receive support (medication or therapy-based), which often requires time to start taking effect, if that support can't be provided in time?

Tanya Shute (RSW, MSW, PhD) is a professor from whom I took a few classes in university, and she has graciously and rigorously built upon the query for this book. Having also worked in the survivors' movement, she says:

"The mental health system is just that, a system. One that is built, designed, resourced, staffed, legislated, regulated, evaluated, and other things systems do—from within itself. And just like any other system, it is prone to entropy and decay. When the starting point for a helping system is rooted in the aggressive elimination of difference through cruel "treatment" such as being chained or lobotomized, or removal from society altogether through massive institutionalization of anyone deemed different, there is no doubt that a legacy of stigma and oppression linger and fester within the system unchecked. Sara's emergency department experience is not uncommon.

"Sara is also quick to point out that she had good experiences too, and that she is hesitant to characterize the mental health system as wholly broken. Indeed, many people find the help they need and rely on in the mental health system, whether that be psychiatrist appointments, inpatient or outpatient treatment, occupational therapy or social work, pharmaceuticals or peer support, and any of its combinations. But the system has not been resourced adequately to address the growing complexity and acuity of distress and trauma at its door. The mental health system, unfortunately, is also the system of last resort, where people who could not have their needs supported or addressed in other ways often find themselves. This demand means services offered late or too late because of extensive wait lists, combined with the necessary experimentation required: no one really knows what will work, when, or for whom. There is a certain level of trial and error necessary, and this takes precious time. But a system so complex it requires navigation is concerning. If at people's most difficult times, when they can barely navigate a shower each day because of the enormous pull on their health, how can we expect people to manage their way through these systems of assessment, eligibility, and service remain undaunted by sometimes less than humane responses to what they are disclosing experiencing, and continue to ask for help (because a system is neither proactive or preventative in nature – but must wait to be approached). Imagine the experience for those who are not connected to reality or context and therefore incredibly vulnerable to the system's response (because they experience something that might be called delusions or hallucinations), or who smell bad or look scary because they have been outside for too long without help, or who can't speak enough in either of the official system languages to detail what they are experiencing for appropriate intervention.

"The mental health system is not the answer to crises related to mental/emotional pain; it is not a panacea, and neither are drugs or talk therapy (for those with the resources to access them and the capacity to engage in them consistently). People who consider themselves psychiatric survivors, a large movement of people across the world seeking change in the mental health system and policy based on their experiences, consider themselves having survived what they endured in a system meant to "help." Often what people need in order to heal is remarkably simple, but just not widely available: adequate income, private health care benefits, adequate housing, meaningful roles in life and community, love, relationships, intimacy, friends... Imagine a system that prescribes safe housing instead of drugs.

"Mental health recovery, a new paradigm in the mental health system, is not yet fully realized; the idea that all people can and do recover from mental health problems and what are often labelled as disorders by the mental health system challenges a lot of the pathology and disease model the mental health system was designed upon. We all recover to some degree, and often fully. People get themselves back from these experiences—sometimes with the system's help and sometimes despite it. But the mental health service safety net we have is definitely not enough if we only have the medical and the clinical and the drugs; we need so much more to recover and maintain our health that the system does not have the awareness and capacity to address."

The bottom line is, we can sit and talk about how stigma isn't that large of a matter until we're blue in the face, but it's out there. It's decreased, but it still seeps through cracks and crevices. It lives on the streets and in-between the walls of some healthcare facilities. It sneaks into day-to-day conversations, and I, too, sometimes catch myself creating unjust opinions based off assumption. Usually it's because I don't fully understand what's in front of me. I will do better with this.

Now, every stigmatizing barrier can't be erased in this very hour, but every day can certainly be taken on with a means of continuing to minimize them. The conversation starts here. Bringing ends to turning our heads away from the hurting starts here. Acceptance and understanding continues on here. Today. In the streets. In the grocery store. At the coffee shop. At home. On social media. In the hospital. On the bus. In the lobby. We can be supportive by doing things like reminding someone how much they mean to us, spending time with each other but also allowing for space, being a friend instead of a doctor to our loved ones who are struggling, offering to help them with things around the house, and being patient. We can talk more openly about mental health while taking care of our own so as to not pour from an empty cup. We can listen and try to understand before placing our thoughts or opinions in the arms of pride. We can choose empowerment and educate ourselves. We can choose tolerance and compassion over shame. We can be mindful of the language we use before making remarks like, "kill me now," and "I could just kill myself." Bear in mind that what may be outwardly shown by those standing next to us may not mirror what's being felt on the inside.

Had I been asked ten years ago if I wrestle with my mental health, I'd have likely said no. Given how unsightly I was at certain points over my teenage years, I'd have probably thought I could never "get those" kinds of issues because they're what "sad or restless people have." As if they were some kind of viral diseases to which pride somehow held me immune. I'm agitated towards this because it just couldn't be further from the truth. It's noteworthy how perceptions change because I now find myself hard-pressed to jump on whichever wagon believes only a few people are affected by a form of one related to mental health, be it through themselves or someone they know. Someone doesn't have to be depressed to have their life be touched by depression, just as people I know don't have to be an alcoholic for addiction or alcoholism to affect them. Some form of struggle lives, has lived, or will live, in everyone at some point in our lives and it's nothing to be embarrassed about.

To the same extent, there is nothing wrong with talking about mental illness. I think a fine line exists between romanticizing the experience, as sometimes happens on social media, and building a more resilient society around it. The social media piece drives me up the wall sometimes because of the times I saw it almost glamorize the hardship that can reside in putting one foot in front of the other through mental health difficulties. On it we see others' lives and are drawn to thinking their lives are perfect, or that they've gotten through or "conquered" their demons. I've read and heard many stories voicing life from "the other side" of depression, as in the healed, "conquered" side. I'm glad for those who share their stories of "success" in leaving it behind and I wish it were possible for everyone. However I think some stories of this kind, as inspiring as they may, were a small part of what worsened my own depression and hope that I'd too get through it at times because, well, if all of these people could conquer it and leave it behind them, why wasn't I able to?

The larger picture may suggest these circumstances could be partially linked to why some do end up following through with taking their own lives. Perhaps they see, hear, and read about others coming to find supposed permanent harmony or happiness in their minds and never slip back down inside their depression because they've seized it as though it is a "one-time" mountain unlikely to be climbed again. Sometimes, depression is situational; for many, though, it's not like that.

A mental health struggle does not define a person, nor does it make up the entirety of a person. Behind every illness is a person; a human being with a soul, a story, and very real emotions and feelings. Any extent of difficulty experienced with mental health is not a sign of weakness, deficiency, or worthiness. The weakness is rooted in the stigma, shame, bias, and everyday jargon that circles it and waters down these very real struggles. Michelle Obama wrote, "At the root of this dilemma is the way we view mental health in this country. Whether an illness affects your heart, your leg or your brain, it's still an illness, and there should be no distinction."

Pain of any kind is as universal as love and we are no better than the first crisis worker I saw if we cannot stand alongside one another in times of darkness and struggle with the same harmony as we do in times of joy and celebration. With it, we have the means to pull on the strengths of the system and within ourselves in unity and acknowledge the gaps that create distance from the provision of compassionate care, to help change the conversation and delivery of mental health. In the face of feeling the urge to turn our backs to difficult conversations, we must do the opposite. Lean in. Address the elephant in the room. Help raise a voice to things being left unsaid and unchanged.

The feeling that rushed through my entire body that afternoon is one that will remain with me always, and although it was a test of dignity and worth, it will inform my future by serving as a reminder of the reach of empathy, and of listening more to those who matter. Moreover, this strange version of Jenga magnified my sense of compassion and heightened the value I see in the avenues that can be walked to continue advocating for and creating change. We need to not just think about needed change; like most things, merely thinking about a result or outcome doesn't ensure a follow-through. Just as with the conversation of living and dying, the rigidity around mental health cannot be expected to lessen, nor the stigma contested, if we ourselves are not in a position to acknowledge what's still happening and meet it head on.

Part of the reason I chose to pursue a degree in social work in 2014 was because I wanted to help people. How I wound up stamping hockey pucks during the day and chasing a dream or two at night is another story, but I wanted to provide people the support I was originally in need of. I've always believed everyone has a voice and a story that deserves to be listened to, and if there are the means to turn up the voices of those who are not being heard, we should always attempt to do so.

Sometimes understanding the experience of another does not come easily. A friend of mine shared with me, "For me, personally, it's just something that I don't really understand. Sometimes I don't know what I'm supposed to say, and I think because I can't relate it's hard for me to fully connect. I've just never felt that way, so for me, it's easy to say to myself, *ok, just get over it* and then I move on. I know it doesn't work that way for everyone, so I try my best to be understanding."

There are ways to hold each other up that don't have to end by calling out Jenga. When empathy gets a genuine front seat, stigma tends to destabilize, creating a greater means of building understanding, ultimately shaping the lens through which mental health is seen and the platform from which compassionate care is built. It's much more difficult to judge something as overtly human as mental health once it's better understood.

Today, if someone opens themselves up in an appeal for support, choose empathy. If you aren't sure you heard or are understanding correctly, ask for clarification. Even if you do, clarify anyway—think about how the words you're saying may be landing. I believe that by listening we learn, by talking we clarify understanding, and by sharing we deflate the stigma around mental health. Have the conversations. Talk. Do something. Whatever it is, please don't turn away or rush to judge another's experience. Depression doesn't have a universal appearance, it expresses itself in many ways. Choose empathy. I don't think you can ever go wrong with it.

One Jenga call is one too many.

If You Start a Fire

I feel like I need to disappear
There's fire, rage and pain here
I'll dig my way out before it hits
me just like the first time
Turns out letting go is my kryptonite

Chorus
I keep fighting these fires in my head
Battle scars never let me forget
But there's not enough heat to make me burn
I am a fighter, and being human hurts
But if you start a fire, I'll put it out
If you start a fire, I'll put it out

My armor is on the floor
And I will not surrender my voice to all of this noise
I've touched bottom before, there's nothing to fear
I am here

Chorus
You can throw your stones, make me bleed
Tie me down, take me out at the knees
But if the only way out is through
Then I'll go through
I have to try, I have to try

Chorus
Sara Rose, We Could Be Beautiful, 2019

a difficult mile:
renovations

August 23, 2019, 7:16 p.m.

Ashes from the neighbour's fire are falling into the yard out back. I'm sitting on the patio for the first time since the last ice storm came through and wiped nearly 80 trees down with it. Everyone's property took an impact, but I didn't realize how much more can be seen now without them.

The neighbor below always seems to be working on something outside, like Mom and Dad. He fills his wheelbarrow to the brim with sticks and branches, pushes it across the yard, dumps it clean, and comes back to do it all over again. He's been going back and forth for hours. From where I am, it looks to be a huge job and while he's not that fast, his pace hasn't wavered. Mom says he's out there almost every day in the summer. By the time fall starts rolling in every year, there's a beautiful landscape.

We seem to live in a world where fixing a problem at hand or undertaking a job as quickly as possible is the goal, in order to fix our attention on the next one. It's amazing, though, how much a mindset can

shift just by looking at something from a different spot, taking one thing at a time. When there's a big job or an overwhelming goal to be fulfilled, it doesn't matter the speed, just as long as there's consistency and a suitable pace. Slow and steady wins the race, one piece at a time, one branch at a time, one piece of wood stacked onto the pile at a time...the job gets done. You get where you're going.
- S

There was a huge rainstorm in 2017 that flooded half the town, including the building from which the hospice I volunteered runs their organization. The speed of the water flowing on the inside of the walls only an hour or so prior was a forecast of how quickly the damage was going to set in.

That's the interesting thing about damage, just a few minutes of disaster can take months or years to repair or build anew. Other times, it can create tons of tiny cracks over time before eventually wearing the whole configuration down to the frame. Once it breaks through, the only part you can control is how you choose to respond.

For years, I chose to respond to my depression by suffering in it, in more ways than one. As uncomfortable as it was, I was strangely comfortable simply idling. It wasn't so much that I felt sorry for myself or enjoyed the feeling in the slightest as it was a feeling of familiarity. I was smack in the middle of a disaster while the waters rose, ravaging everything like the waters in the flood, all because I was afraid of pain. I never saw myself as someone who could endure it, so I hid away, held my breath, and shut the door.

In the months leading up to the time I was suicidal, which feels like fighting for your life, I chose avoidance and got quite good at keeping the heaviness at bay so as to avoid falling apart. Dodged it like a bullet; well, as dodged as something woven into every day can be, anyway. Tending to only that which truly needed attention was all I believed I had to do to be strong, and I was my own worst enemy for it. I viewed letting my walls down as only making the situation worse and knew I definitely didn't have the strength to face it. I felt a bit like a shark: they have to keep swimming or they'll die. As a result, everything I'd been tucking away began to demand attention, jumping up and down, forming tiny cracks in my general wellness until I'd worn myself thin and was heading towards the rock bottom I'd been hoping to keep away from.

I was off my face quite a bit in 2019, hiding away and comforting myself with timeworn habits while all my baggage and pains were running amok. I began to feel hypocritical because the outside version I was presenting to the world when I walked out the door didn't nearly match my internal struggle. I would function all day, only to meet the night by quietly leaning on a fake fix that fed my avoidance by dulling the edge and tamping down my stressors. Dust was settling on the advice I was given but had stopped taking, along with cancelled therapy appointments and the medication I hadn't given a chance to work. People waved their fists in my face out of love and frustration and I didn't wince. They wanted to take all the hurt away, but it's hard to support someone who isn't walking the line or working to make the change. I wanted to hold myself accountable, but I'd already convinced myself the clouds would never part and the rain would never stop.

The race away from myself was far from new. I knew the tools and techniques to help myself, and could help everyone else, but couldn't apply them to myself. Not to mention, I also seriously needed to sift through the crap I'd been toting around like the stuff that piles up at the bottom of a purse. You know, when you don't even really know what's down there and while you can feel the weight it bears on your neck and shoulders every day, you keep carrying it anyway. (Mind you, some of the things in my actual purse are snacks, which are fine.) You can get a sore back from carrying the weight of things for so long without pausing and throwing the damn bag on the floor for five minutes every once in a while, but I was scared to go through it. It seemed as if I were waiting for some magic wand to make everything better but in truth, what I was up against just felt so much bigger than what I was equipped to handle, In my head, falling apart or facing my struggles would only serve to create an even bigger mess, making everything worse.

Then, someone I least expected to hear had spent the greater part of 20 years battling depression said something that in a single moment made me start to believe I could put my elbow into the work and become a functioning human being again.

"Sometimes you make a big mess before you rebuild," she said.

"I'm not sure I'm picking up what you're putting down," I countered.

"Think of a renovation," she continued. "You tear out walls, rip up floors, all the way back to the foundation. Then you get new wiring, more insulation, new drywall, brighter lights, and bring it back to a new, whole better version."

I admire this friend's resilience for how determination resonates with her. If something isn't working, she recognizes that and looks for a different strategy. I wonder if it's true how there's always something else to try.

Soon I began to understand that the renovation she spoke of wasn't a representation of an actual house, it was about me and where I was. It was about descending into the deepest parts of ourselves that we fear the most, and that may hurt to feel, so we can work them out in our heads, deal with them, heal and learn from them, and march on. It flicked some light on long enough for me to pick myself up off the floor and find the iron will I needed to get back in and see my doctor.

It seems silly to speak of the apprehension I had about something as simple as showing up to a doctor's appointment—I still feared the system failing me again if it got to the point of my needing it. There was difficulty in answering the doctor's questions at times. Following an honest answer, the conversation moved to exploring why I felt the way I did and how we'd ensure no tragic or sorrowful actions would be pursued while working on my wellness.

Overall, the doctor's appointments weren't as bad as I'd worked up in my head. She was kind and compassionate, and provided me with a referral to both a therapist and a psychiatrist. There remained a lingering uncertainty of who I was under my depression and anxiety, but ultimately we do what we must to brave the storm, we don't know how things will work out until we try, and we start rebuilding. From the foundation up.

So, I kept breaking the destructive cycle and showed up for the appointments. To my surprise, the social worker and psychiatrist were two of the kindest, gentlest professionals I've met. The psychiatrist took the time to draw diagrams of how antidepressant medications work, reminding me how they help to balance the brain chemicals that bring on depression and anxiety (neurotransmitters). After seeing my apprehension in taking them in case they didn't work, or had side effects that may cause me to feel emotionally or physically worse, she was very straightforward. She didn't gloss over the fact that it takes about four weeks for medication to take effect, that there may be side effects and some will fade, and how it's trial-and-error when it comes to finding the right dosage. Some haven't worked at all, and some have worked and then lost their efficacy. It can take time to notice them take effect and there may be side effects that aren't so great, which is when you have to decide if you want to accept the good they're doing and just deal with any accompanying unpleasantness. In response to my comment about possibly gaining weight on my current medication, a good friend who's presently on his own recovery journey said something that resonated quite deeply with me.

"It's natural," he said. "Try not to worry too much about it. Just stay in a routine. Without mental health there is no physical health."

The therapist was non-judgemental and had a welcoming and empathetic approach in learning the truths that had brought me in to see him. It's amazing to feel the difference in working therapeutically with someone who has a genuine regard for both you and the process versus someone who seems not to.

The way the sessions unfolded has helped to shed light on the truth that mental health difficulties present themselves in very subjective ways and at different times and places for everyone, and I learned the broad interpretation and meaning the words "depression" and "anxiety" hold. I think it all comes down to who experiences those feelings and at what age, how and from where they may derive, how they're expressed, and the ways in which they're best treated. In all honesty, I think one of the most humane and supportive things that can be done is seeking to gain a true understanding of the patient sitting in the chair. The connection established by feeling heard, understood, and valid is both strong and enduring.

As time went on, my inner frustration at a lack of progress grew. I was spiralling downhill again as a result of not being totally honest with the social worker and my doctor; telling them what they wanted to hear never served me well. It wasn't for lack of trust or rapport, it was just easier than doing the work to heal, finding short-term comfort by leaning into fake fixes on my own time. I was comfortable, despite the overwhelming discomfort.

The epiphany that they wouldn't be able help unless I was honest came down on me like a ton of bricks when asked how I was rationally expecting changes to happen when I wasn't telling the whole truth and therefore not doing the appropriate work. Withholding truth only narrowed their understanding of my important issues, causing them to provide inaccurate treatment methods.

So, I chose then and there to be honest and have been ever since: my voice shaking at times, but I've been straightforward and it's helping to save my life. There's such value in being straightforward with one's feelings; the moral is that the truth must be told in order to receive the proper tools to then get well.

The devil is certainly in the details when it comes to how suffering impacts us and what works and doesn't work. Therapy, medication, consistency, and a good support system is the method that's been helping to pull me though. Two approaches to therapy I've benefitted from are mindfulness and Cognitive Behavioural Therapy (CBT).

I learned about both while in school, but it wasn't until my therapist raised the concept of mindfulness and I tried it that I believed in its efficacy. There's a real serenity that comes when your path is taken one moment at a time rather than travelling the whole road at once. When I think I have to do everything at once, anxiety thrives; it puts one foot in the future and one in the past, making me do the splits instead of simply holding on to the moment. One aspect of mindfulness has to do with tuning into your mind and body from the tip of your toes to the top of your head. Becoming aware of my breath and what I'm doing to pull back the reins on those anxious and sad feelings helps to give space for positive thoughts.

Going for a run outside, reading a book, journaling, or writing a song can kick anxiety out of the mix. It really is splendid how tuning into a healthy outlet can shift a mindset. It's the commitment piece, I guess. Sometimes the ol' noggin just needs a break from thinking—warm pajamas and funny movies are definitely good for that.

I was gifted a weighted blanket last year and find they're a calming avenue to reduce anxiety, insomnia, and combat stress...it feels like a good hug. I actually read the other day that hugs lift oxytocin and serotonin levels. Those are the neurotransmitters that relieve anger and loneliness. I also learned that the average time for a hug to emit health benefits is about 20 seconds. The other one I like to use, which eases the nervous system, is pressing one hand securely on my heart and the other on my stomach.

Mindfulness also helps with panic and anxiety attacks. It doesn't always curb them, but I do find it's helped me to ride them out. A few years ago, clients were at hospice for a weekly group when a volunteer who was making rounds with ice cream offered me a cone. I thanked them and said I would pass this time.

"Why? You're not the one dying!" someone said.

"Yeah, just eat it! You have the rest of your life ahead of you. What are you planning to do with it, anyway?" another person piped up.

Obviously, the question came from a place of genuineness and probably had to do with career paths or something but that wasn't where my brain went; I was thinking about the place I was trying to hold back from.

It took a minute or two, with the sole warning being my increasing anxiety, until an overwhelming amount of worry and dread flooded from the top of my body, cutting through me like a knife. Negative thoughts and fears clawed their way up from the back of my hips, making it hard to swallow and sending me into a tailspin. It was like between every blink I was trying to catch my breath and remind myself I was alright. After excusing myself, I had barely reached the bathroom before numbness overtook my limbs.

I'd experienced a few anxiety and panic attacks before then so I knew I wasn't having a heart attack or dying, but being curled up in a tight ball on the floor with my heart pounding and feeling the weight of a boulder on my chest sure made it feel like I was. I learned (after the fact) that hyperventilating increases the severity of symptoms. The physical symptoms were as wearing as the emotional ones and even though the human body can't typically sustain this for very long, it felt like an eternity before the symptoms began to subside.

A friend shed some light on how unnerving it is to watch someone, especially someone you love, experience one. Reflecting on the helplessness that comes from not knowing how to help or even if it's possible, she reported that it's heartbreaking.

> *"You just want to wrap your arms around them and make it better, but sometimes they [panic attacks] don't work like that. My brother needed to be held tightly, whereas I don't want to be touched and need space. Deep breathing and weighted blankets help sometimes but it's just not a pleasurable experience in the slightest."*
> *-Anonymous*

What I try to do now, in general, is turn towards what I'm feeling with acceptance, identify the trigger, notice where I feel it in my body, give the emotion a name, and let my body help me. Because oxygen infusion is calming, bringing focus back to the breath and breathing slowly from the stomach helps. Focus on the rise and fall of your chest, the current moment, and breathe. Counting the duration of a breath in and out while deep breathing to make the breaths equal, weighted blankets and grounding techniques are all useful for preventing or working through an attack. When you really tune into your senses you begin to notice things like your feet on the ground and the temperature of the air. Listening to music or self-soothing by thinking something like, *everything is going to be ok, this will pass* in order to recognize what's happening and being aware that it will end, or relaxing your muscles as best you can so stress hormones don't fire as easily are all helpful. Diving into music, going for a walk and taking in nature and the colour of the leaves or the feeling of a brilliant sun beating down on your skin can shift a mindset almost instantly. In a music care training course I took a few years ago, I learned about entrainment; from my understanding, it's the synchronization of two rhythms. For instance, the rhythm of a song can influence a person's heart rate. It's really cool and can be helpful to bringing anxiety down or matching an emotion to help validate it. One of the clients I worked with in the music program at hospice experienced severe anxiety around going to appointments. Tapping her foot in slow, steady beats of four while waiting for the doctor actually brought her heart rate down, which made getting through the appointment much more manageable. There are also apps such as Calm or grounding techniques like concentrating on finding five things you can touch, hear, smell and feel.

Mindfulness is the skill and practice of mindfully dealing with emotions, to be used on an as-needed basis, not 24/7, and it has helped me because it brings awareness to where I want it and anchors it to the senses. It takes practice and, just as habits are formed and broken, requires repetition but the benefits are immeasurable. It should be utilized in the times when we are overwhelmed with stress or pain that is difficult to manage, and in those good moments when we want to feel and remember every detail and sensation.

Cognitive Behavioural Therapy builds on the idea that the way we think often indicates how we feel and what we do, what we do often indicates how we think and feel, and what we feel often indicates how we think and what we do. When I really examine this theory, I can see patterns that have etched themselves into my life. More or less, pieces of depression and anxiety can be contributed to by pattern of thought.

As human beings, the ways in which we've become accustomed to thinking are reflexive. Similar to making a fist with your hand, you just do it. There really isn't much thought put toward folding our fingers in and squeezing, our brains just do it by way of developed familiarity. Thoughts are similar; those that tailgate life as it unfolds create the inner dialogue that ultimately shape perspective. If years are spent responding in a certain way to a certain kind of situation (take conflict, for instance), the response to it often becomes habitual. As one would expect a smoker to feel combating their habit, challenging my thinking patterns came with its own specific stressors. Sifting out the negative in order to see the glass half-full initially reminded me of what I'd imagined trying to reshape long-hardened handprints in cement would feel like. That, or trying to teach an old dog a new trick.

Thought records are a helpful exercise to identify a more equalized way of approaching situations. While there are many formats, the one I'm most familiar with follows this general suit: One column lists the situation to be identified and explained, the next the emotions that occurred as a result (e.g. happy, sad, frustrated, guilty, anxious etc.). Following this are the automatic thoughts (e.g. "I'm never getting through this," "I'm such an idiot," or "He must hate me.") Of all the automatic thoughts listed, the strongest are acknowledged. Next, evidence that supports the strong thoughts can be written out (i.e. if the thought is, "I'm never getting through this" credible evidence may be, "There are a lot of difficulties filling this day." Or, if the thought is "He must hate me," credible evidence may be, "He seemed quite standoffish.") Once those are identified, the evidence that is unhelpful to the automatic thoughts are recognized (e.g. "I'm having a bad day, I've had them before, and I'll get through this one just the same. I have good days more often than I have bad days" and, "I wonder if he has a lot going on right now.") Lastly, evidence from both sides are weighed to arrive at amended, unbiased thoughts that better represent a more realistic perception (e.g. "I'm going to have bad days, I'm only human. I'm doing the best I can" and, "I can't control the way others act, but I can control how I respond to them."

Dec 2, 2019, 8:14 a.m.

2016 Entry: "I want to be happy and live as largely and bravely as I can. But depression is slumped in front of me, between myself in the door, like giant pile of manure and is stinking up the whole room."

Interesting, seeing where we once were from a bit of a different time and place. I bought a car this weekend (new to me) and until I got it, I rarely noticed that model on the roads. I suppose it's easy to spot a navy-blue Mazda hatchback when you're always thinking of a navy-blue Mazda hatchback. When I got home, the first thing I noticed was a pile of cat poop on the living floor. Smudge (my cat) sat on the stairs and watched me clean it up. He looked proud and amused.

After finding the entry from 2016 a few hours later, I gathered that if focus is placed on the shitty, difficult parts of life, not much else is going to be noticed. What about the carpet it's on? What about the colour of the walls? What about all of the ground that isn't covered in shit? If you tell yourself you can't see anything except the bad parts of something, all of the good, more positive things that are also happening at the same time will go fade out of view. "If you focus on the hurt, you will continue to suffer. If you focus on the lesson, you will continue to grow." We become versions of that on which we constantly place attention.

My mom is good at finding optimism in things. It would drive me nuts as a teenager when she would spin whatever I was venting about into something less horrible. I thought she just didn't understand what I was saying when she was really just reframing it. I appreciate it now.

Who would have thought that a new car and cat poop would lead to learning that if you focus on the problem, it only grows? If the problem is watered more than the solution, it would only make sense

that it wouldn't bloom. Focusing on the solution pulls
you out of rumination and shrinks the problem.
-S

I remember learning in a university lecture that a build-up of negativity impacts happiness. A helpful tool to organize thoughts is by looking at the larger picture. Dividing a piece of paper down the middle and writing down all of the good and bad things that happened each day for a week helps. If there's a recurring negative, it will show and I can consider the pros, worth, and cons in keeping or eliminating it.

Starting and/or ending my days differently by contributing to a gratitude journal rather than jumping right onto social media focuses the larger picture and serves to clear my head. It takes only a few seconds but the impact is lasting. Also, because I try to do it before I pee my pants; it's like a dangerous competition. Or I try and get to the gym, one or the other.

Trainer and nutritionist Tim Walcott offers some insight: "Maintaining a healthy lifestyle routine can help to give purpose, confidence, and structure to an otherwise unpredictable and erratic existence. Life is full of things we can't know or control, so making the small but consistent effort to intentionally create positive routine around your life can be an effective way to build a strong self-image and improve your overall outlook on life. Having a regular exercise routine to look forward to, as well as healthy eating habits, can be incredibly powerful in fostering general motivation particularly in people that would otherwise find themselves falling prey to the grips of depression or just general restlessness. This isn't to imply that eating healthy and exercising are a cure for mental illness, but rather they act as a form of support and maintenance."

Given the illness, the idea of one giant overhaul was a bit short of realistic; as in one day I would be depressed and the next day I would not. It takes just as long to heal as it did to hurt and that journey is a process with no set time frame. There are steps forward, backward, and forward again, given that healing of any sort is rarely linear. I used to get stuck in the thought that if I'm struggling it must mean I'm failing, while the only failure happening was an inability to see that as long as there is consistency with direction and I've got some hope and bravery in my back pocket, speed doesn't matter. A bad day does not equal disaster and to tear oneself into shreds over one tough day doesn't do anything except add guilt and more hurt.

"You need to keep being busy and productive in order to keep your mind busy. And you need to be kind to yourself," my friend said.

"What's the line between being patient and kind to myself but still being productive, and being patient and kind but not trying hard enough?" I asked.

"Being patient and kind to yourself means not beating yourself up for having a bad day but saying tomorrow is a new day. Let's start again. Get in your jammies, climb into bed with the dog, put on a funny movie, close your eyes and get some rest. Tomorrow is a new day."

I know I've got to let go of what is comfortable to make new habits. I'm trying to acknowledge whatever is unfolding and keep going by learning from it. A solid base of consistency, alongside a higher purpose for that base, is what carries healthy behaviours to their follow through. As is often as the case when learning something new, effort and practice are required before it eventually becomes second nature. Discomfort always comes first but a snowball effect inevitably occurs the more those healthy behaviours are applied and utilized. I'm finding that my motivation and desire to practice them often increases the more I see results. Just like learning to ride a bike or drive standard. Hard, but not impossible.

Jan 5, 2020, 7:04 a.m.

> *"What am I supposed to do with the good feelings?" I asked.*
> *"You just feel them."*
> *They didn't happen often, initially. But when they did, they were significant.*
> *-S*

Accepting depression and anxiety as a part of me has taken patience, bravery and effort in my path toward self-acceptance. I'm realizing that when you change the way you look at things, the things you look at change. In his book "Spontaneous Happiness," Andrew Weil speaks to how rumination is an underlying characteristic of creativity. He states: "When we view depression as inherently bad and automatically traumatic—which is easy to do when the symptoms are so difficult—we immediately form a relationship to our mood that chips away at our resilience."

It suggested depression offered an opportunity to learn and grow in the things that bring purpose and bliss to my life rather than a factor that chips away at them. The attention to detail and the ease that has come with rumination are turning into major concepts that help heighten creativity. I think everyone was glad for that revelation.

A decent therapist and support system will look over an issue and hopefully hand out a helpful remedy for it. An honorable therapist and support system are receptive to that same issue, but teaches you how to solve it. Healing, to me, means arriving at a place where pain's power decreases, not to the point of never hurting, but to the point of not being able to hold control over our lives. I believe what hurts can be healed. Human beings are extraordinary, and if we can survive rock bottom, so can we survive the recovery. I don't mean to sound off here, but falling apart isn't always all that bad. It hurts, and that part sucks; however, it's not a double-edged sword because it also gives us time to process and learn from things that may otherwise be swept under the rug.

Healing has also meant letting go of bitterness and electing to forgive. I think many of us are so hard on ourselves over being who we were at some point. I need to elect to forgive myself for the survival patterns, behaviors and qualities I collected when I knew no better at the time.

Pain and adversity of any kind are unavoidable; they sort of come with being alive. As said by John Green, "That's the thing about pain. It demands to be felt." When they do wrap us up like burritos in their arms, damn, can it hurt like hell sometimes. But even throughout it, there are moments when we realize, "wow, things are good and I'm ok." If you're continuing to do the best you can in the face of any struggle, I'm proud of you. It's unbelievably brave to face each day with depression, anxiety, addiction, or any struggle of similar nature that holds the potential to fall within or near the hourly or minute-by-minute fight. I hope you lean enough into self-compassion to recognize this. Lana Rafaela says it best in her poem "I Think It's Brave."

I'm still no expert, but one thing of which I'm becoming certain is that retreating to the part of you that scares you the most, sitting with the ugly, painful feelings in order to start healing them, is much safer than emotionally crashing and suffering. As it turns out, holding in or running away from emotions or pain of any kind with no place to go is sort of like pressing on the gas and brakes of a car at the same time; you just end up overheating and burning out your engine. And then what? Even if it won't happen for miles down the road, it only makes for a longer fall and a harder crash in the end.

The details that have contributed to my depression seemed to work like a kidney stone more often than not; can't run, hide, or win through resistance because they're going to push through anyway. For anxiety, I suppose it's similar to the monster under your bed; until you get down and see what is – or isn't – there, the idea of how frightening what's underneath is will continue to build. The more I allow myself to be vulnerable to what I feel, even if it hurts and especially when my flight response kicks in and I want to hide away in old habits, the easier those emotions run their course and pass through. In facing and dealing with the emotions that come with healing, I've been doing things I never imagined myself doing and achieving some truly meaningful insights.

Serenity and content have started inching their way back into my life as the darkness that coated the lens through which I grew to see the world has been lightening shade by shade. Kind of like an onion, except therapy and consistency with new habits don't burn as much. The familiar sting that comes when I face an unmaintained part of this mile I'm destined to walk reminds me I'm still in the fight, perhaps not to the degree spoken of in previous pages, but I'm grateful to have found a few avenues that continue to somehow hold me up and ground me at the same time. I wouldn't be sitting in this chair feeling a beat come down in my chest if it hadn't been for the support system with which I've been blessed.

Therapy isn't all that bad, either. Just over a year has passed since re-establishing my sessions; I actually look forward to it now because it helps to educate me on how to work healthily and productively with emotions to facilitate action and further growth. Medication helps. The balance and steadiness it offers allows the tools I learned in therapy to be utilized, but it too is a two-way street. I could put a toolbox smack dab in the middle of the floor, but until I put the tools to use and want to apply them, they're not going to do any work.

During the times I felt I had little to offer this world, it had usually originated from the inside; how I see myself and my worth and purpose and whether or not I believe in it. I could've been reminded of my worth 1,000 times over but until I believed it for myself, showed up for help, and believed in it enough to put it to use, it wouldn't have made a deciding difference. When I didn't believe things would ever get better, all chances of healing became wilted and warped. Maybe it will end up awful, but maybe it won't; it's always worth trying and it is never too late.

Oct 8, 2019, 10:48 a.m.

Saturday was one of those days, centre stage in a lull, where taking on the day ahead seemed like an impossible task. I was scheduled to play a show at a bar in downtown Brampton at night but spent the morning trying to convince myself to get up, pull up my socks, and push through rather than duck under the covers and back out of the gig. My friend called to wish me good luck.

"I'm probably not going. I can't," I said.

"Music always makes you feel good. Why don't you feel like you can go?" she asked.

"I just can't go. They're going to take one look at me and know how anxious and close I am to falling apart."

"I know it's hard but you need to get up and get to that show. You committed yourself to do it and you will. Get going," she said.

The idea I might have found myself feeling a bit better once I got going and would feel a sense of accomplishment after it was done seemed a tad short of realistic when I was nailed to the couch. Tough love ended up being enough to force myself to pull my socks up, drag my ass out of the house, and go. I played the show and it went well. My friend was right. It's the same as how spending time with people helped take my mind off things.

After one of my sets, a gentleman came up and asked if I had a tip jar. I hadn't put one out, but he handed me $80 and thanked me for my music. When I said I couldn't possibly accept that much, he went on to share that he discovered my single, 'Never Forget You,' a song I wrote for National Bereavement Day a few weeks prior and was grieving the recent loss of his dear wife.

Gratitude overwhelmed me and left me a bit shocked in a full-hearted kind of way. To have this person come all this way, be standing in front of me thanking me for songs I wrote and for the comfort they were bringing him and his family, was nothing short of gratifying.

It's always the "getting there" or the "starting" of anything that's most difficult. Sometimes instead of waiting until you feel motivated or inspired to start, you have to create your own motivation and inspiration by picking yourself up and just starting to dig your heels in anyway. Standing up is a good place to begin. Usually, I find myself feeling a little better once I get going. And too, you never know what the day ahead may bring when you walk out

*the door. In this case it was following through with
something to which I had committed myself, even
though it was hard starting, and I (well, my music)
was even able to be of help to somebody along the
way. That never doesn't feel good.*
-S

Renovating has meant piecing together a resolve to
live fully and devotedly by working on maintaining a
healthy state of mind, heart, and soul. Sometimes this
calls for embracing change and other times it's simply
owning the things that make me human and being where
I am with no self-judgement. It's also meant having the
willingness to let go of certain things that were holding
me in the spot and perspective I was in. Perceiving
emotions as information and trying to learn and grow
from them helps with processing them and letting them
go with greater ease. Then, if the not-so-good feelings
come around again in the future they may not be as
powerful or last as long and I'm able to respond to them
better. The more I let go of, the freer my hands are and
the more open my mind and heart become to mapping
out more of a blueprint and keep building while healing.
They seem to go hand in hand.

I'm going to build a big front window with a view of
that which makes me happy and remind me of goodness.
I'm going to hang the good memories from the past
on the new walls and keep pulling on strength and
digging up bravery to use the lessons learned from the
rougher times to continue building a new, sturdier and
more resilient foundation. With every brick I lay, I'm
reminded that I'm braver than I sometimes think I am

and can get through and do more than I believe I can. I'm going to keep turning pain into purpose. Depression has been the hardest adversity I've ever encountered, but it's showing me how bold I am and that when it pushes hard, I can push back harder.

Some days are wonderful and others downright suck and I have to dig my heels a little deeper into the belief that I can always keep moving forward. I try to look at the hard days as just having "a day" and believe better ones are to come, as they do. Truth be told, some of the greatest days of my life have been scattered among the worst. The more I choose consistency over inconsistency, so long as it doesn't entail pulling out the bricks I've already laid, the further I get into my inner renovation and ultimately cultivating the life I'd like to lead. On those days where building a whole room feels too big, instead I'll paint a picture for the wall that will eventually be there. If taking a rest means avoiding a lifetime of defeat, I'll take a rest. The house will still be there when I decide to pull myself back together and continue building. As for the days that feel unbearably overwhelming even after trying to face them, well, sometimes you just need to put your phone away and shut your brain off. Or, you just need to scream, cry, or blast your favourite music and not give a shit about anything for a little while. What you always need to do is keep facing forward.

Every day I try to take the part of me that wants to curl up in a ball by the hand and carry on marching by remembering why I started in the first place. Doing the work is hard and I've thought about giving up a lot, but what if that next approach or method works and is the one that brings me further forward?

In a recent therapy session, I was advised to be open in considering how even when you're sitting still focusing on breathing, you're still moving forward. Even on the wickedest, hardest days, every minute I get through is a minute I'm moving forward and progressing.

"Every accomplishment is a victory," he said.

"I didn't do anything except eat and get through the day," I said.

"Did you think you could?"

"Not really."

"Then tell me the evidence that suggests that isn't an accomplishment."

There is importance in giving yourself credit that you're doing the best you can with your best foot forward, even if it's just breathing some days. No matter how small or silly it seems, celebrate those victories. A baby step may seem insignificant on its own, but when just a few are linked together, the distance gained grows tenfold. You find things that bring light into the dark. A change. Gratitude. A new friend. Love. A choice. Hope. You realize a day or a week has gone by that you haven't fought through a bad day and the person looking back in the mirror is someone who is making it through and is damn brave and resilient to boot.

To say managing depression and anxiety is hard especially without a suitable remedy is an understatement. The time others have taken to fully understand the details of my story and the kinds of effort that have been put forth to keep the wheels turning on this journey have been such an uplifting factor. A solid approach to treatment is like a good set of shoes: if you want to get any miles in, it has to suit you and you have to try out a few different options. Then, if you find one that will work, you start working them into your days and molding them into your steps. Some past approaches have felt comparable to receiving physiotherapy on my knee when it was really my wrist that needed attention, which is why I'll always be appreciative of hearing, "let's see if this technique works. If it doesn't, we'll rework it. If it does work, we build from it." Each time I walk out the door now, it's with a therapeutic tool in my back pocket to add to my therapeutic toolbox that can be pulled from when needed.

On the same page, I think as important as a good support system is, standing on your own two feet and believing you can apply yourself are just as vital. The person we undoubtedly spend our whole lives with is ourself. Perhaps, then, we should strive to ensure our internal dialogue is warm, comfortable, forgiving, kind, and peaceful.

Living a life of wellness in concert with depression and anxiety and their sometimes-untimely schedules and surprising façades is an ongoing journey I'm still trying to figure out and am tripping through a lot of the time. I'd like to think their existence is only in the rear-view mirror, but they live quietly in the back of my mind and in the depths of my heart. Perhaps they'll find their own way down their own road one day, and maybe they won't. If they decide to stay, that's all right too. It's an ongoing renovation taken moment by moment, one day at a time, but I'm finding my way. We always do. Even if it means tearing down walls, gutting the bad stuff, or rebuilding from the bottom up, the quietest part of us always knows what we need. Sometimes we just have to slow down a little or be still enough to hear it.

I'm falling in love with living again and with the small joys that are actually proving to be quite large. Things like sunlight bouncing off a window while I enjoy my morning coffee, laughing and singing my favourite song at the top of my lungs in the car with my friends, being a good daughter, granddaughter and friend, or absorbing the wisdom those in my life generously choose to impart. I'm glad I'm alive to realize how the more I lean into the good things every day, the more prevalent and widespread they become and the easier it is to stand up to the harder ones.

As for the delicate piece of me that believed bringing my road to an end was the best plan, it has yet to shrink away into nothingness. However, the size and strength of it began diminishing when I stopped defying it and started trying to understand it. I don't crumble beneath it anymore and am not so afraid of how its occasional tug feels on my sleeve. I know there are threads that may fray once and a while, but I know better now than to yank so unkindly on them. There are also aspects contributing to my depression that I have yet to let go of, though eventually I will. For now, I'll allow the parts that have taught me resilience, empathy and bravery to rise to the surface and fold the others as neatly as I possibly can, tucking them away as a reminder of the place I once was and am no longer at; mere memorabilia, like a few of the grass-stained dresses I outgrew as a little girl.

I put much contemplation into which angle would best outline my approach to the struggle for better mental health. I told myself to take my time and to be delicate so as to not make the experience seem too raw or "too real." Ultimately, I realized that's what depression is. It's raw. It's real. It's valid. It's proven to be a chapter in my life that has highlighted the ugliest parts of itself from my head, down through my heart, and out my feet. There have been times I almost bowed to the belief that I wasn't going to endure it, but every morning I try to greet every theoretical brick I lay and remember that depression is a difficult mile to tread, but it can be managed.

Alive

They said that some days
You'll feel it more than others
Some days I don't feel it all

Hated to admit it
I wasn't so proud
My heart was beating against these
walls and the pain was loud

Chorus
I don't have answers and I sure
as hell don't have a key
But I'm ok, I'm alright
Jumped out of a plane to feel alive

What do you say
When all the words have been spoken
And what do you do
When you're lying in pain

There's a whole damn world
Out there to save you
Thought I had to leave this town
To let my walls down

Chorus
I wanted this all to end, but I can't pretend
That with a friend to know and a hand to hold, I know

Chorus
Sara Rose, 2018

flight kicks in

Jan 28, 2018, 9:09 p.m.

I learned to drive standard when I was 17. Dad always used to say, "no kid of mine isn't going to know how to drive standard." Despite not really having a great interest in learning, I actually prefer it now.

We drove out to a side road and I hopped into the driver's seat. On the middle of a hill Dad told me to push the clutch in and put it in neutral; he released the emergency brake and we started rolling. Even though I knew he'd never put us in danger I nearly lost my mind due to not knowing what I was doing, my mind instantly became flustered trying to remember which pedal was which and how to control it. After stalling more times than I could count, I finally managed it and we made it back up and over the hill.

Sometimes the best way to figure something out, even when you're scared, is to throw your entire self out into the open and do it. Unless you're naked. Don't do that. Rolling back down the hill that way may hurt a bit.

-S

ou're supposed to trust your gut, right? When instinct kicks in and says to run in the opposite direction, do we run? Or are we supposed to find the courage to stand our ground and fight like hell? What defines the line between a time to fight and a time to take flight? I'm sure there's one drawn in the sand somewhere between logical and illogical. Or self-growth and probable disaster.

I've chalked up fear as a variety of uneasy physical and emotional feelings or sensitivities, like a jar of mixed jelly beans, rising up in the face of something intuitively deemed dangerous or threatening, like watching a scary movie or skydiving. Or chipmunks. Or being startled by a bear. Or the thought of something glimmering with grief or anticipated angst like the thought of losing someone close to you or sifting through the intricate details of an ordeal that brought about a large amount of trauma or grief.

A small part of me wishes I could neglect being afraid. I'd like to go back to being a little girl, playing Barbies and house and not having to face the scary parts of life we have no option but to face as adults. Not facing the things or circumstances where fear is potentially life-saving, but the fears that limit growth. The idea of inhaling and exhaling each day or night without a single worry or never having to sense a tiny, sharp fear tiptoeing into my mind is a soothing thought. As an adult I've thought about running away more than I ever did as a kid. Emotionally, there exists this gravity-like blanket in which we want to wrap ourselves when it comes to facing those things we fear. Certainly, it's made of safety at times, given that fear is so normal and natural for us; it's quite literally woven into our DNA. As if it's so normal that it almost isn't even there. Fear is an emotion as old as human existence. Given it kicks in our physiological ancient fight-or-flight response when something's not right, its importance to our survival is there for good reason, I suppose.

For a moment or two, imagine not being afraid of anything—what super-humans we would be! For a short while, anyway. I'm sure the odds of heightened confidence, thrill, and adventure to be bold and do the things usually outside the realm of comfort or general human reach would be quite high, and maybe we would all become skydivers or scaffold workersor better yet, courageous enough to become our greatest selves. A friend who's on a recovery journey once told me that the fears we don't face eventually become the limits within which we live our lives, holding us in a position of stasis.

People speak about being as brave as a lion or as emotionally strong as an iron band. Me? Well, I see myself as a cross between a scared pigeon and an anxious chihuahua. Beneath my tough talk I've been and sometimes still am afraid of a lot of things, likely more than I can possibly count in one breath. I'm scared of having something to lose. Of starting over. Of speaking my mind. Of being happy. Of the depths to which depression is capable of reaching. Of spiders. Of being confident. Sometimes of succeeding. Of getting stuck in a dress in a store change room again. Of losing the people I love and care about. Of pronouncing the dish on the menu wrong (it's pronounced pen-nay, not pen). Of not understanding in time. Of not being understood. Of not finding love. Of not using my voice. Of staying the way I am forever. Of hurting someone. Of contracting an illness that effects the conscious use of my brain. Of perfection. Of suffering. Of not being good enough. Of becoming my depression and anxiety. Of pouring my cereal in a bowl to find out I have no almond milk in the fridge. Of the unknown. Of oblivion. Of hunger and poverty. Of misused power in the world. Of alcoholism. I'm scared of all of these things and in some cases I haven't yet figured out why. I do know that without bravery, a human's flight response kicks in like there's no tomorrow every single time we're faced with a fear.

I don't know why we run. If I had to guess, I'd say it's got a fair amount to do with fear. Having been cursed with timidity for a lot of my teenage years, I suppose it makes sense to have found greater ease in the idea of running from challenges than in confronting them. I think it's normal to feel this to some degree, but reaching a level of comfort with my bashfulness becomes tedious and narrows the scope of your life. It's like the constant drip of a tap; the more you turn away from it, the closer the sink gets to filling and possibly overflowing.

For a long time, when I got scared, I ran. Like bloody hell. I ran emotionally until the soles of my shoes wore through completely and my feet bled. I thought if I stopped running, I would feel the weight of all that from which I was running, but it turns out things tend to run with you. So as far away as I got at times, in the end I didn't get very far.

You can run for miles, days, or years and still experience the push against what you are running from or are reluctant to let in. The problems you're running from will still be there when you get back, or they'll resurface in that new town or at the bottom of that glass of hooch. I suppose it only made sense that all of the running would eventually catch up with me, and just let me say, it's really something to look into the same dusty mirror you've been getting ready in front of every goddamn morning for years, only to one day know with your entire being that something needed to change. That no matter what, you can't keep going on the way you are or some part of you is going to shatter and fall apart, if it doesn't feel like it has already. I hardly recognized the person looking back in the mirror by the time I'd finished school.

March 12, 2019, 3:12 p.m.

Fear comes and goes now, but I'm ok with that. It's not so much of an adversary to me anymore as it is an ally because it opens the palm of a hand to courage; one full of opportunity and instinctively instructive to the places providing room for personal growth and expansion. Speaking of which, the more it's faced, the braver you become. I think, anyway. Remember when you were behind the wheel of a car for the first time and everything felt scary? Look at you now, driving with your knees, drinking a coffee, eating a piece of cake, shifting gears, singing along to the band on the radio, all while going the speed limit.

I'm not saying I'm always brave and never submit to paralyzing fear. Some days are a hot mess. The only difference is I'm no longer running from it because while fear is healthy, panic is the point at which it becomes detrimental. We can only try to overcome fear by facing it. Because more often than not, facing it is a lot less grim than running from it our whole lives.
-S

Fear is a good thing. A damn good thing, in fact. The way it can instruct and motivate the meeting of a goal by beckoning courage is healthy. The way it can provide insight when it's explored is worthy. It bends and warps and reshapes as we grow older. I know people who seem much more fearless than they did when we were kids and I know people who are living as if trapped in a spiral of caution. I suppose living with fear quite simply comes down to a working balance between growth and self-preservation.

Keeping the phrase "I can't" in my vocabulary has seen me up to my eyeballs in the feeling of running a never-ending marathon with my gut literally screaming, "abort mission!" So, I made a decision this year to change how I relate to fear. I'm finally starting to slow it down and chip away at the power it's historically had over me and my decisions. When I'm about to do something that scares me, I remember my first skydive and of the sensation I get while performing. Right now, I'm also thinking of the day my friend's seven-year-old daughter was standing on the platform facing the monkey bars a few summers ago, absolutely petrified to jump out to grab onto them but also determined to do it. She was scared but she did it anyway and it was an eye-opener.

I look at the fears above and the one that overrides all of them is that of not trying in the first place. I'm going to do things and be brave despite my misgivings. Sometimes it takes effort to not give in to my trepidation, but I know now the only problem with fear is how you respond to it and that when you live in a constant state of fear, the resulting survival mode no longer allows you to fully live your life. Respect fear. Listen to it to figure out its underlying message so its root can be deemed logical or illogical and it can be conquered. This doesn't mean each time I'm being brave that in that very second I'm not afraid at the same time, it's just now it motivates me more than anything and I get a little bit stronger every day from throwing my arms into the air and leaning into the wind instead of closing my eyes and taking flight.

I'm not afraid of anyone and have dismantled a few walls, started letting my heart out, believing I can do hard things, and telling some fears that I just don't fucking care because the moment fear is shielded away is that moment it wins. I'm not saying go up to a bear and hug it, but if you're fearful of something or frightened to do something, be scared. You just have to face up to it and do it while afraid because sometimes the fear doesn't go away until you do. Show up and say "I'm scared, but I'm here." It's why I keep a red bandana on the top of my guitar. The colour red has always seemed to me a bold and brave colour. It reminds me to march on, even when I'm petrified. Accordingly, eat fear like a candy bar today so that tomorrow you can look back and say, "I wouldn't believe what I did today, yesterday."

So, when the floodgates of our deepest fears open, do we run or dare fright to bend by standing tall with our shoulders back? More or less, is the world going to end if you do?

Weight of it All

What heart lets down its guard to
fight a fire rising with desire
I will not lay my head down or run
when my feet touch ground
Are you willing to risk it all
Willing to fall, willing to dream
Willing to wear your heart on your sleeve

Chorus
It's the break in the wind
When you feel the weight of it all
And the crumpled-up letters
Staring at me all night all
But everybody thinks it's the fall
Everybody thinks it's the fall

I've got the sense to realize I set my bar a little high
There's a distant voice inside my
head, one I can't hide or forget
Are you willing to try
Willing to fly, to stand tall
To fail if you gain it all

Chorus
Bridges burned, lessons learned
I stopped to feel it all
Kindred hearts wrapped in empathy
Wrinkles show just where we've been

Chorus
Sara Rose, Until Now, 2018

a rare rush

2018

During a rare rush of confidence in February 2017, I booked the Opera House in Orangeville as the concert venue for my debut album *Until Now*. I didn't know if I would be able to fill 270 seats in the theatre, or break even in the end but I wanted to take the chance; I guess the strange feeling I had that it might all work out in the end was enough to jump on board.

Newspapers soon reached out to cover the story on the album and ticket sales started picking up shortly after that. I think it's really cool to be part of a community inspired by art and supportive of local artists.

My friends and I went out for wings and beers on the night before the concert and when I got home, I wrote *Alive*. I ended up deciding at the last minute to open the show with it. After sound check a few close friends showed up with Mom and we went up to the dressing room to get ready. One of my best friends emceed the night and did an incredible job, a friend I've known since Kindergarten who went on to become a dancer opened the show, followed by my first ever guitar student who played some of her own songs at 14 years of age.

I felt terrified yet completely empowered stepping out onto the stage. It was delightfully lit and I could hardly believe I was singing my songs to a crowd of people who had paid to come to my show. It felt really nice, but at the same time strange to believe people wanted to hear me play and listen to what I had to say. The entire evening was one I will never forget and it wasn't just because I filled the venue and broke even, it was because of the love of the people who I was playing to brought into that room. I saw music's impact and how 'at home' it felt to play in my hometown and with the guys who, 14 years ago as a young kid, started sharing their in-depth knowledge and love for music with me, teaching me pretty well everything I know.

The support and engagement in my community, both locally and online, continues to be an unflagging force behind my continuing to pursue what I love. Everybody starts somewhere when they're chasing their dream and that encouragement may be one of the reasons the person writing songs in their basement until 3 a.m. and playing in small bars on weekends is spurred on to continue creating and performing. Plus, music is something to be enjoyed without reservation and always serves as an avenue toward cultivating connection and understanding.

June 1, 2018, 10:12 p.m.

No words. Just so grateful.
-S

we could be beautiful

There's a feeling deep inside my heart that I've long spent trying to figure out. The more I analyzed it, the more it eluded me when it turns out the answer was quite simple all along. Funny how easy it is to take straightforward things and pile on the complications.

This feeling started breaking down when the set for the music video for *Dancin'* was being created and I was standing on the stairs with the owner of the venue, an elegant celebration of life centre called In Memoriam. Being the genuinely humble and down-to-earth guy owner is, he wouldn't accept any money for lending the team the space.

"You have to make money, too," I said, still trying to pay him.

"I know. I'm not looking to with this. Just remember us when you hit the charts," he said, smiling.

As the chat continued, I learned he was an emergency responder before opening his funeral business. Having been on the receiving end of questions as to why I stayed involved with hospice work at the time, I was interested to hear about his interest in this work.

"Lives should be celebrated. I'm all about that. You know, I've served the richest man in town and I've served the poorest man in town. One had a lot to his name, the other had nothing more than the shirt on his back. And they both ended up in the same place," he said.

A few months went by after filming before a man approached me in a Starbucks, during a wicked Toronto snowstorm. I'd arrived in the city that morning and had time before an appointment, so I was there writing.

"Excuse me, ma'am?" the man asked.

I looked up from my laptop to see him standing a few feet away and took quick notice of a plastic ring on his fourth finger. He must have been at least in his late seventies and he had an unkempt, rough look about him. I took my headphones off and he immediately apologized for interrupting before going on to ask if I had a few bucks I could spare for him to buy something to eat. Embarrassed, I said I was sorry but I didn't.

"Alright. Thanks for your time."

He tilted his head forward and as he turned toward the door I watched his shoulders fall. I immediately thought to myself, now with pure shame, that I hardly had enough money to keep myself afloat let alone feed a stranger. Nearing the door, pulling the neck of his long sleeve shirt above his ears, I noticed how thin he was.

I thought about the warm bed waiting for me under my roof and the food in my fridge. Shame washed over me like a tidal wave. Soon after thinking about the clean clothes I was wearing, the warm boots on my feet, a computer, phone, and warm drink in my hands, I thought, *How awful is this of me? How could I be so blind, distant, and resistant?* I took a breath, got up from the table and went out the door. He was already outside and from the look on his face when he turned to see me sliding down Bloor Street, for a second I think he thought I was running after him with no intent to stop (oops).

I bought him a sandwich and a hot chocolate and we sat together. What surprised me most was immediately after he thanked me for the small $9 meal, he asked how my day was going and offered some of it to me. How could someone in his position with not much reason to give half a damn about how a seemingly well-off stranger's life may be, be selfless enough to offer some of what was probably his first full meal in God knows how long? Over the brief half-hour we sat together, I came to learn this man's story. He was a veteran.

He was so grateful, yet the hand I extended contained only nine dollars. Nine stinking dollars that made his day a little less bare. I guess sometimes doing something so seemingly small is all it can take to carry someone a little further through their day. When I offered to buy him a few extra snacks, he politely declined. When I insisted, the tears that filled in the corners of his eyes broke my heart.

"I wish I could do something to say thank you," he said.

"You already have," I said.

Once he left, I sat for a while in contemplation. This man had not a dollar to his name, a soul purer than my own, and was one of the noblest human beings I've met; just a genuinely well-meaning person who demonstrated how putting goodness out to the universe with zero expectation of compensation makes life all the more grand. It tends to be those small, unimportant and irrelevant pieces that, when held up against the bigger picture, are actually of the utmost significance. Not to mention the plastic ring on his finger in place of a silver band, proving that a plastic ring can reflect the same sentiment as a 24 karat diamond; love isn't grounded in materialism but in emotion and inner truth.

In all instances, hate and arrogance are heavy and don't serve anyone. They create and fuel ugly circumstances and probably have a negative impact on overall health. Release them when you breathe out, because at the end of the day it doesn't matter how much better you are than someone, how many zeroes are in your bank account, how many letters follow your name, or how many achievements you've got under your belt. We may lead different lives, but we're literally floating on a giant spinning rock and we may not know exactly where, how, or when we'll go, but we do know we'll pass away at some point, and it's not like we're taking the fancy car, diamond ring, or anything materialistic for that matter, with us. We take the experiences. We take the memories. We take the moments of kindness, those both given and received, we take the life that's been lived, and we take the love. I think that's what the owner of the venue was implying. Those things are what colour humanity in the most fulfilling, beautiful ways. We're all human, and no matter the shell on the outside or the storied filling, we all want and need the same things on the inside: to love and be loved. Almost, I reckon, as much as we need air to breathe.

I must also recognize that people likely wouldn't still exist if there weren't goodness. The world is full of beautiful places, graciousness, and more faith than you can possibly wrap your arms around; however, there still exists suffering of many kinds, sometimes mild and other times too horrific to name. Having said that, even though circumstances may make it difficult, in a world where you can be anything, try to be good to others. Choose compassion and empathy. Choose love. Remain humble and kind as you live out your days. Help someone even if you know the favour can't be returned. If someone falls behind, go back and walk with them. Listen for a minute longer. Give a friend a hug, buy a stranger a coffee. Share. Be a good friend. Hold the door and smile at someone even if they don't acknowledge it; they'll likely think about it all day. Strive to be kind-hearted even to those who aren't good to you and even on the days where your patience is tested and you have to grit your teeth and take a breath to see where you are because integrity is all and time is too precious to put into anything other than love, connection, and kindness and love.

One of the most meaningful things we can do is meet today as an opportunity to stand on the shoulders of who we were yesterday. There will never be a better place, time, or avenue for spreading good and truth than here and now, nor will there ever be too much of either of them. So, sprinkle that shit everywhere and then keep on sprinkling it. You may actually feel your heart grow. We're only here for a short while, and not pulling the wool over our eyes where there are opportunities to hold each other tight helps goodness prevail. I don't know a whole lot about anything, but I'm confident in the fact that even in brief moments of exchange such as this one, we're meant to be there for each other. After all, we're all we have.

With just a little more love and a little less hate, we could be beautiful.

We Could Be Beautiful

Got a feeling in my heart tonight
So far down inside
I wanna break it down, but it's still so raw
The usual pull engraved in our hearts

There's something about how they say
Trust isn't that simple and pile
complication on it anyway
Oh, we had it all but we bent it until it broke
I'm so scared of what happens next, where we'll go

I'm sitting on glass trying to work this out
When did we get so distant now
And how did we become so resistant
I'm dying to know

Chorus
I believe, I believe
We could be, we could be beautiful
With a little more love, a little less hate
We could be beautiful

I'm not worried about fancy cars or diamond rings
We are only human and on the inside,
we're wanting the same things
To love and be loved, oh isn't that the point of it all
Starting to think the answer is clear,
or maybe I'm just naïve

Pre-Chorus
Chorus
What's the truth about love?
Can we just hold on, hold on
If this anger's a hiding place for fear
Hold on, hold on
Can we work it out and stop paying the price
It's time to wake up tonight

Chorus
Beautiful

Sara Rose, We Could Be Beautiful, 2019

bubble baths and lattes

Nov 3, 2019, 9:18 a.m.

> *I learned a few days ago that when you're worn thin and choose to not listen to the signs your body gives you to ask you slow down or take a break, it will eventually make you stop and listen and take a break. Go figure.*
> *-S*

While 2020 took to the backstage to await its debut, the regular rush of familiarity around New Year's resolutions set in. By December 31st the majority of people I know, including myself, will have said, "new year, new me" and by the morning of January 1st, newsfeeds flow with posts about newly-set goals and tossed habits.

Even though I don't think we need formality or tradition as cause to make new resolutions, I did make a few for 2020. For instance, I was going to live by the mantra of, "2020 is the year where clothes are folded as soon as they come out of the dryer." I was going to attempt to keep my life from spiralling out of control by making the mental note to keep my purse Chapstick where it belongs so that my nightstand Chapstick doesn't end up in my car and my car Chapstick doesn't end up in my purse. Others came down to eating healthier and exercising more frequently and consistently. Typically, as history will out, by the time lunch rolls around on January 1st I'll be hungry again, eating bread and the leftovers or pie from New Year's Eve. The last but most sincere resolution was to engage in more self-care.

The only thing is, the self-care I was imagining didn't bring the outcome I was hoping for. Not saying that maxing out a credit card on a shopping spree or binge-watching Netflix and eating horrible food in place of going for a run, or lounging in a relaxing bath wouldn't make me feel a little better, but I'm talking more about the care that goes further. The perception I had of what care for the self means, changed after having the pleasure of hearing a gentleman by the name of Rami Shami speak at a 2019 annual general meeting. The impact of his message about the importance of taking time for ourselves really resonated, especially the intention to maintain emotional, spiritual, and physical well-being.

Sitting there listening, I suddenly realized I hadn't stopped for much more than a breath since starting university. Between 2014 and the start of 2020, I hadn't stopped until I'd hit a wall of emotional and physical exhaustion that had made me stop. Up until then, I'd been working at hospice during the day, juggling part time jobs to make ends meet, attending university lectures or writing papers at night. I was either eating too much or not at all, wasn't sleeping enough, was letting old flames burn me more than once, trying to please everyone and bend for some who didn't even notice until I broke and wasn't there anymore, processing the onset of Grandma's illness and subsequent death, working on albums, writing, moving into different roles with hospice, supporting a friend in a family member's approach to end of life, and trying to manage my own plummeting mental and physical health. There was always something else forcing me to push through exhaustion and meet what I thought were achievable standards but were actually unrealistic expectations.

Reluctant to believe an empty cup can't be poured from, I fought with the need to put my wellbeing on the front burner and kept pushing, despite being in an obvious state of exhaustion. Putting myself first felt selfish. I wasn't respecting the break my body was asking for or the rest my mind was looking for and the mental and physical exhaustion of burning my candle on both ends for that long finally caught up with me, causing the kind of circumstances one would assume as a result.

The root of it now, for me, is becoming more about maintaining wellness on all fronts and making decisions that further me along in making a life for myself that comes without a need from which to escape. Caring for oneself doesn't mean never putting anyone else first, it just means taking care of yourself, too. Even if it's just an hour a day set aside for no one except yourself, even if it lets someone else down. The importance of your wellbeing overshadows the tolls pouring from an empty cup may take.

Rami adds, "care for the self is more than simply dissipating activities such as lattes and bubble baths. To garner resiliency, intentional actions must be put forth that are practiced and regular. One such practice involves the awareness and recognition of how the daily engagements...are affecting our becoming who and what we are, as well as how we operate. The most effective and simple way to achieve this is to pay attention to our own story, daily, and in fact, in every moment, for it is in the moment that the capacity to stay present in the work is built."

Sometimes I wish we could sit in rice for an hour like a soggy cell phone and be fixed, but something tells me this approach to self-care is going to work a little better.

Listen to your body and mind when it feels like it needs a rest. Feed your mind positive things like truth, hope, and love. It'll trust in whatever you offer it. Engage in self-reflective practices. Give yourself permission to care for yourself. Work hard and set goals while remembering a break is not a defeat. Drink water and go for a walk. It clears your mind and keeps your body moving. Try to get a good night's sleep because we don't operate properly when we don't. Eat well, but eat the cake, too. Doing things that keep you grounded, happy, and well are nothing short of showing self-empathy and a way to keep your cup pleasingly full. And definitely get some sunlight because, as has been said time and again, we're basically plants with more complicated emotions.

The human body and mind are magnificent, beautiful, and complex. What they can do for us, helping us to feel, endure and heal, is simply miraculous; they usually sustain us well.

Take care of yourself.

It's Ok

It's ok to miss someone who was once there for you
It's ok to say no
It's ok to forgive yourself
It's ok to speak up
It's ok to amend the standards you set
upon yourself if they are impossible
It's ok to take a break
It's ok to change your mind
It's ok to cry
It's ok to change
It's ok to take time
It's ok to do what makes you happy
It's ok to let whatever you do today be enough
It's ok to ask for help
It's ok to move on
It's ok to start over
It's ok to let steam out; sometimes
you just have to scream
It's ok to be where you are

Sara Rose, 2014

235

backwards

$\mathcal{I}$ f you could live life backwards, would you? I was asked this question by a man nearing the end of his life. I never noticed anyone with him when I would pass him by and it broke my heart every time. Walking down the hallway of a hospice facility, he hollered "Hello" from his room.

"Me?" I asked.

"Yes," he replied.

Part of me thought he was going to ask me to call a nurse over for him, as we had only ever exchanged a smile if we made eye contact at all. Needless to say, it took me by surprise when he extended his hand, though lightly trembling, and asked if I would sit for a minute.

I took a seat in the lone chair adjacent to his hospital bed and noticed his breathing was a bit labored. The same aged hand he had extended moments before fell to the edge of the bed in which he was slightly propped up. His eyes were a cloudy blue, but looked like they'd seen a lot of life.

Once he'd caught his breath, he asked how old I was.

"I'm 23," I said.

"I was your age almost 80 years ago," he said, a smile teasing the corner of his mouth.

"Do you mind if I ask a question?"

"Would love to answer," he said.

"Are you here on your own?"

"Yes," he paused.

"Do you mind if I stay with you for a few minutes?" I asked.

"I would be more than glad."

After a little while, my friend came back inside and needed an extra set of hands.

"You must have an old soul to be willing to sit and listen to an old guy like me," he said.

I told him it was an honour, which it truly was.

As I rose he said with a sense of urgency, "One more thing?"

"Sure, anything," I said.

"If you could live life backwards, would you?"

"Like start out old and grow young?" I asked.

He nodded. Ironic, as my friend and I'd had this exact conversation just a few months prior.

"I'm not sure. Might need to think on that one. Would you?"

"I would," he answered with no hesitation, as if he'd reflected upon that thought many times before.

Over the next few days, the question of whether I would, whirled around in my head. It's an interesting one to ponder, living backwards. I imagine if that were the way life worked, the question I'd be asking instead would be if we could choose to live life as we do now, would we?

I asked Dad this question and he said yes, with a speed similar to the gentleman at the hospice. When I asked why, he said he imagined there would be less emotional and physical pain as we grew younger. That of course would depend on whether or not we would maintain the wisdom and knowledge we'd acquired as we grew young. Would we assume there'd be less pain because we'd be growing less aware of what life is? *That question came up when I talked with a friend.*

"I don't know if it would change a lot," she mused.

"What do you mean?" I asked.

"People would still die or get sick, and even though our bodies might work better with time, I'd be scared to lose what I know. You know?"

I think what she meant, more or less, was that despite the fear often associated with the unknown, we spend our whole lives gaining knowledge and wisdom from experiences and leave the world with them. To see that unwind may bring about a lot of unknowns and possibly confusion and fear. Though I'm not an expert in illnesses such as Alzheimer's or dementia, I wonder if it would be like that. She had a point, though.

By the time I went back to the hospice, I had composed my answer to his question. He gave a wave that was wobbly but serene when I walked by.

"Got an answer?" he asked.

"I think I do, but I'd love to hear yours first," I said.

"I've accepted that my life's been lived and my time is coming, but by the time I had life figured all out and was wise enough to recognize the important things, value the lessons, and enjoy life with wisdom, I was too old and am now too frail and sick to run with it and live with the knowledge I have now. I also think dying would be less of a scary thing," he said.

I would like to live life backwards if I could. We spend our whole existences learning, growing, and working hard to get to retirement so life can be enjoyed, which is an honour and I think a really large part of what makes life the journey it is. It's a privilege to grow old. However, if we started out old and wise with a future that saw us grow younger and more agile instead of one that saw us age and grow more frail, the zest to live would only heighten. Those hard lessons would be learned and the wisdom gained from them would lay the grounds on which we could live more fully, widely, freely and wisely.

Before I could share this, a nurse came to the door to provide care and my friend was ready to head out. About a week later, when I turned the corner towards where my friend's family member was, the gentleman's bed was there but someone else had moved in, and it hit me that he had passed. My heart sunk. I hoped that he hadn't passed alone and I'm saddened to know that there are some who do. The dying process is something we go through alone, but the thought of not being with people when it's my time frightens me. It makes me think about how, regardless of which way we live our lives, young to old or old to young, there remains this deep-seated part of us that needs that human connection. Whether it's touch, presence, or whatever comfort we sought as a child, it never quite leaves us.

I'm so glad I met him.

I began thinking afterward how if I won the lottery and could do something not job-related that would make me happy, I would help my family and friends but I would also visit those of all ages in hospices, hospitals and nursing homes who don't have someone and just be there to listen to their stories, give them a hug, read stories, or just let them recollect old times. I would try to help alleviate their loneliness and give them a space where they can express themselves during what can be such a vulnerable time. I would also want to help those experiencing both homelessness and end of life, as that's a population growing more vulnerable. No one should be alone, hungry, cold, sick, or have to go through those things alone. I would love to just donate to help fund programs that would allow more volunteers to do this, too.

Try to find the time to sit with someone who's alone today. One hour of your time could mean a hell of a lot to someone who spends the majority of theirs alone. What amounted to one small day in the rest of my life was one of the last of his entire life. In his 80-some-odd years, I spoke to him twice and he taught me something that may have otherwise taken years to realize. I think the world would see a lot less suffering if people just took the time to listen and think. He's given me a lot to think about.

elastic band

August 14, 2019, 9:02 p.m.

I've always loved listening to the rain. The constant fall of raindrops is almost a complimentary sister to silence. It's pouring cats and dogs right now and the lightning is illuminating the house every few minutes. It's reminding me of when I was younger, how Mom and Dad and I would eat lemonade popsicles in the garage while we watched a thunderstorm pass through. Back then, even though the storm could sometimes be loud and damaging, to me it still brought about this innate sense of hopefulness that the sun or a rainbow would always come around again afterward.

My hope has worn thin after some of the events that have occurred this year, but the way it can reveal its depths in the subtlest of ways never fails to appear at just the right time. Perchance, it's reason to embrace the storms in life, as nothing grows without rain.

-S

*I*s hope a tactic? A feeling of anticipation or desire for something to be or not to be? A state of being that allows adversity and hard-hitting situations to become more bearable? An ability to innovate as human beings and contribute to a future? What is it that helps us bear the weight loss, hardship, and those unanswered questions I find myself brooding about while staring at the ceiling at night, listening to the sound of my breath; surely it's not the be-all and end-all that dictates an outcome, but I think it might act as a main ingredient in many different aspects of life.

Maybe it's the tiny bit of anticipation located in the bottom of your stomach, gently placing encouragement or faith ahead of an uncertainty, fear, grief, doubt or worry. Maybe it is the sound of rain or the quietest part of us cheering us on from the soundest room inside of our hearts. Maybe it's all of that, none of that, or more than that.

Hope wasn't something I believed a whole lot in until it that which kept me going after questioning whether or not a tomorrow would, could, or should ever come for me. I went through moments believing I wouldn't see the sun again or feel confident enough to breathe, hear the beauty of a bird's song, or put flowers in my hair because I couldn't find it in any part of me to crouch down and find one. I saw how when hope fades, so does the feeling of being alive. Self love fades, too.

Then, after giving it a chance, it has started weaving its way back into my perspective and life in the tiniest and subtlest of ways. I think that to have it sitting, waiting in your corner, in your heart, or in your pocket is to still own the desire for an outcome that improves life in some way, shape or form, and still have the will to get there.

Oct 3, 2016, 12:14 p.m.

> *Should you become weary, remember good*
> *things can come out of the bad*
> *And that in every breath of air that fills your*
> *lungs you've ever had*
> *Is the potential for more hope than you can*
> *possibly wrap your loving arms around*
> *To close the door to this is to be blind*
> *For one can be adrift and hopeful at the same*
> *time.*
> *-S*

Hope is really like an elastic band. It changes, bends, reshapes, or stretches thin to open up new or rigid places and let light back in...sometimes it snaps. Whether it's in the face of personal adversity, political unrest, or somewhere between having everything and nothing to lose, there's always room for it and it's the very thing that reminds us it's never too late.

It's bigger than I am and reminds me to believe things will get better, even when they don't seem like they will. It sits at the front of my chest like armour and is a core part of what keeps me here, because like some kind of magnet it pulls me into actions that mirror desire, change, imagination, and even into facing fear and adversity more than courage ever has on its own.

Even when I've found it shaken or the ground has almost given way, it's never been completely lost. I just had to look harder for it or move a little to see things dissimilarly. Sometimes you have to create your own version of hope and while it may look unalike every time, it's always persistent. Sort of stubborn, now that I think of it.

While you can't skip over the bad, shitty parts of life, you hope that ultimately the joys will outweigh the bad and that the bliss sticks. You have trust that things will work out how they are supposed to, because even on your worst day, there is still hope for better things to come. The fact that we don't know what tomorrow will bring is all the reason you need to hang on and give it a chance. It's pretty cool, too; just as a seed doesn't need to be taught how to grow, it doesn't have to be taught to do its work beyond letting it in, and it loves it when you let it.

Hope

Sometimes it's just inside when you feel like letting go
You reach the line where it feels
like the end of your road
Everything seems that it's at its worst right then
But it's getting yourself right out of that
and reaching way around the bend
And remembering forever

Chorus
You'll make it through the night if you
believe with all your might
If you go the extra mile life will bring you a smile
Gotta have hope and believe in yourself
Cause every day can be a new way
For tomorrow is a brand-new day

You've come a long way and things are
tough but you'll make it through
Just believe in yourself and forward you'll move
And no matter what life brings your way
my heart and I will always pray
It kills me to see what you're going through
Pushes me over the edge and hurts me too
And I won't let you stand alone again
I'll be by your side even when you're alright

Life can be tough but I won't let you give up
You're staying strong and I'll be there all along
But you gotta have hope and believe in yourself
Gotta have hope, oh yeah

Chorus
Sara Rose, 2010, Grade Nine
Written for a dear friend.

In loving memory of Ashton Kimberley
August 18, 1996 – May 21, 2020

Ashton, I've been staring at this page for the last
forty-five minutes trying to know where to even
begin. Every word I go to write seems not near full
enough to match what it feels like inside to try to
believe and accept that you're gone. This feels like an
awful dream. One of the first things you said to me
at 14 was that hope is something a person just has
to have. I know the various battles fought by many
can make keeping our heads above water profoundly
difficult, though from that moment on you reminded
me just how far, deep and wide that four letter
word could span to reach. You were someone who
faced adversity and came out stronger on the other
side. You were the kind of friend who lifted those in
your life when their fall may have generally gone
unrealized. You would help hold others up, even in the
midst of your own challenges and hard times. It takes
an incredible kind of person to do that and you did it
in such a manner as if it were no question and merely
second-nature to you. Not that long ago, you told me

how you were planning on going to school someday to be a social worker. You would have thrived in that field and would have been the social worker I only wish everyone, including myself, could have had. One gone, and so young with so much life to live, is far too many and I am so sorry. Never in a thousand years did I think the last time we hung up the phone and I heard that incredible, contagious laugh of yours would be the last time. Your beautiful heart and spirit will live on in the hearts and minds of all who knew and love you and will forever light the way for every life you touched. I'm so grateful to have known you. Thank you for the unforgettable memories and the irreplaceable friendship that will live on in my heart and forever remind me of the wonderful person you will always be to me. Rest peacefully, watch over Luca, protect us, and spread your wings, my loving and wonderful friend. You are loved immensely. So long, until we meet again. I love you.

an army

---

*"Our friendships are like an ocean; we ebb and flow;
we raise each other up like a wave and yet we remain
the same with a sturdy ocean floor. A floor that is
always there to catch us; a relationship that is forever
changing but solid underneath."*

-Cindy Glassford

To have a friend and to be a friend in return is an extraordinary thing. I'm not certain there are many things of greater significance than encouraging, authentic people and genuine connections in this life. Some of us seem satisfied living in a state of disconnect and some need to establish many connections; nonetheless, whether that connection is based on the mind, soul, or emotions, I feel like it's rare to come by and common to hope for.

Dec 17, 2019, 2:11 p.m.

> *Grateful for the fact that my friends and I can be doing anything or absolutely nothing at all and still have the greatest time doing it.*
> *-S*

I've often wrestled with the truth that friendships morph as life goes on. We find those which only worked on a situational basis, or only for certain life phases, while others have arrived and stay with us for a lifetime. Some get stronger and some are lost to time, leaving behind memories that are cherished forever. The rhythmic pattern of such a tide has something to do with growing and becoming your own person, I think anyway.

June 15, 2019, 4:09 p.m.

I think I learned a few of the most prized lessons to be learned about friendships and relationships in general today.

How someone treats you while you're not on the greatest of terms tells a lot about character and will show who matters and who doesn't.

The good times will show you who's there and times of difficulty truly show who isn't.

If someone expects you to put in the work for both sides of a relationship, they're not worth fighting for. Nothing long-lasting or significant works like that.

Pay attention to those who are genuinely happy for you and who makes more withdrawals than deposits in your life.

Those who say things like "take care," "text me when you're home," and wish you a good day or night, they are really saying they love you.

-S

As I get older I find I just want to be surrounded by good people: People who see, love, and accept me for the person I am without pointing out insecurities.

People who I can say anything to at any time regardless of the consequences and who I can laugh with, cry with, and call no matter what. People who cheer my accomplishments, stand by me through the good, the bad, and the shitstorms of life and who have advocated for me when I haven't quite been able to fight for myself. People who love me enough to not let me just slide by without a kick in the ass when it's needed, who point out when I'm stumbling and tell me to get it together, even when I don't want to hear it. I'm only interested in those who are genuinely good for me.

My friends and I are all of these things to each other. We gently pick on each other, flipping the bird if we pass each other on the highway and sharing the same toxic trait of always having room for dessert no matter how sick or full we are. I know there are things I'll go through alone, but should one of us need another, whether we have strength or energy to give or not, we dig deep and show up. I think at times it's definitely easier to be strong for others. After all, whether it's been a week, a month, or a year, we continue to live in each other's pockets, somehow managing to pick up right where we left off, knowing we'll always be there to lift each other up.

There's something special about good friends. Those who can tune into each other's innermost being are few and far between, and are treasures to be cherished indeed. If they don't love you for who you are and choose instead to tear you down, then walk on and establish some distance because they aren't your people. Recognize your people. My friendships, family and chosen family are so important to me and are my greatest success. I will never stop rooting for them. I want them to succeed, prosper, and be happy. They add meaning to my life, keeping me humble, present, and sane. I'm definitely not going to question how I've been so lucky to find them, I'm just going to hold them close because that's what you do when you have an army standing with you.

My army is small but mighty and when we rise, we rise as one.

the view was great

"When you're on top of the world, do yourself a favour and just enjoy the view instead of looking for ways not to fall."

-Author Unknown

About a month after Ashton left us, I went for a walk on one of the trails we spent quite a bit of time on when we were in high school. With each day feeling harder without her, I thought visiting this spot might bring some peace to the day in remembering one of our memories together.

When I arrived, the details of the first time we were there, some of which had fallen to the wayside, resurfaced and played back in my head. I sat on the grass under the big tree and reminisced us being about 15 or 16 coming here for the first time one summer.

We had been having a lazy day when she told me about a nearby trail just off the main road that she wanted to check out. In thinking a change of scenery might be nice for the both of us, we decided to go. We got slushies on the way and shortly into the walk notice was taken to the huge tree at the first turn ahead.

"Hold my drink," she said, handing off her slushy to me.

Heading to the tree my back is leaning against now, I realized she was going to climb it.

"What are you doing? You're gonna fall and break your leg," I said.

"No I won't, my nickname has been Monkey for forever," she told me, already halfway up the tree. "Come up here, let's take a picture," she said, making her way out onto one of the big limbs.

"No way. When have you ever seen me climb a tree? Plus, we're the most clumsy people I know. This is not going to end well," I said.

"You're such a knob. It'll be fine. Get up here and look how blue the sky is," she said, smiling down at me. The sun was breaking through the branches and leaves above her.

She was taking in the view about eight feet above the ground when I put the slushies on the grass and started climbing. She was right about the view. We were just shooting the shit and talking when the sharp crack of a branch snagged my attention. Being a few feet below her, I looked up to see Ashton falling straight down with the branch that had just been holding her up moments ago.

Her feet broke her fall and she fell forward onto her stomach while I felt mine drop to my feet.

"Holy shit!!!" I yelled, jumping off the branch I was standing on.

"I think I broke my leg!" she yelled.

I ran over to her and when she bent her leg upwards from the knee, her shin flopped over to one side. She let out a painful cry and I unsuccessfully masked the gag her leg sent me into, which made her gag, which made me gag, and so went the wheel.

"Oh my God!" she exclaimed, turning her head back around and putting her forehead against her forearms.

"Try to stay still," I said, scrambling for one of our phones.

"Keep breathing through it. Deep breaths. Help will be here soon," I said, dialling 9-1-1.

Squeezing my hand to the point I didn't know if it was now broken too, she mumbled something into her elbow.

"What?" I asked.

"Tell me something funny," she said again. "Please. I need to not think about the pain."

I reminded her of the time we went for a walk at my house after dark a few months before; she turned the flashlight off and snuck away while I was talking because she thought it would be funny to hide and scare me when I was panicking and running back towards the house. Laughter inched its way between the cries and a few minutes later we saw the ambulance lights at the head of the small trail.

"Love you," she said.

"Love you, too. But we're not going on walks together anymore," I said.

"Hey, Sara?" she said.

"Yeah?" I asked.

"Remember that one time you told me not to climb a tree cause I'd fall out and break my leg?"

"Uh...yes..." I said, gesturing the situation with my free hand.

"Yeah. You were right," she said, half-smiling.

"You're the knob. Here come the paramedics. You're gonna be ok," I said.

"Swear?" she asked, with one hand on her forehead and the other still squeezing my hand.

"Swear. Plus, maybe one of them is hot," I said.

"Let's hope not. Look at me," she said, crying and laughing with mascara smeared down her face.

"Ok be my wingman then," I said, jokingly.

When she was able to walk without crutches again she'd always twist her leg and jump around to intentionally send me into a recollective worry and gag of how it bent like a rubber band. She thought it was the funniest thing since sliced bread. Or whatever that saying is.

She had an incredible fighting spirit, even when she thought she was weak, and she was someone who could find the silver lining by standing up in that incredible strength of hers to pull through and keep going. Or find a way to draw one in herself if there wasn't one.

I visit her there on good days and bad days. Or when I just need a reminder to worry less, slow down, and enjoy the view more.

Before the fall, she always said the view was great.

June 27, 2020, 6:14 p.m

I'm sitting under the tree and now my tears are being met with a bit of a smile in thinking about all the memories and good times we had. Even this one. I miss your laugh, Ashton. I had a dream the other night that it makes you laugh when we talk out loud to you because it "looks like we're talking to the air."

I'm thinking it might be nice to bring my guitar back here next time and write a song. We used to do that together.

The sun just broke through the leaves. As much as visiting here breaks my heart, it's also heartwarming. I know you're with all of us still, but I wish I could wake up and you be here taking in this view with me again.

Maybe we can put a ribbon around this tree one day.

-S

shoulder to shoulder

2018

Sept 20, 2018, 8:28 a.m.

Standing in line for my flight to B.C. this morning, I was working on a pep talk that had been waltzing through my head about why I'm going. Just take the first step, it's the hardest one. You can do it, I told myself! Uhm, that's a hard no...you cannot get on that plane and go to that new place. Better get going or you'll miss your chance and never do anything that scares you or is new again. Do you want to look back, wishing you'd gone and done it? Relax...you're young. 22! Ya got time, girl! There's a new episode of Grey's Anatomy on tonight. Stay content in your bubble. Get out there and live while you're alive! What sweet, unending amusement it is to stand, frozen, at one of Pearson Airport's departure gates, hosting a frantic fight between my heart and my head. My head pleaded, "For God's sake Sara, just turn back to the gift shop, get a key chain and some liquorice and go home." But my heart...that thing reminding me I'm alive, of what's important, and that this so-called "ride" only comes around once.

With all that's gone on lately I've been feeling so distanced from myself, basically lost in my own life. Stopping for a few minutes to gaze into the dusty mirror I'd looked into nearly every day for the last ten years was a sure way to feel it. Someone asked me yesterday, "You're either going backwards, sideways or are falling to the bottom; where are you right now?"

Having long since been eager to do something about it, I finally found enough chutzpah to take a leap of faith in this dark time.

Well, my gate was just called, so I suppose I should get on the plane now...

-S

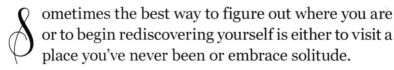 ometimes the best way to figure out where you are or to begin rediscovering yourself is either to visit a place you've never been or embrace solitude.

I managed to land a window seat right beside the wing of the plane. I could see the worn rubber edges of my now-off-white Converse on either side of the ripped bag I somehow managed to squeeze a week's worth of clothes and an armful of faded journals into, mainly to avoid checking any luggage. That frugal student budget and absence of a full-time job thing works wonders in helping a person to pack light. I've got my laptop on and just cracked into a bag of airport chocolate-banana vegan snacks that set me back a whopping 14 bucks. There's also a hole in my left shoe.

There are 80 or so people aboard this plane. Every single one of them is going somewhere, coming from some place, thinking about something, anticipating impending gains or losses and probably just trying to manage their world. Some may be just focussing on breathing or trying not to think at all. I can't fathom the number of stories floating around inside this gigantic metal tube.

My attention would soon be yanked to the fore when the seatbelt light suddenly flashed on against the beige overhead display, and I once again acknowledged the funny feeling in the pit of my stomach that always came with air travel. Seatbelts signify safety and heightened security, yet between each flash of the orange signal I swear I felt equal flashes of unsettling panic and the desire to run away from being alone with myself. Well, there was nowhere to run to at this point, so best find some courage and face it.

September 21, 2018, 1:09 p.m.

I've always loved travelling and though I haven't done it a lot, I am starting to do it more often lately. I love immersing myself in a city or country's culture, trying new foods and meeting new people—life is lived so differently everywhere! The vastness and uniqueness of the world can only be recognized by actually visiting someplace new. It serves as a strong reminder that there's never only one way of seeing the world.

I quickly picked up on the attributes that associated a certain uniqueness to each of the stores along the main drag. No store was the same as another, yet owners and workers were all sweeping yesterday's dirt off the welcome mats outside, groups of elderly men gathered to chat over steaming cups of coffee and read the week's paper outside what looked to be their shops, and the ancient ground beneath my feet looked as though it had guided many travels before me.

The pace of life here is much more relaxed than the hustle and bustle to which I'm accustomed. People stop on the main strip of the town to simply say hello and have a conversation with a stranger. It was a hint that I might want to slow down delivered through a small gesture that insinuates rushing is a resistant state of being that basically serves to take us out of the present moment.

I also ran from a seagull today; it looked like it was on steroids and probably could have eaten me in four bites—seriously huge. It must be something in the water. Like fish or something.
-S

Sidney, British Columbia is a small, beautiful town on the northern end of the Saanich Peninsula on Vancouver Island. My timing in coming here aligned pretty well with an opportunity to make a wonderful personal connection; other than that, I pretty well put my hand on the map with my eyes closed and said "Ok, I'm going here."

I walked down to the Sidney Pier to watch the sunrise one morning and left my phone and laptop in my room, which is unusual for me. Our phones are almost a part of us now; we're committed to them and rely on them so much. Security perhaps? Ensuring we're not missing anything going on in the world? To make sure we can take pictures or videos of noteworthy things? It's definitely an addiction in some form.

From the moment I got outside and fresh air filled my lungs, I felt more relaxed. Content. Freer, more serene, or whatever it is that means the opposite of flustered. Even during the short ten-minute walk down to the water, I noticed a sensation of being less tethered without my devices. There's much beauty and art to see, experience, and feel in the world when you take the time to look up from your screen.

The only sounds at the pier were bird calls and the lapping of the waves. Considering it was still decently dark outside, it was kind of haunting. Apart from those sounds, which grew into sort of a white noise façade, it was quiet. Debilitating thoughts of fear, regret, shame, failure, and sentiments of grief occasionally made themselves known. It was surprising to me how persistent negative emotions can still be, even when you've become so adept at supressing them through the art of distraction.

What I'll remember most, though, is while the unrelenting approach of daylight began cutting open the night sky, robust feelings of gratitude began breaking through at the same time, taking my breath away. Finding the words to describe how large life truly is and how it introduces us to new feelings and moments is nearly impossible. I wanted to soak in everything about this moment: the feeling of solitude and gratitude folding into each other like a pair of hands that have long been apart and how everywhere I turned produced another incredible view.

I kept losing myself in the way the endless blue reflected off the movement of the water. As it moved at its own rhythm, my mind drifted along with it. I thought about home. I thought about worth and forgiveness. I thought about purpose and opportunity, and of thankfulness in being in a position to fulfill it. I thought of Grandma and Grandpa and wondered how Grandma was doing. I worried about where the next few months of her life were going to lead and wondered if the two of them would find another chance to go on an adventure like this again. I thought about my direction and of how lucky I was to have what I have, as I'm aware so many in this world are going without. I pondered how fortunate I was to have so many people around me who truly care, eyes that can see, a working brain, ears that can hear, resources available to me, and a heart that keeps me alive. It's so easy to forget to take the time to be grateful. At that moment I just wanted time to stand still.

I got lunch, brought back a tea, and stayed out until the sun set behind the mountains (the Vancouver Island Ranges.) I felt my shoulders fall down from around my ears in much the same way. My jaw unclenched and I just breathed while the current washed the ocean in below the pier and back out again. I've left some tears in many moments, conversations, and places. Needless to say, this pier was one of those places.

Sept 22, 2018, 8:19 p.m.

> *I can see mountains standing tall from across*
>   *the water*
> *And shells being collected on the rocky shore*
> *It all sort of took my breath away like nothing*
>   *has before*
> *A grandfather holds his granddaughter's hand*
> *While they listen to the waves and watch the*
>   *birds land*
> *There is something about peace that is so full*
> *The kind only an open and eased mind does not*
>   *find overwhelmingly dull*
> *I feel the sun on my face as I collect another*
>   *moment of my life*
> *Remembering that time is precious so not to let*
>   *it slip by*
> *-S*

I had never been so physically far from home on my own before, but no part of me regretted taking this trip. It was only four days, I'd had no money and could barely navigate my own town let alone another province, but it wound up being the best emotional detox and unbelievable taste of solitude I'd ever experienced. I felt as good and recharged as I did when I landed my first skydive and it was an oddly magnificent step of self-growth in which I came to find another piece of my heart, one I hadn't even known existed. I felt good, like I was going to be ok no matter where I ended up going forward. I'd do it again in a heartbeat rather than continue running from solitude. Comfortability in taking such short sabbaticals comes with becoming more at ease within yourself, and I hadn't been at home in my skin for a long time. I'm still not, really—detachment occasionally feels like new territory. But, since this solo trip taught me a whole new way of figuring out how to manage hardship, I think solitude and I are going to become fast friends. I'd have never thought it would be the very thing that recharges me now, allowing for a smoother flow of thoughts and helping me to see myself again.

There's something magnificently full about soaking in a silence that is all but empty. While I don't think silence is full of answers, it would be nice if it were. It certainly allows for a cleaner flow of thoughts and can communicate unbelievably great things if you just learn to listen.

Sept 21, 2018, 12:19 p.m.

> *There's been a light flickering in my heart*
> *One which I've kept my eyes open for when I've*
> *felt lost and confused*

Or maybe, simply hungry for solitude.
When I've felt adrift from my life or alone
It's this light that has guided my soul back home
Of all, wherever I am and the gratifying love in
*   my life*
For what I cannot refuse is that home is not a
*   place*
Longing to be fully embraced.
-S

I've now realized the harmony that exists between solitude and gratitude and how they sit shoulder to shoulder. Embracing and wrapping yourself in genuine silence actually ignites conversation between the heart and head, and finding a pace in this form of connectivity can create serene harmony. I've come to know the two as solid companions lately. As each day ends, solitude allows us to process the information we've received and to reflect upon it, while gratitude allows us to live the conclusions at which we've arrived in meaningful ways.

Sept 23, 2020, 11:12 a.m.

We've reached the mountains now and as they're peeking through the clouds, I'm reminded of how there is never only one way of seeing the world and of how in the absence of taking stock of what we have, we will undoubtedly always feel a need for more. I'm going to go out and live and try not to sensor myself as I venture out into any part of it.
-S

saving place

2005

One of the greatest things about a song is letting it go after it's served its purpose, so it might do the same for someone else. I love how, similar to books, songs offer a mental construct that others can relate to, hold onto, and to some degree be influenced by. It's crazy to think about how a song created by one person with one initial meaning can resonate with others in a thousand various ways. It makes the idea of a creative life grounded on connection sit really well with me.

When someone I worked with shared that I had saved her life with music after the passing of her spouse, I was left with the insight that the creation of all manner of art is probably the most unique expression human beings will realize, and to never undervalue the impact even a single song can have. In this person's circumstance, by stepping into an opportunity to have music reintroduced and listened to, share her memories elicited by chosen songs, and even engage in making music, she says her life was saved.

It's truly marvelous how music is a language of its own yet acts as a universal avenue to connection; it becomes a part of our lives before we're even born. Think about it: our very own hearts pump in a beat of rhythm. Perhaps lullabies become a part of life after we're born. Speaking of which, Dad used to sing "Joy to the World" (Jeremiah Was a Bullfrog) and Mom used to sing "You Are My Sunshine." Nice to reminisce about, except Mom also got me a little sunshine doll to go with the song and it's the creepiest looking thing I've ever seen. I remember dancing in the basement to Shania Twain and Shaggy as a little kid. Mom played piano for a bit but beyond that they don't play any instruments. It's funny, because some of the best advice I've been given about songwriting has come from my Dad. I'm grateful how much it was appreciated by them and greatly admire the many artists to which they've introduced me over the years.

The seed of music really began germinating in my life when I realized writing and playing were becoming my saving grace, and listening to the truth of others' experiences expressed through their songs made me feel less alone. Even if just for a minute or two, a song can manage to put things in perspective and nudge thoughts into the right line, like how sand gets to the banks.

I started writing songs as soon as I got my guitar at ten years of age and seldom shared them with anyone. Going by the lyrics I'd write (the ones I was brave enough to share), most seemed to have one some recognized as an "old soul." I was just writing what I felt.

I think as much as any artist hopes for their work to resonate with others, creating from a true, honest place really remains a significant thing. Being able to listen and write music through all of the stumbles over many obstacles and unexpectedly winding roads, and being able to share it for other people to resonate with in their own ways, is truly significant.

This is, again, where I continue to believe "success" varies from person to person. If my music or words can resonate with just one person, even if I'm not able to do it as a career, I will still consider it successful. I can always write and perform music, which I love and will never stop doing. Whether it's found in the pages of a book, taking in nature, painting, working out, or music, get lost in something that makes you feel good. Music, photography, poetry, gardening, interior design, dance, karaoke at the bar, the hand-drawn photo hanging on your fridge made by your five-year-old child during lunch at school, all of it. Get lost in it.

The first time I sang in front of people was at our trailer park's annual concert. I was 14 and got my first period half an hour before I was supposed to go on stage. Mom gave me a sanitary napkin that felt like a football player's shoulder pad but I went ahead and played "Live Like You Were Dying" by Tim McGraw and had corn on the cob afterward.

2010

Music brings us back to times, places, memories...it's a powerful aspect of our brain's muscle memory. Come to think of it, there isn't one song I've ever listened to that either didn't cause my mood to improve or relate to my life in some way. "Hurt" by Johnny Cash, "Rainbow" by Kacey Musgraves, "Shut Up and Dance" by Walk the Moon, "Glitter in the Air" by P!nk, "Beside You" by Marianas Trench, and "Drowning" by Chris Young are just a few that absolutely dismantled my heart while somehow rebuilding it at the same time. The songs that make me think or that reflect relatable experiences make for the best songs. Or, there are also the ones that knock you off your bloody feet.

I'm grateful to be an artist and to live creatively. Yes, we feel so much so intently and have to retreat to that broken piece of our heart where those raw authentic emotions live in order to write our songs. My first album *Until Now* got me through a lot and my second one *We Could Be Beautiful* is a constant reminder to keep putting one foot in front of the other. I don't know what I'd do without music now. It's the connection that has brought gratitude, grace, understanding, joy, and healing nearer to my heart. It's fun, it feeds my soul, it's an escape, a natural high, and an expressive way of making sense of things. It keeps me moving forward and is the thing that's always there, especially when I don't think I need it. It's my saving grace.

Album Signing, 2019

trust

Trust. Once it's broken, it's hard to get back.

a mark left

I think you pretty well instantly know when you've met a genuinely good person—they have an air about them that's authentically kind. Someone I met a few years ago was one of those people. Just a truly good, humble, and authentic person who, when you looked at them, you would swear to have seen their soul.

One of the first things he told me was that he'd played the violin for nearly 70 years and had been painting even longer. I tried learning the violin once. Mom and Dad were thrilled when I came upstairs after playing a version of "Twinkle Twinkle, Little Star" 1,003 times that sounded more like a screeching version of "Baby Shark" to tell them I was starting to think violin maybe wasn't for me.

Despite his illness, he lived his days with dignity and got around in a wheelchair that didn't slow him in the slightest. It was as if he just made it a part of him and completely owned it. I can still hear his voice proclaiming, "come on up" through the crackly lobby speaker when I would arrive for our weekly visits. The art that hung on his walls portrayed his early, unbelievable talent (given I thought they were actual photographs) and to top it off, he wrote beautiful poems. They were pieces of writing that would blow your heart into a million tiny pieces in the most wonderful way, the kind where you can relate to every line and it causes you to not only think, but reconsider things within, about and around you even hours afterward. I was lucky enough to read a few of them.

I often welled up listening to this man's stories. He lived a rough, yet action-packed and adventurous life and it didn't take long to realize that he had seen quite a lot in his lifetime. Above all, the part that initially took me aback was the way he seemed to build resilience and self-understanding through leaning into passion despite his past hardships. Music, art, and writing poems appeared to have saved him and I often thought they were the ties that held him together even though he couldn't physically play music or paint anymore. Show me someone with a solid passion and you can be assured they've got an unmistakable inner strength, enough to overcome life's many challenges.

The way I related to his perspectives was almost supernatural; he was a man in his 80s, so obviously not all characteristics were kindred. The unmistakable love of art and creation of all kinds, and his approach toward life reminded me a lot of what I'd been coming to understand on my own. I'd give a lot to have another conversation with this man today because although

I was there to support him through his illness, man, did I ever learn a lot about life and artistry from him. I suppose that's the value of positive moments and connecting with good people—it's the kind of interaction that leaves indelible marks on your heart.

dancin'

J love the songs that come around without warning. "Dancin'" materialized halfway through my coffee on a Saturday morning while working on a different song for the album. After writing it, I thought a ballroom dance would make for a cool music video. After running it by the videographer (the brilliant man behind the camera for most of the music videos I've done) and a longtime friend, we moved ahead to the planning stages.

I originally opted to have someone else fill the role in the video given that I'm certainly no dancer. Not a gracious one, anyway. I've started doing the "snapping of the fingers" dance move my mom and my friends' moms do that we swore we'd never mimic. That and the shopping cart. Right off the bat, the choreographer encouraged me to give the dance a try. I figured we could find someone else to play the role if I felt I wasn't getting it, but after the first lesson I thought, *I'm a damn natural at this whole dancing thing—this must be a second calling.* I have no idea where that boost of confidence came from because I've never been a person one would call elegant. I couldn't even pee outside as a kid when we went snowmobiling without having to take all my clothes off and practically getting frostbite.

At the end of each lesson, the choreographer would video us doing the dance so we could see how it looked. I could use it as a reference, and deal with problem areas. After viewing the first video, it wasn't long before I was having second, third, fourth and fifth thoughts on the whole "I'm a natural" thing and the respect I have for dancers increased tenfold.

I didn't want to give up on learning the dance at least well enough to perform it for the video, so between landscaping during the day and working with the producer in the studio a couple of nights a week, the majority of my summer was spent taking lessons and rehearsing. Besides, it felt good to try something new and see my hard work pay off.

That August we shot the video over a day-and-a-half and everyone on the team who made it happen as smoothly as it did was so kind. They were willing to help create something we would be proud of and we all worked so hard. I'm proud of them and still can't believe how generous everyone was with their resources, talents, expertise, and time. I'm forever appreciative of the team I've worked with over the last few years. They are the most incredible group of people.

Dancin'

I still get nervous when you walk in the room
All you do is look my way and I'm
falling in love all over with you
I know I've got a fickle heart and running tendencies
And I'd never ask you to wait for me

Pre-Chorus
But when I think of you and the whole world fades
A single breath is all it takes
You took my hand in yours and said all you have to do
Is trust me and follow my lead

Chorus
You spin me around and around
Like we were the only ones dancin' in this room
This ain't the tequila talking babe or
the courage I'm trying to perfect
Ouuuouuuuouuu
But because of you I found a love
I won't, be letting go of

You look so handsome dressed like that
Lovin' when I can't quite love myself back
Oh, just the way you hold me, how do you do that?
I don't know what I'd do if it weren't for you

Pre-Chorus
Chorus
We're dancin' we're dancin' we're dancin'
We're dancin' we're dancin' we're dancin'

We're dancin' we're dancin' we're dancin'
We're dancin' we're dancin' we're dancin'

Chorus
Sara Rose, We Could Be Beautiful, 2019

the pinecone

January, 2019

December 17, 2019, 5:18 a.m.

Whenever a song would reach its end Grandma would ask, "What's the story behind that one?" I never saw the whole value of it as a kid, but I do now. I suppose it was hidden between the cracks of a realization that these moments, alongside many others, were going to one day be a memory that would grow sweeter with time. We listened to songs from the 40s to the 90s and from the Everly Brothers to Reba, Hank Williams and the Pretenders. As much as I thought I could try and make up a story if I wasn't fully listening, she always got me.

For as long I live, I'll appreciate her showing me that every person and every song has a story to be lived, told, and remembered. You just have to listen for it with your arms and heart open wide.

-S

*G*randparents are a special part of a grandchild's heart. They're an extra layer of protection who hold our hands when we're little, quietly walk behind us to catch us as we fall while we grow up if we're lucky to know them that long or at all, and they live on in our hearts and minds forever. From places of age and experience they convey important things like kind-heartedness and wisdom. To say there's no other special connection from past to future in a person's life like that of a grandparent would be true; it's an irreplaceable garden of love.

When I was a little girl, right up to Grandma Rose's final moments spent together at her bedside at 23 and 73, Shirley Rose was one of the most dignified, strongest women I had ever known. She was the kind of person who you could hear smiling through the phone, she would light up as soon as she saw you, and would never let those she loved go without knowing and feeling that love; you never had to wonder.

The soccer games she and Grandpa came out to when I was a kid turned into the shows I started playing at bars as a teenager. She would always say, "Oh I don't know if we'll make it. It depends," and then they'd walk in with the biggest "we surprised you!!!" Cheshire grins.

She lived with diabetes and a rare blood disease for many years but such trials and tribulations never seemed to interfere with how full she kept her life. The Rose side of the family has seen cancer aplenty, though the onset of her cancer diagnosis that subsequently lead to months of valiant fighting still managed to rock everyone's worlds. As large a part of my life as she always was and will forever be, I'm grateful that we further closed the distance over the last few years because she became one of my best friends and taught me so much about living.

July 3, 2018, 5:13 p.m.

Grandma had just been moved to a room with a window. It's a nice break from the bland, beige walls. She likes watching the world turn. Whichever floor of the hospital she's on, it's never long before she becomes the Gladys Kravitz of the floor. Within a few days she's gathered a general lowdown of every nurse and patient within a mile of her. I'm not sure how, considering she's not left her bed other than for the odd test.

I hadn't seen her for a few weeks, and noticing the change in her coordination and speech was unsettling. There hadn't really been a minute where it was just she and I alone together since she'd been admitted until today when Dad and Grandpa went to get some lunch.

We were sitting back to back on either side of the hospital bed so she could prop herself up with her legs hanging over the side and look out the window. The Price is Right coming from the TV was soaking up the silence in the room. It sort of reminded me of when we would have sleepovers years ago. We would watch game shows and Judge Judy together during dinner and often went downstairs after and listened to music.

Her back was against mine, but her quietness made it feel like she was far away. I could feel her thinking, but I didn't know about what. When I broke the silence and asked, her response caught me off guard.

"How lucky I am," she replied.

"How so?"

"Well I have a brain tumour and masses on my kidney and lungs."

"Yeah, you do," I said, as gently as I could.

"I'm just thinking how grateful I am to be here and where I am," she said, still looking out the window.

"Sorry, I don't know if I totally understand. How so?" I asked

"Well I mean I have tumours, but I have family with me and I'm coherent. I feel awful, but I'm ok. I'm not suffering like my neighbour across the hall," she said, referencing the man who had been in much pain and looked to be further along in his illness than she.

Her ability and bravery to soldier on through her days, even by way of a hospital bed, and still be able to find reasons to be grateful and recognize we're fortunate to be here at all, makes me cry. These aren't the easiest of times and I admire her for the incredible way she's managing it.

As I took a deep breath and prepared to answer, Dad and Grandpa arrived back at the room.

"Look at that pinecone over there," Grandma said, suddenly pointing toward the window where one was hanging off a big pine tree.

I wiped a tear from my cheek and reached around to squeeze her hand. When I got up I saw the pinecone hanging off the tree.

-S

numbered

$\mathcal{I}$t's half past midnight and I'm sitting on a metal cafeteria chair at the hospital, drinking the tea I ordered when I got here around 10 p.m. It's cold now. It's the middle of February and Grandma was readmitted not long ago. I'm glad she was able to be home for Christmas. As is tradition, she loves having everybody over.

It wasn't my plan to come tonight, but I've had a strange feeling in my stomach over the past few days and somehow, I ended up here. Walking down the hallways to her room, I couldn't help but notice how empty the hospital felt. Someone could have dropped a pin and it would have echoed. I find it interesting how hospitals clear as the evening gets longer and, apart from the night shift, become nearly vacant. Then the traffic picks back up bright and early when the sun rises and another day begins.

Grandma's back is to the door when I arrived at her room. I am not sure if she is still awake or not and it is still so dark, I can't tell if she is even in the bed at first.

Grandpa spends every day and most nights by her side, but he must have gone home for the night shortly before I arrived, given that the chair beside her was still warm. I'm glad he's sleeping in his own bed tonight.

"Hi Grandma," I whisper.

A few seconds pass before she shifts and looks over her shoulder. She appears so small lying there compared to a few months ago. Even though it's modest, something seems different each visit, especially if more than a couple of days slip by in between. I'm not sure if she is going to give me a kick in the ass for driving down so late, but the warmest of grins beams across her face upon seeing me.

"Hi Sara," she says sleepily.

"Mind if I sit a while?" I ask.

"That would be great. Turn the light on."

She's always glad to see someone and manages to make every person who comes to her door feel welcomed. Even if it's a tiny, cramped hospital room filled with machines and wires going God knows where, she makes the nurses laugh and finds the good in the day.

When I settle in the chair and could see her a little better, our eyes met and my heart sunk. She looks lost, just for a split second.

"How are you, can I get you anything?" I ask.

"I'm good," she replies as she rearranges herself in the hospital bed that is getting to know her more than I think she was hoping it would.

"Do you want to watch one of your game shows?"

"No, but do you want anything?" she offers.

It takes me a second to realize she isn't kidding. She hasn't gotten around without the assistance of a wheelchair for a while, but I don't think she cares.

"No, I'm good. I've got my tea. Thanks, Grandma."

We sit there and just talk. We were close over the years, but everything was usually kept pretty light. Lately, in these visits when it's the two of us, it seems more and more she reveals a side of herself that I hadn't ever known all that well. Figuratively speaking, it's as if her illness is pouring gas over usual, casual conversation and it's igniting much deeper ones. She has told me how grateful she is for so many things, Grandpa being a major one. The love between them is immeasurable. Even as a young kid, I knew that. I had never seen a more tightly knit couple. She and Grandpa have always been a team. Whatever one went through, the other was always right there jumping the hurdle too. I always had the mental picture of synchronized swimmers when they would call and share what they did together. Their love, from what I saw, was the kind that could have been in a commercial. It is really quite heartwarming.

"I'm so lucky to have him. Every time I look to see if he's there, he's there. When the doctors come in to ask questions or tell me something, he's the one who knows them better than even I do. I just have to look at him. So, so lucky."

I have to ask myself where this is coming from because in imagining myself in her shoes, I don't know if I'd be able to manage such a warm perspective with quite the same graciousness. She goes on to say that when you watch the world go by from a hospital bed day and night, you tend to think about things. You see a lot of people come and go. You see a lot of people with family and a lot of people on their own, sometimes with a photograph on their table. You see some couples walk through the doors arm in arm and some leave holding a jacket and their loved one in their heart. You see pain. You see loss. You see hope stretch thin, change, and wrap tightly around people.

"What did you do today?" she asks.

"I wrote mostly," I reply.

She nods, looking away.

"Why so quiet?" I inquire. My hand is wrapped around hers. It feels smaller and looks withered. The words she says next pull me out of the vortex of loss into which I can feel myself preparing to spiral into and for a few moments, I can feel the ground below my feet begin to steady.

"Don't wait until you're 73," she says.

"What do you mean?"

"Well...just don't spend all your time writing your life away before you live it. Don't wait until you're my age to start living."

"Ok" I nod.

"That's my girl. Thanks for being here," she responds, her voice now sounding increasingly groggy.

I notice myself trying to memorize the sound of her voice because deep down I know the time she had left here was starting to wane. It feels like I am sticking pieces of wet, mushy paper on my breaking heart with scotch tape and praying it holds.

"You don't have to thank me. Get some sleep."

She starts dozing off right after, so I gently kiss her cheek and stop talking. I feel the pull of a strain tighten across my chest, eventually spreading over my entire core as I watch her chest, reluctantly rising and effortlessly falling. She falls asleep in under a minute. Her breathing sounds wheezy as I watch her shoulders rise and fall at an uneven pace, wondering where the time had gone. Where *her* time had gone. The last couple of years felt like they sped by without even pausing for a cold drink and a breather. I can only imagine how she must feel.

We spoke about so many things when I'd visit one-on-one. Our own version of a "Live Like You Were Dying" conversation, if you will. Strange, as that was also the first song I sang in front of a crowd. What a gentle gesture and reminder it was to be mindful of how very small and precious time is in the bigger scheme of things, to not overcomplicate things, to stop playing it so cool. One of the greatest commodities is time; you can't take it back after it's gone, but some wonderful things can be done with it while it's passing by. Even though we can put energy into convincing ourselves there's an unending amount ahead of us, there really isn't an endless supply of time. Respect it by using it wisely. Catch the moments and hours of your life while you're able, and feel all of them; the good and the not-so-good ones. How much we choose to feel can wind up being painful, but it's also one of the most beautiful things that make us human. Seize the precious opportunities to be happy and marvel at the joys and love we have. Spare the few minutes it takes to call your family and friends and tell people how you feel; reflect on your love or gratitude for them. Tell someone you miss that you miss them. Hug for a few seconds longer than you normally would and don't just tell people how much you love them, show them while it's still possible. Life is far too short to stow away our feelings. We only have one life and we don't always know when a piece of it is going to shift or be taken away.

I know I'm only 22 as I'm writing this (which is technically only three years away from being halfway to 50), but sometimes when I stop for a second and look behind me, I realize that my life is moving along a lot faster than I can keep up with. I recognize this when I'm sitting still, usually with my guitar on my lap and a pen in my hand writing about anything and everything or simply trying to make sense of it all. I also sometimes think age should be looked at as levels that reflect the number of years spent learning and growing. To hear someone say they're on their 73rd level of life would be super cool.

I was in such a desperate rush to grow up when I was young but now, I'm not; I'm more restless about it than anything else. I watch the leaves fall off the trees in October and wonder where summer went, I feel the varying degrees of loss and grief society in general encounters, yet, amazingly, people still manage to carry on with their lives. I watch the snow hit the ground and feel it smack me square in the face while I'm brushing off my car in the morning before work and wonder where fall went. Sitting on the school bus playing truth or dare in Grades Five and Six feels like yesterday, not almost 15 years ago.

I move from the chair next to her bed, choosing instead to look up through a skylight in the hospital cafeteria. That chair is so noisy; but then you could scratch an itch on that ward and it would sound like a car slamming on its brakes just next door. I recall how we laughed over Grandpa saying that when he stayed overnight he couldn't move without feeling like he was waking up the whole hospital wing. Suddenly it's 1:03 a.m. and again, I'm not sure where the time is going.

Gray's song "October" plays, travelling from my head down to my heart, then circling back again, the rain and snow falling against the tilted skylight window above my head. Drops slide down and off the edge, some leaving faster than others, some not moving at all. They sort of remind me of lives. I'm sad, but ok.

It feels like there's all this time dancing around that has yet to be taken hold of, but I'm quickly realizing that no, there isn't an endless supply of time and I don't know that I will ever be able to treasure life and moments like the ones I had with Grandma that night enough. What I can do, what we can all do, is ride those moments that make us feel alive. We can move through the bad times, the ugly times, and the ones filled with pain, reflecting on them without living in them. We can wrap ourselves in the time we have left like a vortex, going over the good parts again and again. That is what gets us through. The hard emotions and difficult conversations serve to make us resilient and spirited. The good ones—well, those are what make it all worth it in the end.

I've never heard this song before. I'm glad it came on.

Timing is strange.

Life is strange.

Wear Me On Your Heart

I can still feel it
That same feeling I got when we first met
All the butterflies, they never flew away
And oh when you hold me I know you're here to stay

I can't wait to dance this dance for the rest of my life
I knew I'd found a love when you
said if I'd be your wife
You'll never wear me on your arm
You'll only wear me on your heart

I love how I'm still learning things about you
That I never knew
And every smile that's left a wrinkle
And look that says, 'I love you' oh oh

I can't wait to dance this dance for the rest of my life
I knew I'd found a love when you
said if I'd be your wife
You'll never wear me on your arm
You'll only wear me on your heart

I can't wait to dance this dance for the rest of my life
I knew I'd found a love when you
said if I'd be your wife
You'll never wear me on your arm
You'll only wear me on your heart

Sara Rose, 2018

fear's hiding place

nticipatory grief is almost as complicated and intricate as grief itself. I'd been suspended in a state of it over the last few months; the kind so wide and dismal that it hangs over each day to some degree or another. I'd been scatter-brained, distracted, and with a short fuse that made me angry at a lot of things, from people to cars on the highway, to the weather, to life, at the sense of the helplessness I felt around seeing death inch its way closer to Grandma and not being able to stop it. I'd been looking for something, someone, to blame. Anything to ease the distress of the anticipation of the loss that had become strapped to my back.

Grandma went back into the hospital needing brain surgery, and she hadn't really seemed to come back to us fully since coming out of it. Then again, I hadn't been with her every minute of the day and I'm not a doctor and don't know everything, but I know she's there. She'd lift the corner of her mouth when a song she liked came on or when someone told a funny story. I just didn't think she was there the way she'd wanted to be. It was the end of March now, though I'd been thinking back to a conversation we'd had on another late-night visit last year.

"A lot of people die in one piece. You know, at one time. I feel like I'm dying one piece at a time," she said, looking at the wall across from the bed but with a gaze that seemed like she was looking past it.

Ironically enough, I had been thinking in parallel. When someone you love dies over a period of time, you do lose them in pieces. She grimaced, then broke the silence that had been lingering in the room for much longer than it probably had in reality.

"Why is this happening to me? What did I do to make me get sick? I'm going to die," she said.

I drew in a breath and wanted to cry but nothing came out. I felt the fragile emotions immersed in those questions that had stopped me dead in my tracks.

Despair filled her eyes as if searching the room for respite from the discomfort that filled her.

"There isn't anything you've done in your life to make you become sick. I don't have any answers except that I think sometimes these questions are bigger than we are—they belong to the universe. We just have to go with the flow, fight how and when we can, and deal with whatever comes our way. You're not alone."

"I don't know if I'll get through this one," she said as she shut her eyes, drifting into the nap I think her body had been yearning for all afternoon.

Difficult and shattering don't begin to describe the feeling of seeing someone you love slowly fall apart, be it through a frailness insinuating itself physically, emotionally or spiritually. While you aren't able go through it in the same way they do, you do find a way to go through it with them. One needs to find a steady pace for such slow farewells. Some days we just breathe.

Illness and death confront us, causing us to have to confront the queries and questions none of us really has the answers to. The punishment doesn't always fit the crime. Good people get sick, bad people get by without consequence. Much like depression and anxiety, cancer doesn't care if you're 25, six, or 73. It doesn't discriminate. No one deserves to leave this world in pain through the ravages of disease. It broke my heart to see her living in that hospital bed, feeling vulnerable, trying to understand something that science and medicine can give some answers to, but not the ones she was looking for. All I could do was to reassure her that none of this was her doing and that there were family and workers here for her if she wanted to explore her thoughts and emotions around it.

As best as I could, I tried putting myself in her shoes. To not be able to use the feet she's been using to stand and walk for the last 73 years, struggling to advocate for herself without compromising her ability to breathe, and not wanting to die but also welcoming it to some degree. I don't like the thought that she'd been suffering. I don't know that I'd want to feel trapped in my body, in pain or not, unable to move yet conscious of what's going on. Why can't my legs move? Where did my strength go? Not too long ago it was, "where the hell did my balance go?" Watching death slowly inch its way closer to her all year had been heartbreaking. The feeling of helplessness in not being able to reach out and take the illness that had been starting to outpace her aptitudes and throw them into the deepest, furthest possible place from her had been unnerving to say the least.

Over the course of her illness, I grew mad at the world. I wanted to scream and ask the universe if it was certain it hadn't messed up, because one of the greatest human beings I'd ever known was dying and I couldn't fix her. That's a hard thing to accept when you're a fixer. When I see hurt, I want to bring healing and joy. When I see hate my first instinct is to try and promote love. I don't dislike a lot of things, and I surely don't hate anyone but I hated that feeling of helplessness. It was a 50-pound bowling ball that somehow sat in my stomach and weighed on my heart at the same time. Knowing I couldn't stop death from approaching her door by saying it got the wrong address was a difficult reality to grasp.

I wanted to leave these bland hospital walls behind and walk into her house to the sounds of her talking to the tennis game on TV before she paused it to give me one of her irreplaceable hugs. I wanted to give her my physical strength in order to regain full use of her body again and I wanted to take the exact quality of life she'd known and give it back to her. Instead, I remain sad and angry because I couldn't. I couldn't do any of that. The hope inside all of us seemed to be changing into something more resigned, but I knew if nothing else, I would be there. I would hold her hand and tell her how much I loved her. I could share with her the priceless things she's taught me and revisit the good memories. I could bring her radishes, her favourite snacks, and I could watch her game shows with her because the small things were all of the sudden proving to be far from miniscule. I could listen to her favourite songs with her because Grandpa had them playing in her room most days. I could try to memorize the sound of her voice and the sound of her laugh in my head. I could trace the kind of person she was over top of my heart so I'm constantly reminded of the kind of person I want to be in this world.

Presence, even if little is said, is sometimes more meaningful than not being there at all. It's a call for one to, as Margaret Paan says, "just be there; to not look away, to sit and hold a hand, to help loved ones return from caregiver to family once again and Just. Be. Present. Despite best practices and expertise, we cannot eliminate all suffering as grief is an unavoidable and necessary aspect of the journey, but we can commit to be there."

June 1, 2019, 1:13 a.m.

I'm thinking of the last time Grandma and Grandpa were over for dinner earlier this year, shortly before her illness returned, landing her in the hospital again for the last time. The driveway was slippery from the ice and I had thrown on a pair of Dad's old Crocs to go meet them. Cedar came out with me, as she was always so keen to meet anyone who came by the house. Grandma rolled down her tinted window and, keep in mind, I hadn't heard she was going to be getting a wig, there she was, in a white shirt, black leather jacket, leather gloves, and a salt and pepper wig. She looked like a rock star. She felt good and she loved it. She will always be my hero.

She made me laugh a while ago when we were watching one of those Minion movies while Grandpa went home to cut the grass. She sent me to get chips and pop and I accidentally got the non-diet stuff. I was going to go get the right one when she reached for it.

"Don't tell Grandpa, hehehe," she said, eyes twinkling.

In spite of everything, we laughed. We just laughed. She still found humour in her days. I will always remember this day.
-S

Perhaps anger is really just a hiding place for fear. I didn't want to see a world without her but I knew I soon would. Maybe I was resisting one of the most jarring facts of life when I should have been trying to let it take root by accepting it. I still have some growing to do with this. Now that I think of it, I remember learning in elementary school how one of the most well-known symbols for growth of all kinds is the pinecone. I guess it sort of fits.

March 28, 2019, 12:12 a.m.

Over the past month it's felt like beautifully shaped pieces of life were flying around like fireflies. I was trying to get them into a jar like the butterflies my cousins and I ran after with plastic Fisher nets as kids. I wanted to catch the moments like fireflies but each moment was moving by faster and even though I've been scrambling, I haven't been able to catch them all.
-S

Breathe

I'm out of touch
I'll say it's fine but in truth I'm just
trying to keep it together now
This delicate heart so heavy in my chest
It's breaking all but my fears, they won't rest
One minute I'm fine and the next
I'm holding back tears
Oh, how come I keep looking back after all these years

Chorus
Some days we breathe, we all just breathe
Feel me against the hope making my hands sweat
Some days we breathe, just keep breathing
Hold me, before I lose it all
Hold me, before I lose it all

I'm out of love
I'm scrambling and dropping things trying
to make my heart whole again
But time steals the breath right from my lungs
Please don't say I'm too far gone
I need the ground to steady, I need to breathe
Can I have just a minute please

Chorus
Sara Rose, We Could Be Beautiful, 2019

april 5

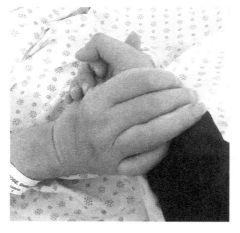

April, 2019

It's strange to see the world continue to turn around you when you're frozen in the middle of a moment – one so still, quiet, wide, and deep, yet somehow filled with an overflowing amount of emotion. I think I'm still thawing out from the moment I stood in with my family on the fifth of April.

To be fair, the mourning we endured on this day had probably begun wrapping itself around us months before. The thought of it had been tucked down pretty far in my head and heart, though the near disbelief that came crashing down when we faced it felt completely unforeseen.

April 1, 2019, 11:19 p.m.

Dad and I went to the hospital to visit Grandma and Grandpa this morning. Neither of us work Mondays and Tuesdays right now, so we usually drive down to the hospital together. Talking, even if it's about trivial or seemingly irrelevant things, is nice. Our relationship has surely seen some rocky points over the years and I think spending these hour-long drives together has been helpful grounds for reconnecting. How something as heart wrenching as an illness can also be a catalyst to untangling and dragging us out of being caught up in the small things that can somehow take precedence, and into the realization and remembrance of the bigger, much more important things in life, lends a mix of feelings.

Silence seemed to accompany the majority of this particular drive and although neither of us acknowledged it, we both knew the reason. Grandma was getting ready to leave us. She'd recently undergone a surgery on her brain that had quickly become a necessity if there were going to be any chance of her health returning and while she made it through it, she was moved to the ICU not long after.

"I feel like we take this view for granted," I said, shortly after we left the house.

The view from the top of the hills near our house is breathtaking. I usually drive it a few times per day, though for some reason I noticed it more this time. Before the same breath left my lungs, Dad agreed with a sureness that suggested he'd given the same idea some thought before, too.

Turning the corner into Grandma's room sent my heart into a tailspin. I found myself unable to believe the person lying there was actually her. Grandpa was facing her and the pain cast over his face when he turned to us was so marked that it hurt to see. In a split second, it echoed onto our own.

They say you can tell a lot by a person's eyes. Pain...joy...fear...peace. I don't know whether that's an old wives' tale or not, but when I looked in Grandma's eyes, the depth of emotion in them went right through me, like a shot straight to the heart.

"Is this what you want?" I quietly asked, though not really meaning to.

The words practically fell out of my mouth with no filter or second thought and I nearly choked afterwards. I'm a granddaughter, bottom of the totem pole, really. It wasn't my place to ask and I didn't mean to, but the tear that fell and the look in her eyes that followed it answered my question. As more tears gathered in her eyes, I felt my own do the same. It was this moment that reminded me of her voice; she had such a soft tone that instantly made you feel calm. Like everything was going to be alright. I wondered if I would hear it again and wished she could have told me what she was trying to convey with her eyes. It pulled at my heart strings to see her this way. I understand now why she said she didn't want anyone seeing her this way when she went into the hospital in June, and that was when she was independent for the most part, not hooked up to any machines.

I saw some meaning of life in her eyes and I looked over to see the handshake between Dad and

Grandpa quickly escalate into an embrace that was filled with love and acceptance of the overwhelming feelings of an anticipated loss. I felt so sad for them. For Grandma. For Grandpa. For Dad. For myself. It's so hard to be unable to take away someone's pain. It's like sitting on glass.

"We're here for you both," Dad said to Grandpa, as my hand met the back of his shoulder.

I don't know what else could have been said. I mean, what could be said? He was preparing to come face to face with the splintering pain of letting the love of his life move onto her next adventure; the person with whom he's spent the greater part of his time here on earth doing everything. And, I mean absolutely everything. There are no words to counterbalance that kind of looming loss. Grandpa looked at me as I was trying to hold back tears, and his expression reminded me of the importance of giving yourself permission to feel the emotions that arise.

"It's ok to cry," he said.

I think the body knows when it's reached its time by beginning to shut down. I had long sensed that the time she had left here was winding down, slipping into a reality into which I wasn't entirely comfortable. The hope I had for her body to heal and for her to make it through her illness never wavered in the sense that I've always known her to be so strong-willed, but that changed when I walked through the door this morning. I realize that I have to start moving towards acceptance of what's likely coming.

"I don't know what I'm supposed to feel," I later said to a friend.

"You feel all of the feelings that accompany anticipated grief and loss. You feel sad. You feel confused, upset, angry, broken..." she said.

"So, when they knock on the door, I let them in?"

"You let them in."

-S

As is usually the case when anything good or bad happens, I picked up my guitar when I got home. I'd been working on the songs for the album and started playing with the intent to tie the final strings (no pun intended) together for the next song that was going into the studio. Within ten minutes, the basis of "You Can Let Go" was there in front of me. It practically wrote itself; it was as if it had just been sitting inside of me, waiting to come out. It caught me off guard, to be perfectly honest. The timing was also strange, in a way I'm still not sure how to put into words, given what would unfold only a scant few days later.

April 3, 2019, 9:17 a.m.

Time is gathering speed and I can't find the brake pedal or the rewind button. I know time is going to have its way. It's the rationalizing concept that a head and heart seem to have difficulty grasping, rationalizing that time moves us forward and it runs out.

Tell me something
Tell me anything
I want to hear your voice one last time
Before I close my eyes

Time isn't on our side
I hear the long seconds hurry by
As much as I want you to stay alive
I pray for mercy while time goes by

It's so hard to see you this way
With your shoulders bearing the weight of the
serenity and complexity woven into your days
If you're getting ready you can go, it's all right
Your heart is always here, we promise to keep it
dignified
-S

A family meeting was called for the Friday of that week, three days before my birthday. I was out for breakfast at a local diner with a family friend the morning of the meeting and one of Grandma's favourite songs, "Bye Bye Love" by the Everly Brothers came on. As it played through the speakers. I wished she was there with us to hear it, too.

Shortly after arriving at the hospital, we were led to one of the many family rooms, the walls of which I'm sure had been seen by many families before us. While waiting for the doctor with Mom, Dad, and the rest of the family, a feeling was settling deep down inside me that the conversation to come likely wasn't going to be one about recovery. The worries that had been on my mind during the drive down hours before hadn't seen anything yet.

Unless death comes unexpectedly, I think it's typically obvious when it's imminent. Still, I don't think any of us were expecting the next few hours to unfold as they did, and as quickly as they did, for that matter.

The doctor and social worker's faces said everything we needed to know and within 20 minutes they were sitting off to the side, awaiting a decision from the family. Regardless of their gentle approach to laying out the reality we'd all hoped would not be the case, that Grandma wasn't in a state of health she could likely recover from, every predictable yet somehow still shocking word landed on all of us like a ton of bricks. I was in and out of realizing what was happening so some moments are blurry, but I remember hearing that some people just don't make it through those surgeries. The lump that grew in my throat choked me, the grip my hand had on the arm of the couch tightened while my stomach and heart did flip-flops. I knew it was bad, but I wanted them to say there was more time or that she was going to miraculously pull through. I didn't want it to be true. I didn't want to believe it. Because if I believed it then it was real, and if it was real then life was never going to be the same.

The question in my head soon moved from *how will I be strong when...* to *I will accept what is best for that person because I love them.* Nobody wanted her to be in pain or to prolong her suffering, so the decision was made to let her go. A 73-year-old soul was being released and in a single second, seven hearts broke. I imagined Grandpa was thinking how it wasn't supposed to be this way or that he was supposed to go first. I think it goes to show how no one really knows how to say goodbye.

I probably never will when it comes to the ones I hold near and dear to my heart. I know I will likely have to face that one day, though, and that's just a reality with which I must come to terms. This day had loomed with some warning but the truth is, no amount of time can fully prepare you to say goodbye to somebody you love. Winnie the Pooh says, "How lucky am I to have something that makes saying goodbye so hard." I've always loved that.

Following the meeting, we went downstairs for a smoke and a breather. As we headed down, in between the attempts to grasp what was happening, I started feeling terrible for not making the trip down to see Grandma the week before. I was working half an hour from the hospital, but had a bad day and chose to go home instead. It would have taken 30 minutes to get there. 30 stinking minutes. 1,800 seconds. And now, well, now I will forever know that I won't ever have that chance again. I know we can't hold ourselves hostage to the choices we've made based solely on what we know in a given moment. There isn't any way I could have known that the next week would be her last, yet I was mad at myself. I knew only as much as I knew at that time and if it were somebody else telling me this, I would say the same thing. Obviously if I knew that was going to be one of her last weeks, I'd have gone.

I also thought about how Mom has said in previous years that she wished her mom was still here, and how she'd called her once a week but wishes she had more often even if just for a minute or two to hear her voice or ask for advice. We'd been butting heads quite a bit, but when we were standing by the emergency doors in the lobby downstairs, an eye-opening thing happened.

"It's moments like this that make the problems and worries I tend to see as world-ending, actually quite small and irrelevant," I said.

"Me, too," she said. "I feel the same way."

I remembered someone telling me over dinner a few weeks prior, "As I get older I've been realizing how even when it may not seem possible, someone always has it worse or is dealing with something much bigger and deeper. Those times are reminders of what's truly important and worth worrying over." Every little worry, frustration, and pile of junk that felt world-ending to me suddenly fell away and became unimportant. Everything I'd thought was huge or detrimental to my survival was actually quite small and paper thin. The stresses and worries I saw in front of me were but grains of sand on the ocean floor. For the last while, someone I loved had been preparing to take her last breath and leave this world, and I'd been thinking life was so hard and unfair over stupid things like rent money and arguments over dishes in the sink.

June 16, 2019, 8:17 p.m.

I would really like to understand why it sometimes takes losing, or almost losing, someone or something, finding oneself shoulder-deep in loss, anticipated loss, or having a near-death experience

*to truly realize the fragility of life. I don't want to
wait until my days are numbered or until someone
else close to my heart is facing their end to realize
this. I'm going to love freely and intensely and keep
this memory in the pocket of my jeans for when
I get distracted by the problems that take on a
monumental façade, or if I get greedy with what I
have, forgetting that all could be lost at the drop of
a hat tomorrow.*
-S

We were all in a thick fog by the time we headed back upstairs. I felt so lost standing outside of her room while we took turns going in to say goodbye. Nurses and doctors were carrying on with their jobs, doing what they were supposed to do. The floor below us saw families welcoming new life into their own. The family in the room next to us was visiting a loved one who didn't look to be as far along her illness trajectory, while we would soon gather around our loved one as she left this world to set off on her next adventure. It was a whirlwind of situations.

When I went in to say goodbye I didn't know if I would be able to come up with the right words to say. I felt like it was going to be impossible to get the words out because I was already feeling like an emotional wreck, but it wasn't about me and I needed to recognize that. As I was talking to her, she grew so still. Calm. As if she were just having a good night's sleep and pleasant dreams. It was as if the universe were hovering over her room, like a cloud that had been waiting for permission to release the rain. The radio played quietly in the background and

I hadn't taken notice of it until it played the same song that had come on the last time Dad and I were here: "Rainbow" by Kacey Musgraves.

I just sat there for a minute, holding her hand in mine, trying to gather the words to tell her how much she meant to me and that I wasn't ready to say goodbye. None of us were. I didn't say goodbye, I said goodbye for now and thanked her for the things she taught me that will carry me through my life until it's my time to move on. I told her how great of a Grandma she was, how much I loved and looked up to her in so many ways, and I promised that I had listened to her when she'd told me to not wait to start living.

They say hearing is the last thing to go. I think she heard us, I believe she knew we were all there, and I hope it was our way of telling her it was ok to let go.

When it was time, my head knew what my heart didn't want to believe was happening. With every passing second I found myself swaying in and out of the moment. Letting go and holding on felt like the same thing and all that could be done was to accept and feel it. I suppose it's easier to tighten your grasp when you know what the ache that's going to follow will feel like. Everyone in the room was experiencing it from their own perspectives. I was holding her hand, my knees on the floor, my head resting softly on her forearm. I wondered if she was dreaming of being on a beach somewhere and hoped that whatever she was going through, she knew she wasn't alone.

People in my family and those I have known have died before. I've seen death and felt the weight bear down on my heart like a boulder, but I'd never seen it while it's doing its work. Dying is a process. It can be fast or slow, and witnessing it is both life-changing and somewhat eerie at the same time. Watching someone take their final breath, with the time between each rise and fall of a chest and stomach growing lengthy and uneven is the worst part; I found myself synching my breath with hers, believing I could make the next breath happen by sheer force of will. I hoped she was going to be ok. I wondered what she was going through and if she knew what was happening. I hoped she was as content and at peace on the inside as she seemed on the outside.

Even though the progression of her illness took more than a year, the beauty in sharing someone's last moments and witnessing a soul leaving the body is otherworldly and nothing short of standing in an intimate, sacred whirlwind. As sad as it was, it was an honour to be there to see her off on her next adventure. Apart from feeling a silent but powerful explosion go off in me, there was no way of knowing if she was ok or had made it to the other side. She was just...gone. Everything suddenly felt so still. The world seemed imperceptibly smaller. She was one person, but the world felt instantly emptier. It still does. I saw how much of a vessel we really are. Sometimes I wish I knew how it worked— where a soul or whatever makes us who and what we are travels to, upon our passing. It was also the first time I'd felt even a sliver of ease around the concept of it, including my own. Everyone has feelings around what dictates or determines a good or noble death. I believe she was ready and I think she had a dignified death. Everyone deserves that.

The world outside of the curtain felt like it could have stopped and we wouldn't even have noticed. It had been a wearying, anxiety-ridden afternoon and the depth of that very quiet moment following her departure was suddenly full of every single emotion humanly possible. I didn't want to look away. Walking out the door meant seeing her for the last time and starting the rest of my life without her in it—a world I didn't know. I thought to myself, *Why can't we say hello again? Did that really just happen? She's gone? Where did her soul go? Is she ok?* Someone who meant the world to everyone in that room had carried on from this life, and everyone in that room had just lost someone important, forcing them to learn how to live without her. A mother. A wife. A mother-in-law. A sister. A grandmother.

I was proud of the way my family advocated for her and stood by each other in accepting that it was her time, even though nobody was ever going to be ready for it. Death seems to be arduous that way. Between the tears that never seemed to stop flowing, I saw an enormous and nearly-immeasurable amount of love for someone who could have been counted on for anything, for a woman who lived with her arms open and her heart open even wider. I saw a son, three daughters and a sister who would never see the world the same again. I saw a husband who stood by his wife's side while she was braving cancer with the fortitude of an entire army. Truly, when I looked at the two of them, I saw a couple who had been a team since long before I was a part of this world. In seeing Grandpa as her caregiver at her life's close, I learned that he's just as much of a rock as she was. Even after he paused to let a few tears out, he quickly regrouped and managed to remain her pillar of strength.

Shirley Rose, from my earliest memory as a little girl to the final moments spent together at her bedside, never swayed by anything put in her path, living her life unafraid and with much love. She was an incredible source of inspiration to me, and that will inform how I try to my life from here on out.

April 6, 2019, 11:23 p.m.

Grandma is gone.

Tears had flowing all afternoon yesterday—they were hurting and I was exhausted, but when I got in the car to drive up to a good friend's house all I could think about was that stupid pinecone.

"Oh, for God's sake," I said aloud, frustrated.

I don't have a clue as to why I felt the need or if whatever I was going to come across would mean something, but I turned around and went back to the hospital where she'd spent so much time in the months before her passing. The pine tree whose branch met the middle of her old window backed onto the now deserted parking lot.

When I walked over to it and looked up, I fell to my knees in grief, my breath gone. I'm surprised there were any tears left. I thought, So now what?

The pinecone had fallen.

-S

It was just a pinecone, an item that frustrated me because I didn't see its relevancy or significance. Until it fell. It became such a symbol for the integrity and dignity of Grandma's direction right up to the end and if there aren't a few shavings of perspective slipped in there, perhaps losing your breath entirely is a way of getting it back. It was an awakening of sorts, seeing how death also manages to be a beautiful teacher.

You Can Let Go

You held my hand when I was little, and
I hold you in my heart forever
I'm wishing for just a handful of minutes
to hug you a few seconds longer
Kissed your cheek, caught a tear on the
way out, you're holdin' on tight
You lived your life never afraid to try,
you held your heart open wide

Oh, I'm in pieces, 'cause no one
teaches us to hurt this way
But it's like you said, of all our days,
it's only on one we'll die
And I wish this goodbye could see another
hello but I can see it in your eyes

Chorus
You can let go, I know we'll be alright
Our worlds will never be the same but you'll
live on in my heart and in my mind
I know you're waiting to fly
You can let go now, it's alright

Grandpa's holding on so tight, he's never left your side
He says it's the little things that bring
his heart to pieces every time
'Cause it's so hard to not be able to take away the pain
Every word catches my breath
because time will have its way

Oh, I'm in pieces, 'cause you taught me
everything except how to live without you
But I know love, and it never dies and
you'll be here, just in a different way
And I don't know if you can hear me,
but I love you and if you're ready

Chorus
Memories of a life that's been loved
are playing over in my mind
And no matter how hard I try I'll
never be ready to say goodbye
Cause if love could have saved
you, I know it would have
But we know life doesn't work that way

You can let go, I know we'll be all right
Our worlds will never be the same but you'll
live on in my heart and in my mind
You're an angel ready to fly
You're an angel

Sara Rose, We Could Be Beautiful, 2019

truth of love

September 9, 2019, 10:16 p.m.

I learned of an analogy for how grief works this morning and I've been spinning it around in my head ever since. It went something like this: Sitting on the floor in front of you is a big box. You own this box. The space inside represents you. A big ball has just been dropped inside. This ball is grief. On a day-to-day basis, the size of the ball may vary. Some days it will be small and will go nearly unnoticed, but when it bounces around and hits a wall, it can catch you off guard and it can hurt for a while after. Other days it will be so large that it pushes up against each side to the point it can barely move.

There are good days and bad days; days where the ball is smaller and days where it is tremendously

huge. Regardless of its presence, we're always reminded by grief that we loved.
Today it's big. I miss her voice most today.
-S

I think that much of our lives centre around remembering. The good, the bad, the love, the heartache. However, generally, I don't think what one dies of solely frames the portrait or turns down the songs that make up one's entire life. So often the painting of a human life can easily be dried into memory by how it's finished. The end of life is just as significant as the living that lead it, but when the final days approach or death has made itself present, it can be difficult to not remember and see those final brushed moments as the focal point of the entire portrait. The experiences. The moments. The mistakes, scars, lessons, and wisdom. The losses. The pain. The hope. The connection. The stories. The journey. The love. Those are all things that are lived, and also the things to be remembered by when we're gone.

I've been sifting through the events of April 5th and certain days that unfolded leading up to it over the last year as if with tweezers and a tiny magnifying glass. I rewind them and play them over again like a VCR tape, working through them until my head hurts. The size of their space in my head and my heart is of equal measure but it's like I'm trying to rearrange each image I have of and with her before her illness began overtaking her to the front, so they are the ones I see first when I think of her. I find this a little ironic too in some ways, given that many people going through an illness speak of not wanting to be remembered "this way" in the end. I've also heard the wishes of the undying may rest around choosing to remember their loved ones by the recollections of how they were when they were well. I didn't quite understand this until I found myself struggling to keep the volume of the memories and images I had of her when she got sick and went through her illness quieter than the ones I have of her from the 22 years prior.

I'm not sure going over and over this day is particularly helpful, or what answers I'm expecting to find in doing so. It kind of feels more like denial in the face of trying to move into acceptance that Grandma is gone and never coming back. Fighting reality is sort of like trying to move an immovable object and I suppose moving forward is accepting what is.

Nevertheless, focussing on the good times and memories as much as I can does help to make me feel better. Especially the ones that didn't initially strike me as noteworthy but over time have become quite significant.

May 18, 2019, 9:58 p.m.

Grandpa was over for dinner a few months ago and seeing the truck back in while knowing Grandma wasn't going to open the passenger side door, nor have Cedar run up to greet her, was emotional. Even harder for Grandpa, I think. They came for dinner a lot and even though I always looked forward to it, I never saw those visits as more than the usual. I never really thought about the depth of their value in terms of how it would feel if they were to change.

After dinner I showed him a couple of songs we finished for the album, one being "You Can Let Go."

"Grandma would be so proud," he said between tears. "She would be so proud of you using your voice and people being able to hear it."

Hearing this meant a lot. It made me think about how often she'd want lyrics in front of her when I sang so she could hear the words because I was too shy to sing loud enough to be heard clearly.

I have her to thank for my music appreciation. I admire her for her ability to connect with pretty well any song she heard and I think that's where my songwriting and writing in general derived from. I can almost hear her voice now.

"I want to hear the lyrics. I want to understand what the song is about and hear the story."

When I went through my first wave of depression in high school, I wrote a song called "Hold On." One of the of the lines was, "we've all got something hidden way deep down and find it sometimes pushing us around." As per normal, Grandma was following along with the words as I sang and plucked along on my first acoustic guitar, an Epiphone. When I was done, she stared at the page.

"It's so true," she said.

"What's so true?" I asked.

"We really do all have something way deep down."

Maybe we'll send "You Can Let Go" to Reba one day. Grandma was always a huge fan of hers. I remember being eight-years-old, downstairs on the computer after dessert, listening to her as we sat. Specifically, paying close attention to the video where she blows up her ex-lover's boat.

"Take notes," Grandma said.

-S

Each memory was a thread of a life being lived and now somehow is keeping the entire sweater held together. The "Live Like You Were Dying" conversation had happened just over a month prior, and was the last one we shared together. There were visits afterward, but it was the last one like that. One precious evening will forever hold more meaning in it than one-hundred casual ones. I guess that's where the significance of memories comes from, they're souvenirs of time and experience. Sometimes they are a guide, a pillar of strength, a lesson, or the aftermath of a stumble, but they are part of the map on my hand that I carry with me everywhere I go.

I know loss is unavoidable. When someone dear is lost, the hole it leaves is hollow yet unimaginably full of ache at the same time. Regardless of how much time has been spent with someone, if they meant a lot to you and pass away, your heart breaks.

Elizabeth Kübler Ross's model of the five stages of grief suggests a framework describing responses to loss that portray the terrain of grief. They include denial, anger, bargaining, depression, and acceptance, though not everybody goes through every stage, nor in a specific order. While at its most profound grief is the greatest rearranger of things, it's not a "one direction fits all" path. Our existence changes when our lives are infused with it, when we're faced with moving through the ebb and flow of destabilizing and aching loss, but it remains unique. I feel grief most in my chest, as if there's a big, heavy bowling ball hanging heavily in the middle of it.

Feb 6, 2020, 9:19 p.m.

They say time makes you bolder, though I'm not sure I'm the biggest believer of that today. Grandma has been gone for almost a year yet it feels like an eternity and only a handful of minutes at the exact same time. Maybe I haven't given myself enough space for the sadness surrounding this loss to ease.

Last night I was going through photos from her last visit to our house and I didn't know that live photos on an iPhone record sound, too. Her voice was in a few of them and I heard her laugh again. Then there are the songs, those that bring us back to the heart of a moment and can make us feel the same feelings as if we never left the moment at all...songs are good at that. "Rainbow" by Kacey Musgraves, "It Matters to Me" by Faith Hill, "Long Gone Lonesome Blues" by Hank Williams, "Love Me Like You Used To" by Tanya Tucker, and "D-I-V-O-R-C-E" by Tammy Wynette are just a few. It's nothing other than bittersweet. The bitterness and the sweetness feel as if they're two ends of the same ribbon, gone in opposite directions to meet back at the top centre of my heart and tying themselves together into the perfect bow.

Every day I feel different. There are days I'm doing ok and there are roller coaster days where the grief seems fresh, wraps its arms around me in a bear hug out of the blue and walking by a picture hanging on a wall is enough to bawl my eyes out. I can be laughing one minute and unable to hold back the tears the next because something has triggered a thought and memories cascades over me as yet another reminder that she's gone up. Other times an entire day or week goes by and I realize I haven't cried.

Clearly, I'm still grieving; does one ever stop weeping for someone loved and lost? There are some things I still need to face, things I need to process and God knows, there are things about which I need to come to a place of firmer acceptance, and I will. If only it were as easy as flicking a light switch. Evenings of music help to lighten my heart a little bit, but mostly I'm distracted, dropping balls, scatter-brained. I'm trying to be present in my life and I am who I am in many ways thanks to her.

I also know she wouldn't want my life to come to a screeching halt or for me to move through every hour sad, spending my days crying and closing myself off to all of the wonderful things life has to offer. She'd likely smack me upside of my head if she could, so I won't.

-S

Just the same as time does not make history obsolete, I don't think it's as much about "getting over" a loss so much as it is about figuring out how to emerge from the fog of intense sadness and live life without them. That's the scary part. I'm finding that truly feeling grief is much less grim than pushing it away, reminding me that the only remedy for grief is to grieve, even though I don't think that process is ever completely over. It's an experience that ebbs and flows on a day-to-day, moment-to-moment basis, and must be moved through at whichever pace is comfortable. You simply feel as well, as awful, as angry, and as sad and as heavy-hearted as you do. Importantly, we do not "get over" grief. We walk through it. While we do, hopefully our hearts are getting a little stronger, too.

My heart hurts for the loss of such a wonderful person and I mourn for the delight and brightness she brought into our world. I wonder where she is and I hope she's ok. I have a feeling she's spreading her wings as far as can be, feeling free, soaring through the sky (and maybe dropping gifts on a few people who pissed her off if she's a bird), but well onto her next adventure. I also have a feeling she's not venturing too far though, because she'd want to wait for Grandpa. Even though she's not here physically she buzzes in my heart, cheering and walking beside all of us every day, pulling strings to bring wholeness to our lives beyond my comprehension. As I sit here, I'm kind of horrified thinking those who have passed might be able to see me naked when I get changed. Hahaha.

A soul that will always be remembered with gratitude left behind a legacy that will never fade. I see Mom and Dad continuing to keep her legacy and spirit alive by playing her favourite music in the house and reminiscing about the times they've had with her. I think about her every day, as I'm sure I will for the rest of my existence. I'm grateful for the almost 23 years I had with her and am so fortunate to have been able to share what hours and days we had, especially in the year leading up to the final brushstrokes of her life's painting and last measures of her song that will continue to play on. I see Grandpa learning to live in a world without the most important person in his life. His love for her will never end; in fact, I think it may even be stronger.

Just because I'm accepting that she's died doesn't mean I don't have bad days and urges to lash out in frustration, sadness, denial, and everything in between. Those stages of grief are moved through interchangeably and I have to remind myself that every journey through loss is difficult and can be jarringly complicated. Sometimes every single one of those steps washes over me at the same time like a tsunami. We feel shattered. We hurt and we cry. We fall to our knees. We scream for understanding. We try to bargain with the universe. We go back and reprocess. We sit in the depths of heaviness that come down on us when someone has been taken. We adjust to the absence and we keep going. We morph and seek to reconfigure ourselves in the face of a beloved one's departure in order to manage the uniqueness of grief's process. Amongst it all, we learn what our heart can and cannot take. Usually, though, it can handle a lot more than we think it can. I'm starting to not mind having a broken heart all that much. Of course, I would trade it if it meant her having more time here, but that won't happen. I say that because the thing about a heart is that it's mighty, influential, and quite resilient. You can't make it stop feeling, loving is what it's good at. It may not fall in love anew, but it will learn to love those things that are lost in a different way. Sometimes taking a leap in the dark must be done so it can have a chance to do what it does best.

Jan 13, 2020, 8:16 p.m.

Crying or sadness isn't always devastating. It can be good. It's cleansing and is a reminder of what laughter is, flushing out stress hormones and other toxins. It assigns value onto emotion and allows for release just as laughter does. The more I push grief away, the more it riles and the more exhausted I get. Sometimes you gotta work through the icky feelings to get to the good ones and move forward. It's like trail mix—you have to dig through the raisins to get to the cashews.
-S

While it's in our nature to mourn, the world doesn't stop turning to grieve with us when we do. The good thing is you can grieve and still live life well. It's still possible to face the day. You can still go out for dinner with friends. It's ok to smile at the good memories and the laughs you had. Laughter isn't betrayal and as Mom has said, "it's ok to be sad but remember, it's ok to be happy, too." We smile because they have lived. We appreciate and celebrate a life that's been lived and loved. We sew the words "to live in hearts left behind is not to die" on our sleeves beside our hearts. We let our hearts overflow for the life that was lived. We sculpt the memories into something we can hold onto and breathe with. We count our lucky stars we had them and work to carry on their legacy. We slowly get back on our feet and continue moving. One of our greatest assets is learning to live in a loved one's absence.

Slowly, that hole becomes full again.

Grief gathers in the corners of my eyes and pushes on the walls of my chest on a daily, sometimes more often than not. Time is healing it, but when its details are rough, I sometimes wonder how many tears there really are inside, given the seemingly unending amount that have the ability to come during a big cry. Every time that grief overflows and its current is strong though, I'm reminded of the love behind it; a love so big, so strong, and the very thing that holds us together in the face of loss and in the journey of grief. Something I noticed in the months following was the hesitancy of others around connecting with me. While many were supportive and completely amazing, I felt that some were walking on egg shells around me and I think it was because people often don't know what to say or they didn't want to make me sad so they simply avoided me. Elizabeth Edwards writes that mentioning the loss of a person is actually quite a wonderful gift because it serves as a reminder that the person lived. All who have suffered great loss usually hope for though, is for you to show up. Don't turn from the dying or those grieving.

Love and loss are so prevalent, and grief knocks on all of our doors at some point or another. When it does, I let it in so it can teach me what it needs to. Love is the point of everything. Love did not dissolve when she died. We will, but love never will. If anything, I think it's expanded and found its way into every corner of our beings. Love is wise and the most powerful force on Earth, exceeding all. Even death.

June 18, 2019, 12:12 a.m.

The other day Grandpa and I were going through photo albums for Grandma's celebration of life. It's pretty crazy to realize how much you can learn about a person after they're gone. It's bittersweet and I almost can't wrap my head around it. I wish I could ask her about the memories the photos captured and hear more about her life, but I can't, though Grandpa told me a lot as we were going through them.

As much as not being able to talk to her or hop in the car and drive to see her hurts, I suppose it's proof of how you know something means something if it hurts when it's gone. It feels like I lost a real ally and this weight sits on me, as if testing its durableness to withstand and heal the sometimes-inevitable ache of losing someone with whom an unconditional love was shared.

Being human hurts, but it's kind of amazing that those who have left were even here. And I'd rather experience this grief from having what I had with her than to not have had it at all.
-S

In the end, perhaps we're all nothing but energy and spirits. While this loss has yet to settle fully in my soul, I'm confident time will help. And while I don't know a whole lot about a whole lot of things, one thing about which I'm confident is that love is, indeed, undying.

And that's the truth of love.

Grandma,

You taught me about love, life, hope, and living. You taught me that every song and every person has a story, you have only to listen for it, keeping your arms and heart open wide. You also told me, when I was eight, not to take people's shit and then showed me Reba McEntire's music video where she blows up her ex's boat, encouraging me to "take notes." I miss laughing with you. You taught me to always test the grapes at the grocery store before buying them to make sure they were hard and fresh enough, though I could never do it as nonchalantly as you. You wrote awesome letters to places like Loblaws and Costco when you were treated poorly by them because you knew your value and didn't take anyone's shit.

You taught me everything except how to live without you.

My head pounds under the weight of trying to accept such a heart-wrenching reality, one I can't run from no matter how far or fast I go. I don't want to see a world without you and I don't want it to be real that you're gone, but you are. I'm glad you're not in pain anymore. You fought for so long and so hard, and if love could have saved you, I know it would have.

We'll be ok and we'll take care of Grandpa. He says he has his hard days but that he walks a lot and tries to keep busy. He mentioned he leaves the light on beside you at night so you're never in the dark.

I know you would want us to soldier on with a strong and true heart, and not settle for anything less than an extraordinary life because not all is material. I saw that in the way you looked at everyone crammed in your living room at Christmas every year, in the way your eyes lit up when you laughed, and in the way you talked about how beautiful the drive to Mom and Dad's is in the fall. I wish you could see the person I'm becoming. Dad says I'm a lot like you. The fact I got 23 irreplaceable years with you is pretty damn great.

I know you're still here. You're in the hearts of all of us and you're in every memory, which will only grow sweeter with the passage of time. You're in songs I sing and write, in the brilliance of a perfect blue sky. I'll think of you when the sun rises and when one of our songs plays on the radio. You'll live on in my heart and mind forever.

I love you.

Sara

Never Forget You

Dear my friend how things have changed around here
I can't quite say my world's the same
I wrap my heart around the memories we shared
And my love will never change

Chorus
It's for you we stand today
Let the candles light the way
As we sing Hallelujah, oh oh
We will never forget you

Though I may not understand the way
the way this world spins around
But I know you're here someway
If I could say something more today
I love you and thank you

Chorus
We've all got someone close to our hearts
And with this love we'll never be apart

Chorus
Sara Rose, National Bereavement
Day Ceremony, 2017

a blanket for an unknown

*N*ot knowing what happens after death is certainly anxiety-provoking. Many religions offer myriad ideas about it and though I am by no means a wealth of knowledge on existing faiths, I see them as avenues for comfort in the face of the unknown. I wasn't raised under any specific religion. I'm more of a spiritual person; I see spirituality as a dynamic concept encompassing many theories. Regardless of the religion, I think engaging in them brings comfort in the face of uncertainties, anticipations, and loss; I sort of see religion as a blanket to wrap ourselves in for comfort in the face of the divine questions that confront us as human beings. The unknown has a history of bringing out rigidity and recklessness in me, mostly because I like trying to understand. I like understanding people, trying to see the world through someone else's eyes and heart, trying to comprehend why we're here at all. I've never done so well with uncertainty.

Honing in on the physical and emotional escalators that move us around and along a human lifespan causes me to become enormously apprehensive in never getting a definitive answer to any of it, resulting in a fairly lengthy period of time tangled up in trying to understand what this life really is. Yes, it sounds cliché, perhaps even a bit trite to say I've been on some kind of venture to "find meaning"; it's a completely normal and human thing to do, to be curious about our very existence and therefore to seek answers. A silly part of me has considered the thought that perhaps technology may reach a point of discovering some new type of medicine or gadget allowing us to "live forever." There isn't a whole lot of logic in that, I know. I do find it thought-provoking though, the kinds of things one bargains for while waist-deep in uncertainty. Especially when that uncertainty has to do with rather large, elaborate things like existence and demise.

I don't know why we have to die. How someone can be here and then suddenly not be turns my stomach, pulls on my heart strings, and makes me feel like I don't understand this life at all. I also don't know why I'm so engaged in this conversation at 23 years of age. The thought usually unfolds along the lines of this: Why we are here? What for? Am I doing everything right? Where does a soul go when it leaves a body? How are snowflakes made? What can I do better as a person if that's one of the only things I can control? Are we a compilation of cells that create a body, in which our souls may reside over the course of a lifetime so we can live, serve a purpose, die, and move onto the next adventure? Who decides how and when someone dies and who gets to live? People sometimes pass away in the wrong order because life and death don't run on a clock based solely on age. When it's our time to leave this body, no one can stop it. The material things we invest in are left behind only to be discarded. As I once saw on an unreferenced image, "No one ever wishes for more money in their last days, but experiences and memories are priceless." It has alarmed me before but I'm trying to reframe it to recognize that no amount of time is promised to us. I could die well before the person being kept alive by a ventilator is, and then again, I may not. I certainly hope I have a lot of years ahead of me. As I and many others have often said, "To grow old is a privilege."

Aug 22, 2016, 8:19 p.m.

Doing laundry was one of my grandma's favourite things to do. When she passed away, our washing machine kept acting up and as time went on, we'd sometimes find it would act up when the family experienced any drama. It's the anniversary of her death today and the laundry machine has been clunking since I put a load in after dinner. Sometimes I wonder if it's her energy or if it's just coincidence.

"We need to come up with a sign we can use if, God forbid, one of us passes away," Mom said.

"Oh yeah like what?" I asked.

"I don't know, switch the lights on and off or something," she said. "Just something to say we're still around and with each other."

Nice thought, but I swear if someone messes with the lights in the house or comes back as a chipmunk and chases me, I'll kick them in the ass.

-S

I'd like to think there's an afterlife of some kind. Whether it's heaven, hell, reincarnation, spirits, a higher power, I don't know. I remember hearing one belief that the time we leave this earth has already been decided by the time we're born. If I could choose what I'd come back as I'd either be an eagle or a quokka, a small cat-sized Australian animal that appears to be smiling all of the time. Eagles bestow courage and symbolize honesty, and quokkas are just so happy. Maybe a seagull to poop on some people. Ok, so I actually don't know what I'd come back as but oh heck, would it be something totally tubular. None of us knows what comes next. We're all just hoping for the best and doing the best we can.

Sometimes I feel like the world is so big, given its physical size and the endless amount of possibility as to what life even is, but then again, it could all be so very small. Maybe this is only the beginning. Maybe earth is some kid's science experiment in another universe, sitting on a shelf like a snow globe.

in tandem

A few months passed between writing "You Can Let Go" and getting into the studio to record it. I held off, worried that becoming rewrapped in the fragile place the song had been left in months prior, the week Grandma died, would evoke a lot of rocky emotion. I was right; it felt as fresh as if it had been written yesterday. Songs are like magnets when it comes to emotion.

Halfway through one of the takes, my producer friend stopped the track. I looked over to see him sitting still and wondered what had made him call cut.

"Look at this song," he said. "When you sing it, close your eyes and put your soul on the line. Make me believe it."

Allowing those resulting emotions to drive the song was cathartic and also made the song believable, which is what I always aim to do with my music. I'm lucky I've been welcomed into a place where I could do that, especially with this song.

After the recording session, I came home with a rough demo of the track and Mom and Dad were eager to hear it. Their CD player inside wasn't working at the time, so we went out to my car to listen. It was a warm evening, so I kept my door open and hit play. Shortly after the second chorus started, the strangest of things happened: a gigantic butterfly flew in and fluttered in front of our faces for a few seconds. It must have hung around for a good 15 to 20 seconds. As soon as the lyric, "I know you're waiting to fly, you can let go" played, it flew back out the door like a bolt of lightning.

Perhaps it was coincidence, perhaps it was Grandma giving us a gentle gesture to let us know she's moving in tandem with us, just in a different way now. All of us looked at each other, equally stunned. I still get goosebumps when I think about it.

where are you looking?

J t seems to be in the heart of those moments of amazing disbelief after something shocking happens that life snaps itself back into perspective. Shortly after finishing the Beautiful Teacher section of this book, I heard the tragic news of the helicopter accident that took the lives of nine people including Kobe Bryant and his 13-year-old daughter. The world's heart broke for each of them and their loved ones, as did my mine, and once again proved the reach and influence each of us has.

Death seems almost surreal until it sinks in as a reality that can't be ignored. People of all ages in all different circumstances die every day. Yesterday, there was someone who woke up with plans for the evening and didn't make it to them and today there's someone who may not make it to their plans tonight. All the money in the world can't stop it, either. Sometimes we see it coming and sometimes it's a surprise, but each passing always weighs in as a reminder to me to remember that when I feel down and out with life and my problems feel monumental, there are many people who didn't have the chance or option to stay here and wish they could have.

We get so busy with life paying bills, running from errand to errand, working, and living that these things are sometimes forgotten because they slip into the back of all of our minds. At times I feel I'm not appreciating life enough or am taking life for granted. Sure, I'm supposed to be out being a normal 24-year-old and sometimes lose sight of these things. As we all do. Then something happens that wakes us up by nudging the very important reminder of what a truly remarkable gift it is to be here and why it's important to cherish and enjoy every day we get by examining what's good in our lives and valuing and riding on them, because life can be taken away in a minute.

I think it's important that wherever you're looking, whatever stress is weighing, see it with the reminder that tomorrow isn't promised, no one really knows what's going to unfold, and the blink of an eye can change everything. All the more reason to live authentically, to not save something for another day, to love greatly with a full heart, to replace counting problems with blessings, to inspire, and to take the time to tell those you love, that you love them.

a beautiful teacher

Charlie Brown: "Someday, we will all die, Snoopy."
Snoopy: "True, but on all the other days, we will not."

Jan 12, 2019, 9:18 p.m.

I had a teacher in grade school who approached lessons in a way that communicated, "I'll just stand up here and talk in a monotone voice while the class sits at their desks and what's being taught fades to a mere distant hum in the back of their heads while they either fall asleep, zone out, or think about what kind of snack they're going to eat after school, oblivious."

The class was dreaded by many, but the funny part of it was if you listened beyond the dry monotone wrapped around the lesson and embraced the time, you would find that what was being said was actually quite profound. Lessons were absorbed like a sponge in water to those who chose to remain aware.

-S

beautiful teacher, much like a good mentor, can change the course of a life. Death, the unavoidable, inevitable part of life that is often elbowed out of the forefront of thought and heart until it makes itself present, is one of those teachers. In some ways, there really isn't an easy way of delving into a conversation about death and as such, living, without risking realism. Life can't be spoken about for its authentic self in the absence of its ending.

When I was younger, I always said, "if I die..." I don't know if it makes a whole lot of sense because at the same time, in the back of my mind, I knew that all living things eventually die. However, as time brought about age and loss, the more that statement moved towards one of "when I die..." And that changed some things. There's something profound about the cycle of a human life. It's pretty black and white, though I've grown an interest in the grey parts that house and highlight the intricate ways spirituality, religion, emotion, and evolving medicine shape an outline of the way we perceive and live as each hour, minute, and second stack up to build the days and experiences that comprise our lives.

It's a weird occurrence, the day you realize you're not immortal. I understood from a young age that people die and that I would also face my time someday. However, my late teens and early twenties saw a period of time where the true realization that life is not forever and that there was nothing I could really do to change that fact came whipping around the bend, smacking me square in the face like the rubber dodgeballs we threw in elementary school gym class. I got hit in the face a lot and looked like a radish during many final periods of school. I would wake up in the middle of the night anxiously gasping for air, firmly ensconced in a dream that either I or someone I knew was dying or had died. Nevertheless, I will always credit it to a card sitting on my kitchen counter, celebrating my 19th birthday.

Buried in the bills, flyers, and coupons yet to be sorted, I recognized the cursive writing the moment my eyes met it. Grandma has the most beautiful writing. By the way, I've yet to understand why cursive isn't taught in schools anymore. It's such an asset. Supposedly, it improves brain development in ways that typing and printing do not. I bet by the time my generation are "old folk" it'll be used as code for those of us who were privy to learning it.

"I'll open this later," I said aloud, though mostly to myself.

"Oh, just open it. It'll take you two seconds," Mom said from across the room.

Frustrated, as I was already late to get on with whatever I was heading out to do, I flipped the envelope over, tore the sticky part off, and opened the card. Signed from Grandma and Grandpa, 14 words managed to bring me to my knees.

"Have a great day and a great life. All our love, Gramma & Grampa xxx."

Suddenly, I wasn't in such a rush to get going anymore. I probably read it five times before I looked up to see Dad standing across the room. He was trying to find his glasses. If my face hadn't already been stricken with worry and sadness by then, it did after he asked what the card said.

I called Grandma without any special news to share, or any reason other than to hear her voice and have a conversation with her. After thanking her, she told me about how excited she was to go to bingo that week.

"You know, I've been playing this game for 50 years and I've never won big. But I just love it because I go with people I love," she said.

We just spoke. About nothing, really—yet it was everything.

September 12, 2016, 5:43 p.m.

I think I'm scared of you, death. Over the course of one inhalation, you can shape and figure me or dismantle me. You nip at my heels while I'm trying to avoid you and the more I strive to create some distance, the more the fear and anxiety around the idea of you being a bigger monster, or alien-like "thing" rises. I'm scared to come face-to-face with you because I don't know what happens next and I don't understand how all of this, whatever "this" is, could just go away.

You remind me of the reality that anyone's life, including my own, could end at any time for reasons beyond our control. It's scary to think of walking this

earth without those I love and care about one day,
and vice versa. The unknown of what happens when
we ourselves meet you leaves my chest heavy and
my throat dry because even if we're surrounded by
loved ones, the point at which we "pass over" is the
one thing we go through alone. I think, anyway. But
what do I know?
-S

There's comfort in a question with an answer, but the experience of moving from life to death and the answer of what comes after life may be one we will never know while we're here. Death is a predestined inevitability we know so well because it's universal to human existence, but it's scary because at some point it will be our turn to go and for certain, it sits beyond our understanding.

At the same time I'm accepting of that, this ambiguity has been the root of my challenge in figuring out how to deal with the unknown while I'm alive. I've raged and cried over how death holds up life's impermanency, wondering what I'm supposed to do and what the point of life is if it's just going to end anyway. At times it's kind of felt like an out of control garden that I've not wanted to acknowledge out of fear.

If I were looking at this state of being from another perspective I may suggest that a fear of life ultimately translates into a fear of emotion. Being human means feeling everything and that sometimes everything, apart from joy, content, serenity and love, involves fear and restlessness. Emotions—they're as human as it gets. I may then go on to place recognition on what a marvelous gift we have, to be able to feel such an array of things, and to do so deeply. Part of a Jake Woodard quote I stumbled across last year just popped into my head:

> *"Imagine your mind like a garden and your thoughts are the seeds. You get to choose what seeds you plant in it. You can plant seeds of positivity, love, and abundance. Or you can plant seeds of negativity, fear, and lack."*

If life were looked at like a garden, I suppose what's in our control is what we make of the life we have. So, either plant seeds of fear and worry that life ends and we don't know what happens next, which just leads to that garden of life becoming overgrown with weeds, or plant seeds of good things that make the flowers grow.

Jan 23, 2019, 7:13 a.m.

> *Last week I had the same dream four nights in a row. I was on a beach with my best friends, in Hawaii, a margarita in one hand, tornado potatoes (deep fried spiral-cut potatoes on skewers) in the other, singing "Red Solo Cup" and "Man! I Feel Like A Woman!" with floaties on my arms. It was fun and perfectly serene. I awoke right after looking down to see a beam jutting from beneath my heels and toes. The beam extended as far as my eyes could see before fading into a fog. It was strange because the conversation I'd had with someone the night before was about how being alive comes with timelines that may not be specifically known.*
>
> *I came to thinking this beam may symbolize one's life. Seen behind are the moments that have brought you to this day. The distance ahead is the remainder*

of life, which likely isn't known. I wonder how much of the way we live would change if we knew when our physical expiration date was? If you knew how many more steps there was room for, right down to the number, date, and time, what would you do differently right now, if anything? How would you like to spend it? When the end is reached, are you glad for all you've done? Did you love with all you had? If this should be it, are you delighted with all you've done? Would you start ticking off the things on your bucket list? Would you love harder? Stress less? Live more intensely and vividly? What would you say? What would you care about, or stop caring about? Would you forgive? Apologize less for who you are? Travel?

Everyone's walking their beam of life and I'm not going to take any more steps or time I have on mine for granted. You can't take time back for a redo after it's gone, but some wonderful things can be done with each moment. We're only here for a short time and every day is precious. I guess that recurring dream was something I'd yet to resolve and still may not have totally undertaken.

-S

I think a lot about death, though not in the ways I have in the past while so tightly wound in depression that I hadn't much desire to be alive at all. It's been a strange whirlwind of change, going from seeing the point of life through such a hazed, depressive lens, to being absolutely terrified to die, to beginning to try and accept dying as a fact of life. I'm envious of those who have an ease about it, mostly because it would be untrue to say that while the thought of my own demise is causing me to live life more fully, it can also bring about a sense of restlessness when I think about it for too long. Part of me feels young to be thinking about these things, and maybe I am, but life doesn't come without death and it likely never will. We all relate to it, even though that relation is unique to our particular stories. It's just as much of a part of life, and of the same importance, as being born is.

Surely, it's natural to push away that which isn't understood, but we don't have to do that. We are alive. We are breathing. The fact we have hearts that beat purpose into life and carry us through our songs while we create the albums of our lives is a damn miracle. I'm not living as passionately and fully as I'd like eventually to be, but I'm working on adding a few centimetres every day by letting the facts of life drive me to live a full, vivid existence. I think the attention death demands is actually a good thing in some ways; its persistence is robust but the multitude of lessons death can teach once given permission to do so is so very intimate and boundless that it's almost inconceivable.

Death is the greatest demander of attention and interrupter of all and in the end no amount of reasoning, cleverness or medicine will permanently turn its inevitable presence off. Not all of its notes are easy to hear and some songs may not come to make sense until our last one is being played. What a revelation it starts to become though, when that realization is not resisted but rather worked with. My relationship with death has been slowly changing over the last while. As a result, the relationship I have with life is also seeing change. I'm trying to work with it by building a richer understanding of how cultivating a rolling awareness of impermanence can make living so very much finer and fuller in its meaning. While death reminds me that time is precious and gives us deeper reason to appreciate, when it's given permission to be our teacher not only at the end of the road but right here and right now, we really learn how to truly be alive. We take action. We risk bringing visions to life. We dive into purpose. We love deeper. A friend once told me about a poem called "How You Live Your Dash." She explained, "The physical markings we leave behind on our stones: the two dates are our time of entry and of our departure. It's the dash in the middle—that's the life we live." What a symbol for the prevalence of purpose and why we're meant to fulfill it. That little dash holds the experiences, adventures, loves, losses, victories, and failures of our lives. Not to mention, as has been proposed in various contexts many times, if one's purposefulness and opportunity as a human being to fulfill it is rendered unusable, what's the point? I guess the whole purpose thing really has purpose.

In the end, what I've learned about life, and as such, death, is that they make you live. As a matter of fact, I'm starting to consider whether I would want to live forever if given the option. If I could permanently freeze myself at this age, I don't know that I'd find myself overly happy in the future. It would also depend on if my friends and family could live forever, too. I may sound like a nut, but if we lived forever, would we appreciate life as much? To appreciate life, you must also appreciate death. Endings serve to allow life to flow, helping give deeper meaning to relationships and reminding me to keep listening to the beat in my chest. So, we follow it. We let death teach the art of relishing the value of a moment, of what really matters, and let it remind us daily to live as widely as possible not only because we're hopefully in a position of being able to, but because there is an end. Death is making me noble and teaching me about making every moment count by living intentionally and meaningfully, by never letting a day go to waste, and by living life while I can.

Oct 13, 2014, 12:13 p.m.

> *There's a student in my first year sociology class. He's in his eighties. I asked him one day what inspired him to come back to school. He said, "I just love learning, and I love people. And, if you think you know everything, then why live? There's nothing left to learn if you know everything."*
> *Something to think about.*
> *-S*

So, for now, I'll let myself continue falling in love with being alive. I've still got a long list of questions but they're the kind that I won't find until my life is over. Dying is a real part of life that school didn't prepare me for and I don't think it could have anyway because life, in general, is first-hand. A person can go stir crazy obsessing over the unknown and then lose out on the life that can be lived and loved, or they can live for the day and not let the inevitability of death dictate the life being lived right now. I try to remind myself of this and that it's ok to ponder the mysteries of life, but I need to remember to rejoice in the time I have, with what I know, and lean into the fact that I'm alive.

Death, albeit a certainty, is conversely full of uncertainty, along with being a beautiful teacher. So, go do everything. Let it impart its knowledge. This is it.

Feb 17, 2020

My favourite season has always been the fall. I love the colours and the temperature. The fact it doesn't last forever is making me appreciate it all the more now.
-S

over your hill

2018

I see such grand similarities between roller coasters and the days that collectively shape our lives. Ups and downs are expected on a ride, you sort of sign up for them when you go to a theme park, unless you're the designated bag-holder for the day. There's something about stepping into the lineup for something you've never ridden, going through the various stages of waiting for the next move regardless of whether you're ready or not, buckling in (or not, and doing it anyway), feeling your stomach drop to your feet during the anticipated yet also unexpected pitches and plummets, screaming and throwing your arms in the air in joy or misery, all while deciding whether or not you want to have another go.

The precariousness amid the two is actually quite invigorating, now that I think of it. The only difference between a roller coaster and living is there isn't really any stepping off of life to examine it. One day we're just suddenly here, on this ever-forward and changing ride to becoming full-on humans. And we just do it, too; we move along through our days, catching moments and packing as much time, hope, and memories as we can into the pockets of our jeans. We fall backwards sometimes, our lungs releasing peals of laughter, we love with all we have, we get scared, we fuck up, we learn as we go and our hearts break yet somehow become whole again, though never in the same way. Most of all, we hope to relish as much of the good as possible because in the back of our minds and hearts we know the roads that we and our loved ones travel can change at any turn, dip, straightaway or incline and will eventually come to an end, sometimes a lot sooner than we can imagine.

Life goes by fast.

I'd like to think the courage and trust I have in myself to throw my shoulders back and stand within a sense of self-worth and comfortability around being in my own skin has coloured a bolder shade over past actions. Still, there is still a quiet, yet slowly fading part of me, sunken deep inside my heart, wandering around a muffled space of doubt and alleged uncertainty that's waiting. To run.

To hide. To let go of leftover aging hurt. To numb myself. To breathe free of all else trying to smoke bravery out of fear. However, if there's an underlying attitude that has set the precedence for putting one foot in front of the other, it's that of recognizing it's a privilege to be able to make the choice to face adversity when it arises. Abraham Maslow carves a theory of choice out well by describing it as either stepping forward into growth or backwards into safety. I wish stepping forward into growth was as easy as it's felt to fall back into some of the things I know so well. I sided with comfort for a long time (whatever "a long time" can be justly deemed by a 24-year-old), and while it kept me safe at times, I recognize it rarely serves me well in the end.

We're gonna have low days. We're gonna have hard days. We're gonna have days where we question our very existence, what we did right, what we did wrong... it's all part of the hills we must climb. Not every single one has to hold the power to set you adrift, though. Surely, as I'm learning in the ups and downs, there are things that happen to us that are beyond our control and sometimes even land outside of our understanding. There is treasure, misfortune, and all else in between that remind us the way to insight is to climb the hills. We get sent curve balls with the good stuff to make sure we're still on our toes and that doesn't mean things won't work out, it just means it won't be easy, and anything really worth it isn't easy. A quote shared by a friend a few months ago just occurred to me: in a near-stop on a climb, he said, "the great thing about this situation is the sun will rise tomorrow either in splendour or behind a mask of clouds, but it will rise. A clean slate. Tomorrow morning you can be whoever you want to be. Change is inevitable, but growth is optional."

We choose the people we're going to be. We're responsible for that. There's a choice to remain stuck in the ruts, anticipated or not, or to get back up when you fall down, lift your chin, dig your heels into the ground, and embrace the ride by buckling in and soldiering through. In all, it means believing you're worth the climb. Sometimes that means asking for help. Sometimes it means throwing your arms in the air and screaming to let out steam or running away for a little while, but always coming back. Maybe it's sitting under the night sky or even stopping for a bag of popcorn or eating a banana while sitting outside for a bit. Whatever keeps you going. Kobe was the one who said, "Have a good time. Life is too short to get bogged down and be discouraged. You have to keep moving. You have to keep going. Put one foot in front of the other, smile and just keep on rolling."

For me, reaching the top of a hill has never signified a reason to stop moving, never looking back. Surely there may not be a "back to the old me," but the versions of ourselves we were should still be celebrated. Every climb has shaped who we are. I still don't know if what I'm doing is "right" half the time but I'm starting to put my entire self out into the world through inner strength and determination to never back down, and in the support from my family and friends who follow behind each climb just to make sure I get there.

While in some ways my world is still so very small, in a lot of ways I'm glad for this. It means there are still more miles ahead on my road awaiting to be walked, run, tripped on, and explored. It means there are still depths of life left to learn. I still have no idea where I'm going to end up or how long I've got in this world, but I sure hope it's full of new things, experiences, and adventures with a whole lot of laughter and love. As for the tough parts, well. The steep hills can't be skipped and for those that make my legs burn, exhaust me, and give me reasons to give up, I know it will only make me better. Life's ride isn't breaking me; it's strengthening me, preparing me, and humbling me. The views I'm starting to see are making me believe life is worth the climb and it's like when my friend said that although I couldn't see it right then, hold fast to looking back on them one day and being able to say that was rough, really painful, it sucked and I didn't think I was going to make it over that hill, but I'm making it and look at where I am now. I'm starting to think that she was onto something there and will indeed give me an "I told you so," someday.

Between these covers sits a few perspectives of an ongoing journey littered with highs and lows; a tangible adventure speaking to the truth of what a rolling effort it can be to remember and believe that the world is still full of beautiful things and places no matter how hard the impact has been from whatever may have knocked you off your feet. The story doesn't have to be over. You never know what's on the other side of the hill until you reach it, and that climb now gives me hope. So, I'm gonna live until I die. And maybe, just maybe, it's in the heart of those moments that we find such strong feelings of uncertainty about keeping the pen on the page, that we should indeed continue writing.

So now what?

Fault Line

Fault lines drawn all over
Your body, your mind, your lost soul
Sitting below the surface
Unseen where truth meets stories untold

Leave me in the centre of my heart
Being someone I'm not never got me far
With every vein screaming "you're right"
Oh, I'm bound to crack this time

Chorus
Arms wide open, heart open wide
I'm teetering on the edge of risk
And breathing to unwind
Love, oh love of mine
Is where weakness and strength collide
This is the fault line

Doesn't matter where I go to feel
The push against the ranges this ride sees
Maybe I just feel too much
But you are never too broken to be loved

I'm afraid to see what's been aging in my heart
But not listening to it is pulling all affection apart
When we're convinced we're broken
We are just broken open
Waver my confidence, stress fracture to my plans
It won't overcome the self-worth
in the map on my hand

Chorus
Love, oh love of mine
Love, oh love of mine
Love, oh love of mine
Love, oh love of mine

Chorus
Sara Rose, We Could Be Beautiful, 2019

Epilogue

$\mathcal{A}$ few years ago, I couldn't really imagine being here today, let alone standing on a stage auditioning for one of my favourite shows in another country. There's no room to deny the presence of change in everyone and everything. It isn't always simple keeping up with variation, let alone managing it even with your hair piled on top of your head, sweat, dirt beneath your nails and a few resulting scars that tell a story of endurance, but I'm sure glad for that in some ways. I'm glad I'm becoming inspired to figure out what to do with each day's blank sheet of paper, for the doors I open letting the future inside, for the situations allowing me to try new things, and for the like-minded people and mentors with hearts as large as all outdoors, furthering my focus on what I want for my future.

Upon starting this book at age 21, albeit sporadically, I learned from a long-time friend that hard work and perseverance, in any capacity, must be matched with passion; a passion to inspire ourselves and others through the sharing of our stories in a form of art that's meaningful to us. I think everyone has a story to tell, learn from, and perhaps write about...it's there somewhere, in some place. If it's difficult to find, perhaps it's wedged into the bottom of your heart; the one thing that truly centres and grounds our very existence.

Eliminating all of our sorrows is not possible. We wouldn't be human if we weren't required to move within the range of our emotions. What we can do, though, is alleviate some of that sorrow creating avenues through which to share pieces of yourselves in a way that says you are not alone in what you are facing, that you're capable of being someone who's true to themselves by living an expressive and honest lifestyle. Similar to what others' music and books continuously do for me, I aspire to also look back on this book years from now and think differently than I do now. In fact, I hope that's the case because it means I'm doing something right.

Not one page of this is intended to be a comparison to someone who's found everlasting happiness, never falls backwards, or eats failure for breakfast, lunch, and dinner. I wanted to express and illustrate not what I've gone through, but that the mere act of getting through the struggles we all face, and finding places to allow the light back in, IS possible even when a million other reasons make it seem otherwise.

When I finished the last notes of the song at that audition, I slowly looked up at the judge. I'd just played *Weak in the Knees*, a classic by Canadian musician Serena Ryder, the best I'd ever played it. My chest felt heavy and my heart was pounding, only now in the utter joy of being in that moment, the moment I'd been waiting for. As the judge delivered the news that I wasn't going to be moving onto the next stage of auditions, I smiled, nodded, thanked everyone in the room, and let out a breath. I felt a touch deflated that I didn't get through, but more inflated in the incredibleness of the entire experience.

I packed up my guitar in the case that accompanies me most places and to my surprise instead of immediately asking, "So, now what?", I thought to myself, *Keep putting one foot in front of the other. You'll get to where you're going.* I hope one day I can personally thank the person who told me that.

Ashton's Song

It was a Friday afternoon about ten past two
I was sittin' at the kitchen table
and the call came through
Didn't know what to say 'cause
no I never saw it coming
Had to take a walk and let the news sink in

Times got hard yet there you were
Using that fighting spirit to reach
the dreams you deserved
And all I'm thinking about is how
you should be here now
I wanna pretend this ain't real but I can't figure it out

'Cause somebody lost a mother,
somebody lost a daughter
Somebody lost a granddaughter,
a niece, and I lost a friend
I'm still waiting for your call
Can't believe you're really gone

Chorus
So until we meet again
I'm gonna live this life for you till the end, till the end
Don't wanna see a world without you
And I pray you'll help us through
Heaven gained an angel when we lost you
Oh but if I had just one wish it'd be
That you didn't have to leave

23 years old with a little boy of your own
I see your shine in his eyes, you'll
always be his strength and home
He just wants to be happy and safe like we all do
How do I catch my breath and
carry on if there's no you

Somebody lost a mother, somebody lost a daughter
Somebody lost a granddaughter,
a niece, and I lost a friend
I'm still waiting for your call
It's killing me that you're really gone

Chorus

Are you living in your favourite memory
Spreading your wings even though
our hearts weren't ready
Lately all I think is how I would've done anything
To turn you back around

Chorus

Sara Rose, 2020

Acknowledgements

---

*Mom and Dad, to merely say thank you for your love
and ongoing support and reminders to
enjoy life's ride would feel far too much
of an understatement. I love you.*

*Chosen family, I will forever be
overwhelmed with gratitude.*

*Erin, for your belief in my story and your gracious
encouragement to speak
directly from the heart, I will never
be able to thank you enough.*

*Ashton, heaven gained a beautiful angel when we
lost you. The memories, laughs, light, and loving
friendship you brought to my life will forever remain
irreplaceable. There is no one like you in the universe.*